SEA AND SARDINIA

First Warbler Press Edition 2023

First published in 1921 by Thomas Seltzer, New York

Biographical Timeline © 2023 Warbler Press

ISBN 978-1-959891-93-2 (paperback)
ISBN 978-1-959891-94-9 (e-book)

warblerpress.com

SEA AND SARDINIA

D. H. LAWRENCE

CONTENTS

I. AS FAR AS PALERMO

Comes over one an absolute necessity to move. And what is more, to move in some particular direction. A double necessity then: to get on the move, and to know whither.

Why can't one sit still? Here in Sicily it is so pleasant: the sunny Ionian sea, the changing jewel of Calabria, like a fire-opal moved in the light; Italy and the panorama of Christmas clouds, night with the dog-star laying a long, luminous gleam across the sea, as if baying at us, Orion marching above; how the dog-star Sirius looks at one, looks at one! he is the hound of heaven, green, glamorous and fierce!—and then oh regal evening star, hung westward flaring over the jagged dark precipices of tall Sicily: then Etna, that wicked witch, resting her thick white snow under heaven, and slowly, slowly rolling her orange-coloured smoke. They called her the Pillar of Heaven, the Greeks. It seems wrong at first, for she trails up in a long, magical, flexible line from the sea's edge to her blunt cone, and does not seem tall. She seems rather low, under heaven. But as one knows her better, oh awe and wizardy! Remote under heaven, aloof, so near, yet never with us. The painters try to paint her, and the photographers to photograph her, in vain. Because why? Because the near ridges, with their olives and white houses, these are with us. Because the river-bed, and Naxos under the lemon groves, Greek Naxos deep under dark-leaved, many-fruited lemon groves, Etna's skirts and skirt-bottoms, these still are our world, our own world. Even the high villages among the oaks, on Etna. But Etna herself, Etna of the snow and secret changing winds, she is beyond a crystal wall. When I look at her, low, white, witch-like under heaven, slowly rolling her orange smoke and giving sometimes a breath of rose-red flame, then I must look away from earth, into the ether, into the low empyrean. And there, in that remote region, Etna is alone. If you would see her, you must slowly take off your eyes from the world and go a naked seer to the strange chamber of the empyrean. Pedestal of heaven! The Greeks had a sense of the magic truth of things. Thank goodness one still knows enough about them to find one's kinship at last. There are so many photographs, there are so infinitely many water-colour drawings and oil paintings which purport to render Etna. But pedestal of heaven! You must cross the invisible border. Between the foreground, which is our own, and Etna, pivot of winds in lower heaven, there is a dividing line. You must change your state of mind. A metempsychosis. It is no use thinking you can see and behold Etna and the foreground both at once. Never. One or the other. Foreground and a transcribed Etna. Or Etna, pedestal of heaven.

Why, then, must one go? Why not stay? Ah, what a mistress, this Etna! with her strange winds prowling round her like Circe's panthers, some black, some white. With her strange, remote communications and her terrible dynamic exhalations. She makes men mad. Such terrible vibrations of wicked and beautiful electricity she throws about her, like a deadly net! Nay, sometimes, verily, one can feel a new current of her demon magnetism seize one's living tissue and change the peaceful life of one's active cells. She makes a storm in the living plasm and a new adjustment. And sometimes it is like a madness.

This timeless Grecian Etna, in her lower-heaven loveliness, so lovely, so lovely, what a torturer! Not many men can really stand her, without losing their souls. She is like Circe. Unless a man is very strong, she takes his soul away from him and leaves him not a beast, but an elemental creature, intelligent and soulless. Intelligent, almost inspired, and soulless, like the Etna Sicilians. Intelligent daimons, and humanly, according to us, the most stupid people on earth. Ach, horror! How many men, how many races, has Etna put to flight? It was she who broke the quick of the Greek soul. And after the Greeks, she gave the Romans, the Normans, the Arabs, the Spaniards, the French, the Italians, even the English, she gave them all their inspired hour and broke their souls.

Perhaps it is she one must flee from. At any rate, one must go: and at once. After having come back only at the end of October, already one must dash away. And it is only the third of January. And one cannot afford to move. Yet there you are: at the Etna bidding one goes.

Where does one go? There is Girgenti by the south. There is Tunis at hand. Girgenti, and the sulphur spirit and the Greek guarding temples, to make one madder? Never. Neither Syracuse and the madness of its great quarries. Tunis? Africa? Not yet, not yet. Not the Arabs, not yet. Naples, Rome, Florence? No good at all. Where then?

Where then? Spain or Sardinia. Spain or Sardinia. Sardinia, which is like nowhere. Sardinia, which has no history, no date, no race, no offering. Let it be Sardinia. They say neither Romans nor Phoenicians, Greeks nor Arabs ever subdued Sardinia. It lies outside; outside the circuit of civilisation. Like the Basque lands. Sure enough, it is Italian now, with its railways and its motor-omnibuses. But there is an uncaptured Sardinia still. It lies within the net of this European civilisation, but it isn't landed yet. And the net is getting old and tattered. A good many fish are slipping through the net of the old European civilisation.

Like that great whale of Russia. And probably even Sardinia. Sardinia then. Let it be Sardinia.

There is a fortnightly boat sailing from Palermo—next Wednesday, three days ahead. Let us go, then. Away from abhorred Etna, and the Ionian sea, and these great stars in the water, and the almond trees in bud, and the orange trees heavy with red fruit, and these maddening, exasperating, impossible Sicilians, who never knew what truth was and have long lost all notion of what a human being is. A sort of sulphureous demons. *Andiamo!*

But let me confess, in parenthesis, that I am not at all sure whether I don't really prefer these demons to our sanctified humanity.

Why does one create such discomfort for oneself! To have to get up in the middle of the night—half past one—to go and look at the clock. Of course this fraud of an American watch has stopped, with its impudent phosphorescent face. Half past one! Half past one, and a dark January night. Ah, well! Half past one! And an uneasy sleep till at last it is five o'clock. Then light a candle and get up.

The dreary black morning, the candle-light, the house looking night-dismal. Ah, well, one does all these things for one's pleasure. So light the charcoal fire and put the kettle on. The queen bee shivering round half dressed, fluttering her unhappy candle.

"It's fun," she says, shuddering.

"Great," say I, grim as death.

First fill the thermos with hot tea. Then fry bacon—good English bacon from Malta, a god-send, indeed—and make bacon sandwiches. Make also sandwiches of scrambled eggs. Make also bread and butter. Also a little toast for breakfast— and more tea. But ugh, who wants to eat at this unearthly hour, especially when one is escaping from bewitched Sicily.

Fill the little bag we call the kitchenino. Methylated spirit, a small aluminium saucepan, a spirit-lamp, two spoons, two forks, a knife, two aluminium plates, salt, sugar, tea—what else? The thermos flask, the various sandwiches, four apples, and a little tin of butter. So much for the kitchenino, for myself and the queen bee. Then my knapsack and the q-b's handbag.

Under the lid of the half-cloudy night sky, far away at the rim of the Ionian sea, the first light, like metal fusing. So swallow the cup of tea and the bit of toast. Hastily wash up, so that we can find the house decent when we come back. Shut the door-windows of the upper terrace and go down. Lock the door: the upper half of the house made fast.

The sky and sea are parting like an oyster shell, with a low red gape. Looking across from the veranda at it, one shivers. Not that it is cold. The morning is not at all cold. But the ominousness of it: that long red slit between a dark sky and a dark Ionian sea, terrible old bivalve which has held life between its lips so long. And here, at this house, we are ledged so awfully above the dawn, naked to it.

Fasten the door-windows of the lower veranda. One won't fasten at all. The summer heat warped it one way, the masses of autumn rain warped it another. Put a chair against it. Lock the last door and hide the key. Sling the knapsack on one's back, take the kitchenino in one's hand and look round. The dawn-red widening, between the purpling sea and the troubled sky. A light in the capucin convent across there. Cocks crowing and the long, howling, hiccuping, melancholy bray of an ass. "All females are dead, all females—och! och! och!—hoooo! Ahaa!—there's one left." So he ends on a moaning grunt of consolation. This is what the Arabs tell us an ass is howling when he brays.

Very dark under the great carob tree as we go down the steps. Dark still the garden. Scent of mimosa, and then of jasmine. The lovely mimosa tree invisible. Dark the stony path. The goat whinnies out of her shed. The broken Roman tomb which lolls right over the garden track does not fall on me as I slip under its massive tilt. Ah, dark garden, dark garden, with your olives and your wine, your medlars and mulberries and many almond trees, your steep terraces ledged high up above the sea, I am leaving you, slinking out. Out between the rosemary hedges, out of the tall gate, on to the cruel steep stony road. So under the dark, big eucalyptus trees, over the stream, and up towards the village. There, I have got so far.

It is full dawn—dawn, not morning, the sun will not have risen. The village is nearly all dark in the red light, and asleep still. No one at the fountain by the capucin gate: too dark still. One man leading a horse round the corner of the Palazzo Corvaia. One or two dark men along the Corso. And so over the brow, down the steep cobble-stone street between the houses, and out to the naked hill front. This is the dawn-coast of Sicily. Nay, the dawn-coast of Europe. Steep, like a vast cliff, dawn-forward. A red dawn, with mingled curdling dark clouds, and some gold. It must be seven o'clock. The station down below, by the sea. And noise of a train. Yes, a train. And we still high on the steep track, winding downwards. But it is the train from Messina to Catania, half an hour before ours, which is from Catania to Messina.

So jolt, and drop, and jolt down the old road that winds on the cliff face. Etna across there is smothered quite low, quite low in a dense puther of ink-black clouds. Playing some devilry in private, no doubt. The dawn is angry red, and yellow above, the sea takes strange colors. I hate the station, pigmy, drawn out there beside the sea. On this steep face, especially in the windless nooks, the almond blossom is already out. In little puffs and specks and stars, it looks very like bits of snow scattered by winter. Bits of snow, bits of blossom, fourth day of the year 1921. Only blossom. And Etna indescribably cloaked and secretive in her dense black clouds. She has wrapped them quite round her, quite low round her skirts.

At last we are down. We pass the pits where men are burning lime—red-hot, round pits—and are out on the high-way. Nothing can be more depressing than an Italian high-road. From Syracuse to Airolo it is the same: horrible, dreary, slummy high-roads the moment you approach a village or any human habitation. Here there is an acrid smell of lemon juice. There is a factory for making citrate. The houses flush on the road, under the great lime-stone face of the hill, open their slummy doors, and throw out dirty water and coffee dregs. We walk over the dirty water and coffee dregs. Mules rattle past with carts. Other people are going to the station. We pass the Dazio and are there.

Humanity is, externally, too much alike. Internally there are insuperable differences. So one sits and thinks, watching the people on the station: like a line of caricatures between oneself and the naked sea and the uneasy, clouding dawn.

You would look in vain this morning for the swarthy feline southerner of romance. It might, as far as features are concerned, be an early morning crowd waiting for the train on a north London suburb station. As far as features go. For some are fair and some colorless and none racially typical. The only one that is absolutely like a race caricature is a tall stout elderly fellow with spectacles and a short nose and a bristling moustache, and he is the German of the comic papers of twenty years ago. But he is pure Sicilian.

They are mostly young fellows going up the line to Messina to their job: not artizans, lower middle class. And externally, so like any other clerks and shopmen, only rather more shabby, much less *socially* self-conscious. They are lively, they throw their arms round one another's necks, they all but kiss. One poor chap has had earache, so a black kerchief is tied round his face, and his black hat is perched above, and a comic sight he looks. No one seems to think so, however. Yet they view my arrival with a knapsack on my back with cold disapprobation, as unseemly as if I had arrived riding on a pig. I ought to be in a carriage, and the knapsack ought to be a new suit-case. I know it, but am inflexible.

That is how they are. Each one thinks he is as handsome as Adonis, and as "fetching" as Don Juan. Extraordinary! At the same time, all flesh is grass, and if a few trouser-buttons are missing or if a black hat perches above a thick black face-muffle and a long excruciated face, it is all in the course of nature. They seize the black-edged one by the arm, and in profound commiseration: "Do you suffer? Are you suffering?" they ask.

And that also is how they are. So terribly physically all over one another. They pour themselves one over the other like so much melted butter over parsnips. They catch each other under the chin, with a tender caress of the hand, and they smile with sunny melting tenderness into each other's face. Never in the world have I seen such melting gay tenderness as between casual Sicilians on railway platforms, whether they be young lean-cheeked Sicilians or huge stout Sicilians.

There must be something curious about the proximity of a volcano. Naples and Catania alike, the men are hugely fat, with great macaroni paunches, they are expansive and in a perfect drip of casual affection and love. But the Sicilians are even more wildly exuberant and fat and all over one another than the Neapolitans. They never leave off being amorously friendly with almost everybody, emitting a relentless physical familiarity that is quite bewildering to one not brought up near a volcano.

This is more true of the middle classes than of the lower. The working men are perforce thinner and less exuberant. But they hang together in clusters, and can never be physically near enough.

It is only thirty miles to Messina, but the train takes two hours. It winds and hurries and stops beside the lavender grey morning sea. A flock of goats trail over the beach near the lapping wave's edge, dismally. Great wide deserts of stony river-beds run down to the sea, and men on asses are picking their way across, and women are kneeling by the small stream-channel washing clothes. The lemons hang pale and innumerable in the thick lemon groves. Lemon trees, like Italians, seem to be happiest when they are touching one another all round. Solid forests of not very tall lemon trees lie between the steep mountains and the sea, on the strip of plain. Women, vague in the orchard under-shadow, are picking the lemons, lurking as if in the undersea. There are heaps of pale yellow lemons under the trees. They look like pale, primrose-smouldering fires. Curious how like fires the heaps of lemons look, under the shadow of foliage, seeming to give off a pallid burning amid the suave, naked, greenish trunks. When there comes a cluster of orange trees, the oranges are red like coals among the darker leaves. But lemons, lemons, innumerable, speckled like innumerable tiny stars in the green firmament of leaves. So many lemons! Think of all the lemonade crystals they will be reduced to! Think of America drinking them up next summer.

I always wonder why such vast wide river-beds of pale boulders come out of the heart of the high-rearing, dramatic stone mountains, a few miles to the sea. A few miles only: and never more than a few threading water-trickles in river-beds wide enough for the Rhine. But that is how it is. The landscape is ancient, and classic—romantic, as if it had known far-off days and fiercer rivers and more verdure. Steep, craggy, wild, the land goes up to its points and precipices, a tangle of heights. But all jammed on top of one another. And in old landscapes, as in old people, the flesh wears away, and the bones become prominent. Rock sticks up fantastically. The jungle of peaks in this old Sicily.

The sky is all grey. The Straits are grey. Reggio, just across the water, is white looking, under the great dark toe of Calabria, the toe of Italy. On Aspromonte there is grey cloud. It is going to rain. After such marvelous ringing blue days, it is going to rain. What luck!

Aspromonte! Garibaldi! I could always cover my face when I see it, Aspromonte. I wish Garibaldi had been prouder. Why did he go off so humbly, with his bag of seed-corn and a flea in his ear, when His Majesty King Victor Emmanuel arrived with his little short legs on the scene. Poor Garibaldi! He wanted to be a hero and a dictator of free Sicily. Well, one can't be a dictator and humble at the same time. One must be a hero, which he was, and proud, which he wasn't. Besides people don't nowadays choose proud heroes for governors. Anything but. They prefer constitutional monarchs, who are paid servants and who know it. That is democracy. Democracy admires its own servants and nothing else. And you couldn't make a real servant even of Garibaldi. Only of His Majesty King Victor Emmanuel. So Italy chose Victor Emmanuel, and Garibaldi went off with a corn bag and a whack on the behind like a humble ass.

It is raining—dismally, dismally raining. And this is Messina coming. Oh horrible Messina, earthquake-shattered and renewing your youth like a vast mining settlement, with rows and streets and miles of concrete shanties, squalor and a big street with shops and gaps and broken houses still, just back of the tram-lines, and a dreary squalid earthquake-hopeless port in a lovely harbor. People don't forget and don't recover. The people of Messina seem to be today what they were nearly twenty years ago, after the earthquake: people who have had a terrible shock, and for whom all life's institutions are really nothing, neither civilization nor purpose. The meaning of everything all came down with a smash in that shuddering earthquake, and nothing remains but money and the throes of some sort of sensation. Messina between the volcanoes, Etna and Stromboli, having known the death-agony's terror. I always dread coming near the awful place, yet I have found the people kind, almost feverishly so, as if they knew the awful need for kindness.

Raining, raining hard. Clambering down on to the wet platform and walking across the wet lines to the cover. Many human beings scurrying across the wet lines, among the wet trains, to get out into the ghastly town beyond. Thank heaven one need not go out into the town. Two convicts chained together among the crowd—and two soldiers. The prisoners wear fawny homespun clothes, of cloth such as the peasants weave, with irregularly occurring brown stripes. Rather nice handmade rough stuff. But linked together, dear God! And those horrid caps on their hairless foreheads. No hair. Probably they are going to a convict station on the Lipari islands. The people take no notice.

No, but convicts are horrible creatures: at least, the old one is, with his long, nasty face: his long, clean-shaven, horrible face, without emotions, or with emotions one cannot follow. Something cold, sightless. A sightless, ugly look. I should loathe to have to touch him. Of the other I am not so sure. He is younger, and with dark eyebrows. But a roundish, softish face, with a sort of leer. No, evil is horrible. I used to think there was no absolute evil. Now I know there is a great deal. So much that it threatens life altogether. That ghastly abstractness of criminals. They don't *know* any more what other people feel. Yet some horrible force drives them.

It is a great mistake to abolish the death penalty. If I were dictator, I should order the old one to be hung at once. I should have judges with sensitive, living hearts: not abstract intellects. And because the instinctive heart recognised a man as evil, I would have that man destroyed. Quickly. Because good warm life is now in danger.

Standing on Messina station—dreary, dreary hole—and watching the winter rain and seeing the pair of convicts, I must remember again Oscar Wilde on Reading platform, a convict. What a terrible mistake, to let oneself be martyred by a lot of canaille. A man must say his say. But *noli me tangere*.

Curious these people are. Up and down, up and down go a pair of officials. The young one in a black gold-laced cap talks to the elder in a scarlet gold-laced cap. And he walks, the young one, with a mad little hop, and his fingers fly as if he wanted to scatter them to the four winds of heaven, and his words go off like fireworks, with more than Sicilian speed. On and on, up and down, and his eye is dark and excited and unseeing, like the eye of a fleeing rabbit. Strange and beside itself is humanity.

What a lot of officials! You know them by their caps. Elegant tubby little officials in kid-and-patent boots and gold-laced caps, tall long-nosed ones in more gold-laced caps, like angels in and out of the gates of heaven they thread in and out of the various doors. As far as I can see, there are three scarlet station-masters, five black-and-gold substation-masters, and a countless number of principalities and powers in more or less broken boots and official caps. They are like bees round a hive, humming in an important *conversazione*, and occasionally looking at some paper or other, and extracting a little official honey. But the *conversazione* is the affair of affairs. To an Italian official, life seems to be one long and animated conversation—the Italian word is better—interrupted by casual trains and telephones. And besides the angels of heaven's gates, there are the mere ministers, porters, lamp-cleaners, etc. These stand in groups and talk socialism. A lamp-man slashes along, swinging a couple of lamps. Bashes one against a barrow. Smash goes the glass. Looks down as if to say, What do you mean by it? Glances over his shoulder to see if any member of the higher hierarchies is looking. Seven members of higher hierarchies are assiduously not looking. On goes the minister with the lamp, blithely. Another pane or two gone. *Vogue la galère.*

Passengers have gathered again, some in hoods, some in nothing. Youths in thin, paltry clothes stand out in the pouring rain as if they did not know it was raining. One sees their coat-shoulders soaked. And yet they do not trouble to keep under shelter. Two large station dogs run about and trot through the standing trains, just like officials. They climb up the footboard, hop into a train and hop out casually when they feel like it. Two or three port-porters, in canvas hats as big as umbrellas, literally, spreading like huge fins over their shoulders, are looking into more empty trains. More and more people appear. More and more official caps stand about. It rains and rains. The train for Palermo and the train for Syracuse are both an hour late already, coming from the port. Flea-bite. Though these are the great connections from Rome.

Loose locomotives trundle back and forth, vaguely, like black dogs running and turning back. The port is only four minutes' walk. If it were not raining so hard, we would go down, walk along the lines and get into the waiting train down there. Anybody may please himself. There is the funnel of the great unwieldy ferry-object—she is just edging in. That means the connection from the mainland at last. But it is cold, standing here. We eat a bit of bread and butter from the kitchenino in resignation. After all, what is an hour and a half? It might just as easily be five hours, as it was the last time we came down from Rome. And the *wagon-lit,* booked to Syracuse, calmly left stranded in the station of Messina, to go no further. All get out and find yourselves rooms for the night in vile Messina. Syracuse or no Syracuse, Malta boat or no Malta boat. We are the *Ferrovia dello Stato.*

But there, why grumble. Noi Italiani siamo così buoni. Take it from their own mouth.

Ecco! Finalmente! The crowd is quite joyful as the two express trains surge proudly in, after their half-a-mile creep. Plenty of room, for once. Though the carriage floor is a puddle, and the roof leaks. This is second class.

Slowly, with two engines, we grunt and chuff and twist to get over the break-neck heights that shut Messina in from the north coast. The windows are opaque with steam and drops of rain. No matter—tea from the thermos flask, to the great interest of the other two passengers who had nervously contemplated the unknown object.

"Ha!" says he with joy, seeing the hot tea come out. "It has the appearance of a bomb."

"Beautiful hot!" says she, with real admiration. All apprehension at once dissipated, peace reigns in the wet, mist-hidden compartment. We run through miles and miles of tunnel. The Italians have made wonderful roads and railways.

If one rubs the window and looks out, lemon groves with many wet-white lemons, earthquake-broken houses, new shanties, a grey weary sea on the right hand, and on the left the dim, grey complication of steep heights from which issue stone river-beds of inordinate width, and sometimes a road, a man on a mule. Sometimes near at hand, long-haired, melancholy goats leaning sideways like tilted ships under the eaves of some scabby house. They call the house-eaves the dogs' umbrellas. In town you see the dogs trotting close under the wall out of the wet. Here the goats lean like rock, listing inwards to the plaster wall. Why look out?

Sicilian railways are all single line. Hence, the *coincidenza*. A *coincidenza* is where two trains meet in a loop. You sit in a world of rain and waiting until some silly engine with four trucks puffs alongside. Ecco la coincidenza! Then after a brief *conversazione* between the two trains, *diretto* and *merce*, express and goods, the tin horn sounds and away we go, happily, towards the next coincidence. Clerks away ahead joyfully chalk up our hours of lateness on the announcement slate. All adds to the adventurous flavour of the journey, dear heart. We come to a station where we find the other diretto, the express from the other direction, awaiting our coincidential arrival. The two trains run alongside one another, like two dogs meeting in the street and snuffing one another. Every official rushes to greet every other official, as if they were all David and Jonathan meeting after a crisis. They rush into each other's arms and exchange cigarettes. And the trains can't bear to part. And the station can't bear to part with us. The officials tease themselves and us with the word *pronto*, meaning *ready!* Pronto! And again Pronto! And shrill whistles. Anywhere else a train would go off its tormented head. But no! Here only that angel's trump of an official little horn will do the business. And get them to blow that horn if you can. They can't bear to part.

Rain, continual rain, a level grey wet sky, a level grey wet sea, a wet and misty train winding round and round the little bays, diving through tunnels. Ghosts of the unpleasant-looking Lipari islands standing a little way out to sea, heaps of shadow deposited like rubbish heaps in the universal greyness.

Enter more passengers. An enormously large woman with an extraordinarily handsome face: an extraordinarily large man, quite young: and a diminutive servant, a little girl-child of about thirteen, with a beautiful face.—But the Juno—it is she who takes my breath away. She is quite young, in her thirties still. She has that queenly stupid beauty of a classic Hera: a pure brow with level dark brows, large, dark, bridling eyes, a straight nose, a chiselled mouth, an air of remote self-consciousness. She sends one's heart straight back to pagan days. And—and—she is simply enormous, like a house. She wears a black toque with sticking-up wings, and a black rabbit fur spread on her shoulders. She edges her way in carefully: and once seated, is terrified to rise to her feet. She sits with that motionlessness of her type, closed lips, face muted and expressionless. And she expects me to admire her: I can see that. She expects me to pay homage to her beauty: just to that: not homage to herself, but to her as a *bel pezzo*. She casts little aloof glances at me under her eyelids.

It is evident she is a country beauty become a *bourgeoise*. She speaks unwillingly to the other squint-eyed passenger, a young woman who also wears a black-rabbit fur, but without pretensions.

The husband of Juno is a fresh-faced bourgeois young fellow, and he also is simply huge. His waistcoat would almost make the overcoat of the fourth passenger, the unshaven companion of the squinting young woman. The young Jupiter wears kid gloves: a significant fact here. He, too, has pretensions. But he is quite affable with the unshaven one, and speaks Italian unaffectedly. Whereas Juno speaks the dialect with affectation.

No one takes any notice of the little maid. She has a gentle, virgin moon-face, and those lovely grey Sicilian eyes that are translucent, and into which the light sinks and becomes black sometimes, sometimes dark blue. She carries the bag and the extra coat of the huge Juno, and sits on the edge of the seat between me and the unshaven, Juno having motioned her there with a regal inclination of the head.

The little maid is rather frightened. Perhaps she is an orphan child—probably. Her nut-brown hair is smoothly parted and done in two pigtails. She wears no hat, as is proper for her class. On her shoulders one of those little knitted grey shoulder-capes that one associates with orphanages. Her stuff dress is dark grey, her boots are strong.

The smooth, moon-like, expressionless virgin face, rather pale and touching, rather frightened, of the girl-child. A perfect face from a mediaeval picture. It moves one strangely. Why? It is so unconscious, as we are conscious. Like a little muted animal it sits there, in distress. She is going to be sick. She goes into the corridor and is sick—very sick, leaning her head like a sick dog on the window-ledge. Jupiter towers above her—not unkind, and apparently feeling no repugnance. The physical convulsion of the girl does not affect him as it affects us. He looks on unmoved, merely venturing to remark that she had eaten too much before coming on to the train. An obviously true remark. After which he comes and talks a few common-places to me. By and by the girl-child creeps in again and sits on the edge of the seat facing Juno. But no, says Juno, if she is sick she will be sick over me. So Jupiter accommodatingly changes places with the girl-child, who is thus next to me. She sits on the edge of the seat with folded little red hands, her face pale and expressionless. Beautiful the thin line of her nut-brown eyebrows, the dark lashes of the silent, pellucid dark eyes. Silent, motionless, like a sick animal.

But Juno tells her to wipe her splashed boots. The child gropes for a piece of paper. Juno tells her to take her pocket handkerchief. Feebly the sick girl-child wipes her boots, then leans back. But no good. She has to go in the corridor and be sick again.

After a while they all get out. Queer to see people so natural. Neither Juno nor Jupiter is in the least unkind. He even seems kind. But they are just not upset. Not half as upset as we are—the q-b wanting to administer tea, and so on. We should have to hold the child's head. They just quite naturally leave it alone to its convulsions, and are neither distressed nor repelled. It just is so.

Their naturalness seems unnatural to us. Yet I am sure it is best. Sympathy would only complicate matters, and spoil that strange, remote virginal quality. The q-b says it is largely stupidity.

Nobody washes out the corner of the corridor, though we stop at stations long enough, and there are two more hours journey. Train officials go by and stare, passengers step over and stare, new-comers stare and step over. Somebody asks *who*? Nobody thinks of just throwing a pail of water. Why should they? It is all in the course of nature.—One begins to be a bit chary of this same "nature", in the south.

Enter two fresh passengers: a black-eyed, round-faced, bright-sharp man in corduroys and with a gun, and a long-faced, fresh-colored man with thick snowy hair, and a new hat and a long black overcoat of smooth black cloth, lined with rather ancient, once expensive fur. He is extremely proud of this long black coat and ancient fur lining. Childishly proud he wraps it again over his knee, and gloats. The beady black-eyes of the hunter look round with pleased alertness. He sits facing the one in the overcoat, who looks like the last sprout of some Norman blood. The hunter in corduroys beams abroad, with beady black eyes in a round red face, curious. And the other tucks his fur-lined long coat between his legs and gloats to himself: all to himself gloating, and looking as if he were deaf. But no, he's not. He wears muddy high-low boots.

At Termini it is already lamp-light. Business men crowd in. We get five business men: all stout, respected Palermitans. The one opposite me has whiskers, and a many-colored, patched traveling rug over his fat knees. Queer how they bring that feeling of physical intimacy with them. You are never surprised if they begin to take off their boots, or their collar-and-tie. The whole world is a sort of bedroom to them. One shrinks, but in vain.

There is some conversation between the black-eyed, beady hunter and the business men. Also the young white-haired one, the aristocrat, tries to stammer out, at great length, a few words. As far as I can gather the young one is mad— or deranged—and the other, the hunter, is his keeper. They are traveling over Europe together. There is some talk of "the Count". And the hunter says the unfortunate "has had an accident." But that is a southern gentleness presumably, a form of speech. Anyhow it is queer: and the hunter in his corduroys, with his round, ruddy face and strange black-bright eyes and thin black hair is a puzzle to me, even more than the albino, long-coated, long-faced, fresh-complexioned, queer last remnant of a baron as he is. They are both muddy from the land, and pleased in a little mad way of their own.

But it is half-past six. We are at Palermo, capital of Sicily. The hunter slings his gun over his shoulder, I my knapsack, and in the throng we all disappear, into the Via Maqueda.

Palermo has two great streets, the Via Maqueda, and the Corso, which cross each other at right-angles. The Via Maqueda is narrow, with narrow little pavements, and is always choked with carriages and foot-passengers.

It had ceased raining. But the narrow road was paved with large, convex slabs of hard stone, inexpressibly greasy. To cross the Via Maqueda therefore was a feat. However, once accomplished, it was done. The near end of the street was rather dark, and had mostly vegetable shops. Abundance of vegetables—piles of white-and-green fennel, like celery, and great sheaves of young, purplish, sea-dust-colored artichokes, nodding their buds, piles of big radishes, scarlet and bluey purple, carrots, long strings of dried figs, mountains of big oranges, scarlet large peppers, a last slice of pumpkin, a great mass of colors and vegetable freshnesses. A mountain of black-purple cauliflowers, like niggers' heads, and a mountain of snow-white ones next to them. How the dark, greasy, night-stricken street seems to beam with these vegetables, all this fresh delicate flesh of luminous vegetables piled there in the air, and in the recesses of the windowless little caverns of the shops, and gleaming forth on the dark air, under the lamps. The q-b at once wants to buy vegetables. "Look! Look at the snow-white broccoli. Look at the huge finocchi. Why don't we get them? I *must* have some. Look at those great clusters of dates—ten francs a kilo, and we pay sixteen. It's monstrous. Our place is simply monstrous."

For all that, one doesn't buy vegetables to take to Sardinia.

Cross the Corso at that decorated maelstrom and death-trap of the Quattro

Canti. I, of course, am nearly knocked down and killed. Somebody is nearly knocked down and killed every two minutes. But there—the carriages are light, and the horses curiously aware creatures. They would never tread on one.

The second part of the Via Maqueda is the swell part: silks and plumes, and an infinite number of shirts and ties and cuff-links and mufflers and men's fancies. One realises here that man-drapery and man-underwear is quite as important as woman's, if not more.

I, of course, in a rage. The q-b stares at every rag and stitch, and crosses and re-crosses this infernal dark stream of a Via Maqueda, which, as I have said, is choked solid with strollers and carriages. Be it remembered that I have on my back the brown knapsack, and the q-b carries the kitchenino. This is enough to make a travelling menagerie of us. If I had my shirt sticking out behind, and if the q-b had happened merely to catch up the table-cloth and wrap it round her as she came out, all well and good. But a big brown knapsack! And a basket with thermos flask, etc! No, one could not expect such things to pass in a southern capital.

But I am case-hardened. And I am sick of shops. True, we have not been in a town for three months. But *can* I care for the innumerable *fantasias* in the drapery line? Every wretched bit of would-be-extra chic is called a fantasia. The word goes lugubriously to my bowels.

Suddenly I am aware of the q-b darting past me like a storm. Suddenly I see her pouncing on three giggling young hussies just in front—the inevitable black velveteen tam, the inevitable white curly muffler, the inevitable lower-class flappers. "Did you want something? Have you something to say? Is there something that amuses you? Oh-h! You must laugh, must you? Oh—laugh! Oh-h! Why? Why? You ask why? Haven't I heard you! Oh—you spik Ingleesh! You spik Ingleesh! Yes—why! That's why! Yes, that's why."

The three giggling young hussies shrink together as if they would all hide behind one another, after a vain uprearing and a demand why? Madam tells them why. So they uncomfortably squeeze together under the unexpected strokes of the q-b's sledge-hammer Italian and more than sledge-hammer retaliation, there full in the Via Maqueda. They edge round one another, each attempting to get back of the other, away from the looming q-b. I perceive that this rotary motion is equivalent to a standstill, so feel called upon to say something in the manly line.

"Beastly Palermo bad-manners," I say, and throw a nonchalant "Ignoranti" at the end, in a tone of dismissal.

Which does it. Off they go down-stream, still huddling and shrinking like boats that are taking sails in, and peeping to see if we are coming. Yes, my dears, we are coming.

"Why do you bother?" say I to the q-b, who is towering with rage.

"They've followed us the whole length of the street—with their *sacco militario* and their *parlano inglese* and their *you spik Ingleesh*, and their jeering insolence. But the English are fools. They always put up with this Italian impudence."

Which is perhaps true.—But this knapsack! It might be full of bronze-roaring geese, it would not attract more attention!

However, and however, it is seven o'clock, and the shops are beginning to shut. No more shop-gazing. Only one lovely place: raw ham, boiled ham, chickens in aspic, chicken vol-au-vents, sweet curds, curd-cheese, rustic cheese-cake, smoked sausages, beautiful fresh mortadella, huge Mediterranean red lobsters, and those lobsters without claws. "So good! So good!" We stand and cry it aloud.

But this shop too is shutting. I ask a man for the Hotel Pantechnico. And treating me in that gentle, strangely tender southern manner, he takes me and shows me. He makes me feel such a poor, frail, helpless leaf. A foreigner, you know. A bit of an imbecile, poor dear. Hold his hand and show him the way.

To sit in the room of this young American woman, with its blue hangings, and talk and drink tea till midnght! Ah these naïve Americans—they are a good deal older and shrewder than we, once it nears the point. And they all seem to feel as if the world were coming to an end. And they are so truly generous of their hospitality, in this cold world.

II. THE SEA

The fat old porter knocks. Ah me, once more it is dark. Get up again before dawn. A dark sky outside, cloudy. The thrilling tinkle of innumerable goat-bells as the first flock enters the city, such a rippling sound. Well, it must be morning, even if one shivers at it. And at least it does not rain.

That pale, bluish, theatrical light outside, of the first dawn. And a cold wind. We come on to the wide, desolate quay, the curve of the harbour Panormus. That horrible dawn-pallor of a cold sea out there. And here, port mud, greasy: and fish: and refuse. The American girl is with us, wrapped in her sweater. A coarse, cold, black-slimy world, she seems as if she would melt away before it. But these frail creatures, what a lot they can go through!

Across the great, wide, badly paved, mud-greasy, despairing road of the quay side, and to the sea. There lies our steamer, over there in the dawn-dusk of the basin, half visible. "That one who is smoking her cigarette," says the porter. She looks little, beside the huge *City of Trieste* who is lying up next her.

Our row-boat is hemmed in by many empty boats, huddled to the side of the quay. She works her way out like a sheepdog working his way out of a flock of sheep, or like a boat through pack-ice. We are on the open basin. The rower stands up and pushes the oars from him. He gives a long, melancholy cry to someone on the quay. The water goes chock-chock against the urging bows. The wind is chill. The fantastic peaks behind Palermo show half-ghostly in a half-dark sky. The dawn seems reluctant to come. Our steamer still smokes her cigarette—meaning the funnel-smoke—across there. So, one sits still, and crosses the level space of half-dark water. Masts of sailing-ships, and spars, cluster on the left, on the undarkening sky.

Climb up, climb up, this is our ship. Up we go, up the ladder. "Oh but!" says the American girl. "Isn't she small! Isn't she impossibly small! Oh my, will you go in such a little thing? Oh dear! Thirty two hours in such a little boat? Why no, I wouldn't care for it at all."

A bunch of stewards, cooks, waiters, engineers, pan-cleaners and what-not, mostly in black canvas jackets. Nobody else on the ship. A little black bunch of loutish crew with nothing to do, and we the first passengers served up to be jeered at. There you are, in the grey light.

"Who is going?"

"We two—the signorina is not going."

"Tickets!"

These are casual proletarian manners.

We are taken into the one long room with a long table and many maple-golden doors, alternate panels having a wedge-wood blue-and-white picture inserted—a would-be Goddess of white marble on a blue ground, like a health-salts Hygeia advertisement. One of the plain panels opens—our cabin.

"Oh dear! Why it isn't as big as a china-closet. However will you get in!" cries the American girl.

"One at a time," say I.

"But it's the tiniest place I *ever* saw."

It really was tiny. One had to get into a bunk to shut the door. That did not matter to me, I am no Titanic American. I pitched the knapsack on one bunk, the kitchenino on the other, and we shut the door. The cabin disappeared into a maple-wood panel of the long, subterranean state-room.

"Why, is this the only place you've got to sit in?" cried the American girl. "But how perfectly awful! No air, and so dark, and smelly. Why I never saw such a boat! Will you really go? Will you really!"

The state-room was truly rather subterranean and stuffy, with nothing but a long table and an uncanny company of screw-pin chairs seated thereat, and no outlet to the air at all, but it was not so bad otherwise, to me who have never been out of Europe. Those maple-wood panels and ebony curves—and those Hygeias! They went all round, even round the curve at the dim, distant end, and back up the near side. Yet how beautiful old, gold-coloured maple-wood is! how very lovely, with the ebony curves of the door arch! There was a wonderful old-fashioned, Victorian glow in it, and a certain splendour. Even one could bear the Hygeias let in under glass—the colour was right, that wedge-wood and white, in such lovely gold lustre. There was a certain homely grandeur still in the days when this ship was built: a richness of choice material. And health-salts Hygeias, wedge-wood Greek goddesses on advertisement placards! Yet they *weren't* advertisements. That was what really worried me. They never had been. Perhaps Weego's Health Salts stole her later.

We have no coffee—that goes without saying. Nothing doing so early. The crew still stands in a gang, exactly like a gang of louts at a street-corner. And they've got the street all to themselves—this ship. We climb to the upper deck.

She is a long, slender, old steamer with one little funnel. And she seems so deserted, now that one can't see the street-corner gang of the casual crew. They are just below. Our ship is deserted.

The dawn is wanly blueing. The sky is a curdle of cloud, there is a bit of pale gold eastwards, beyond Monte Pellegrino. The wind blows across the harbour. The hills behind Palermo prick up their ears on the sky-line. The city lies unseen, near us and level. There—a big ship is coming in: the Naples boat.

And the little boats keep putting off from the near quay, and coming to us. We watch. A stout officer, cavalry, in grayey-green, with a big dark-blue cloak lined with scarlet. The scarlet lining keeps flashing. He has a little beard, and his uniform is not quite clean. He has big wooden chests, tied with rope, for luggage. Poor and of no class. Yet that scarlet, splendid lining, and the spurs. It seems a pity they must go second-class. Yet so it is, he goes forward when the dock porter has hoisted those wooden boxes. No fellow-passenger yet.

Boats still keep coming. Ha-ha! Here is the commissariat! Various sides of kid, ready for roasting: various chickens: fennel like celery: wine in a bottiglione: new bread: packages! Hand them up, hand them up. "Good food!" cries the q-b in anticipation.

It must be getting near time to go. Two more passengers—young thick men in black broad-cloth standing up in the stern of a little boat, their hands in their pockets, looking a little cold about the chin. Not quite Italian, too sturdy and manly. Sardinians from Cagliari, as a matter of fact.

We go down from the chill upper-deck. It is growing full day. Bits of pale gold are flying among delicate but cold flakes of cloud from the east, over Monte Pellegrino, bits of very new turquoise sky come out. Palermo on the left crouches upon her all-harbour—a little desolate, disorderly, end-of-the-world, end-of-the-sea, along her quay front. Even from here we can see the yellow carts rattling slowly, the mules nodding their high weird plumes of scarlet along the broad weary harbour-side. Oh painted carts of Sicily, with all history on your panels!

Arrives an individual at our side. "The captain fears it will not be possible to start. There is much wind outside. Much wind!"

How they *love* to come up with alarming, disquieting, or annoying news! The joy it gives them. What satisfaction on all the faces: of course all the other loafers are watching us, the street-corner loungers of this deck. But we have been many times bitten.

"Ah ma!" say I, looking at the sky, "not so much wind as all that."

An air of quiet, shrugging indifference is most effectual: as if you knew all about it, a good deal more than they knew.

"Ah si! Molto vento! Molto vento! Outside! Outside!"

With a long face and a dramatic gesture he points out of the harbour, to the grey sea. I too look out of the harbour at the pale line of sea beyond the mole. But I do not trouble to answer, and my eye is calm. So he goes away, only half triumphant.

"Things seem to get worse and worse!" cries the American friend. "What will you do on such a boat if you have an awful time out in the Mediterranean here? Oh no—will you risk it, really? Won't you go from Cività Vecchia?"

"How awful it will be!" cries the q-b, looking round the grey harbour, the many masts clustering in the grey sky on the right: the big Naples boat turning her posterior to the quay-side a little way off, and cautiously budging backwards: the almost entirely shut-in harbour: the bits of blue and flying white cloud over-head: the little boats like beetles scuttling hither and thither across the basin: the thick crowd on the quay come to meet the Naples boat.

Time! Time! The American friend must go. She bids us goodbye, more than sympathetically.

"I shall be awfully interested to hear how you get on."

So down the side she goes. The boatman wants twenty francs—wants more—but doesn't get it. He gets ten, which is five too much. And so, sitting rather small and pinched and cold-looking, huddled in her sweater, she bibbles over the ripply water to the distant stone steps. We wave farewell. But other traffic comes between us. And the q-b, feeling nervous, is rather cross because the American friend's ideas of luxury have put us in such a poor light. We feel like the poorest of poor sea-faring relations.

Our ship is hooting for all she's worth. An important last-minuter comes surging up. The rope hawsers are being wound clankily in. Seagulls—they are never very many in the Mediterranean—seagulls whirl like a few flakes of snow in the upper chill air. Clouds spin. And without knowing it we are evaporating away from the shore, from our mooring, between the great *City of Trieste* and another big black steamer that lies like a wall. We breathe towards this second black wall of steamer: distinctly. And of course an individual in an official cap is standing on the bottom of our departure ladder just above the water, yelling Barca! Barca!—shouting for a boat. And an old man on the sea stands up to his oars and comes pushing his clumsy boat with gathering speed between us and the other black wall. There he stands away below there, small, firing his clumsy boat along, remote as if in a picture on the dark green water. And our black side insidiously and evilly aspires to the other huge black wall. He rows in the canyon between, and is nearly here.

When lo, the individual on the bottom step turns in the other direction.

Another boat from the open basin is sweeping up: it is a race: she is near, she is nearer, she is up. With a curvet the boat from the open rounds up at the ladder. The boat between the gulf backs its oars. The official individual shouts and waves, the old man backing his oars in the gulf below yells expostulation, the boat from the open carries off its prey, our ship begins slowly to puddle-puddle-puddle, working her screw, the man in the gulf of green water rows for his life—we are floating into the open basin.

Slowly, slowly we turn round: and as the ship turns, our hearts turn. Palermo fades from our consciousness: the Naples boat, the disembarking crowds, the rattling carriages to the land—the great *City of Trieste*—all fades from our heart. We see only the open gap of the harbour entrance, and the level, pale-grey void of the sea beyond. There are wisps of gleamy light—out there.

And out there our heart watches—though Palermo is near us, just behind. We look round, and see it all behind us—but already it is gone, gone from our heart. The fresh wind, the gleamy wisps of light, the running, open sea beyond the harbour bars.

And so we steam out. And almost at once the ship begins to take a long, slow, dizzy dip, and a fainting swoon upwards, and a long, slow, dizzy dip, slipping away from beneath one. The q-b turns pale. Up comes the deck in that fainting swoon backwards—then down it fades in that indescribable slither forwards. It is all quite gentle—quite, quite gentle. But oh, so long, and so slow, and so dizzy.

"Rather pleasant!" say I to the q-b.

"Yes. Rather lovely *really*," she answers wistfully. To tell the truth there is something in the long, slow lift of the ship, and her long, slow slide forwards which makes my heart beat with joy. It is the motion of freedom. To feel her come up—then slide slowly forward, with a sound of the smashing of waters, is like the magic gallop of the sky, the magic gallop of elemental space. That long, slow, waveringly rhythmic rise and fall of the ship, with waters snorting as it were from her nostrils, oh God what a joy it is to the wild innermost soul. One is free at last—and lilting in a slow flight of the elements, winging outwards. Oh God, to be free of all the hemmed-in life—the horror of human tension, the absolute insanity of machine persistence. The agony which a train is to me, really. And the long-drawn-out agony of a life among tense, resistant people on land. And then to feel the long, slow lift and drop of this almost empty ship, as she took the waters. Ah God, liberty, liberty, elemental liberty. I wished in my soul the voyage might last forever, that the sea had no end, that one might float in this wavering, tremulous, yet long and surging pulsation while ever time lasted: space never exhausted, and no turning back, no looking back, even.

The ship was almost empty—save of course for the street-corner louts who hung about just below, on the deck itself. We stood alone on the weather-faded little promenade deck, which has old oak seats with old, carved little lions at the ends, for arm-rests—and a little cabin mysteriously shut, which much peeping determined as the wireless office and the operator's little curtained bed-niche.

Cold, fresh wind, a black-blue, translucent, rolling sea on which the wake rose in snapping foam, and Sicily on the left: Monte Pellegrino, a huge, inordinate mass of pinkish rock, hardly crisped with the faintest vegetation, looming up to heaven from the sea. Strangely large in mass and bulk Monte Pellegrino looks: and bare, like a Sahara in heaven: and old-looking. These coasts of Sicily are very imposing, terrific, fortifying the interior. And again one gets the feeling that age has worn them bare: as if old, old civilisations had worn away and exhausted the soil, leaving a terrifying blankness of rock, as at Syracuse in plateaus, and here in a great mass.

There seems hardly any one on board but ourselves: we alone on the little promenade deck. Strangely lonely, floating on a bare old ship past the great bare shores, on a rolling sea, stooping and rising in the wind. The wood of the fittings is all bare and weather-silvered, the cabin, the seats, even the little lions of the seats. The paint wore away long ago: and this timber will never see paint any more. Strange to put one's hand on the old oaken wood, so sea-fibred. Good old delicate-threaded oak: I swear it grew in England. And everything so carefully done, so solidly and everlastingly. I look at the lions, with the perfect-fitting oaken pins through their paws clinching them down, and their little mouths open. They are as solid as they were in Victorian days, as immovable. They will never wear away. What a joy in the careful, thorough, manly, everlasting work put into a ship: at least into this sixty-year-old vessel. Every bit of this old oak wood so sound, so beautiful: and the whole welded together with joints and wooden pins far more beautifully and livingly than iron welds. Rustless, life-born, living-tissued old wood: rustless as flesh is rustless, and happy-seeming as iron never can be. She rides so well, she takes the sea so beautifully, as a matter of course.

Various members of the crew wander past to look at us. This little promenade deck is over the first-class quarters, full in the stern. So we see first one head then another come up the ladder—mostly bare heads: and one figure after another slouches past, smoking a cigarette. All crew. At last the q-b stops one of them—it is what they are all waiting for, an opportunity to talk—and asks if the weird object on the top of Pellegrino is a ruin. Could there be a more touristy question! No, it is the semaphore station. Slap in the eye for the q-b! She doesn't mind, however, and the member of the crew proceeds to converse. He is a weedy, hollow-cheeked town-product: a Palermitan. He wears faded blue over-alls and informs us he is the ship's carpenter: happily unemployed for the rest of his life, apparently, and taking it as rather less than his dues. The ship once did the Naples-Palermo course—a very important course—in the old days of the General Navigation Company. The General Navigation Company sold her for eighty thousand liras years ago, and now she was worth two million. We pretend to believe: but I make a poor show. I am thoroughly sick to death of the sound of liras. No man can overhear ten words of Italian today without two thousand or two million or ten or twenty or two liras flying like venomous mosquitoes round his ears. Liras—liras—liras—nothing else. Romantic, poetic, cypress-and-orange-tree Italy is gone. Remains an Italy smothered in the filthy smother of innumerable Lira notes: ragged, unsavoury paper money so thick upon the air that one breathes it like some greasy fog. Behind this greasy fog some people may still see the Italian sun. I find it hard work. Through this murk of Liras you peer at Michael Angelo and at Botticelli and the rest, and see them all as through a glass, darkly. For heavy around you is Italy's after-the-war atmosphere, darkly pressing you, squeezing you, milling you into dirty paper notes. King Harry was lucky that they only wanted to coin him into gold. Italy wants to mill you into filthy paper Liras.

Another head—and a black alpaca jacket and a serviette this time—to tell us coffee is ready. Not before it is time, too. We go down into the subterranean state-room and sit on the screw-pin chairs, while the ship does the slide-and-slope trot under us, and we drink a couple of cups of coffee-and-milk, and eat a piece of bread and butter. At least one of the innumerable members of the crew gives me one cup, then casts me off. It is most obviously his intention that I shall get no more: because of course the innumerable members of the crew could all just do with another coffee and milk. However, though the ship heaves and the alpaca coats cluster menacingly in the doorway, I balance my way to the tin buffet and seize the coffee pot and the milk pot, and am quite successful in administering to the q-b and myself. Having restored the said vessels to their tin altar, I resume my spin chair at the long and desert board. The q-b and I are alone—save that in the distance a very fat back with gold-braid collar sits sideways and a fat hand disposes of various papers—he is part of the one-and-only table, of course. The tall lean alpaca jacket, with a face of yellow stone and a big black moustache moves from the outer doorway, glowers at our filled cups, and goes to the tin altar and touches the handles of the two vessels: just touches them to an arrangement: as one who should say: These are mine. What dirty foreigner dares help himself!

As quickly as possible we stagger up from the long dungeon where the alpaca jackets are swooping like blue-bottles upon the coffee pots, into the air. There the carpenter is waiting for us, like a spider.

"Isn't the sea a little quieter?" says the q-b wistfully. She is growing paler.

"No, Signora—how should it be?" says the gaunt-faced carpenter. "The wind is waiting for us behind Cape Gallo. You see that cape?" he points to a tall black cliff-front in the sea ahead. "When we get to that cape we get the wind and the sea. Here—" he makes a gesture—"it is moderate."

"Ugh!" says the q-b, turning paler. "I'm going to lie down."

She disappears. The carpenter, finding me stony ground, goes forward, and I see him melting into the crowd of the innumerable crew, that hovers on the lower-deck passage by the kitchen and the engines.

The clouds are flying fast overhead: and sharp and isolated come drops of rain, so that one thinks it must be spray. But no, it is a handful of rain. The ship swishes and sinks forward, gives a hollow thudding and rears slowly backward, along this pinkish lofty coast of Sicily that is just retreating into a bay. From the open sea comes the rain, come the long waves.

No shelter. One must go down. The q-b lies quietly in her bunk. The state-room is stale like a passage on the underground railway. No shelter, save near the kitchen and the engines, where there is a bit of warmth. The cook is busy cleaning fish, making the whiting bite their tails venomously at a little board just outside his kitchen-hole. A slow stream of kitchen-filth swilkers back and forth along the ship's side. A gang of the crew leans near me—a larger gang further down. Heaven knows what they can all be—but they never do anything but stand in gangs and talk and eat and smoke cigarettes. They are mostly young—mostly Palermitan—with a couple of unmistakable Neapolitans, having the peculiar Neapolitan hang-dog good looks, the chiselled cheek, the little black moustache, the large eyes. But they chew with their cheeks bulged out, and laugh with their fine, semi-sarcastic noses. The whole gang looks continually sideways. Nobody ever commands them—there seems to be absolutely no control. Only the fat engineer in grey linen looks as clean and as competent as his own machinery. Queer how machine-control puts the pride and self-respect into a man.

The rain over, I go and squat against the canvas that is spread over the arched sky-lights on the small promenade deck, sitting on the seat that is fixed to the sky-light sides. The wind is cold: there are snatches of sun and spits of rain. The big cape has come and is being left behind: we are heading for a far-off cape like a cloud in the grey air. A dimness comes over one's mind: a sort of stupefaction owing to the wind and the relentless slither-and-rearing of the ship. Not a sickness, but a sort of dim faintness. So much motion, such moving, powerful air. And withal a constant triumph in the long, slow sea-gallop of the ship.

A great loud bell: midday and the crew going to eat, rushing to eat. After some time we are summoned. "The Signora isn't eating?" asks the waiter eagerly: hoping she is not. "Yes, she is eating," say I. I fetch the q-b from her berth. Rather wanly she comes and gets into her spin chair. Bash comes a huge plate of thick, oily cabbage soup, very full, swilkering over the sides. We do what we can with it. So does the third passenger: a young woman who never wears a hat, thereby admitting herself simply as one of "the people," but who has an expensive complicated dress, nigger-coloured thin silk stockings, and suede high-heeled shoes. She is handsome, sturdy, with large dark eyes and a robust, frank manner: far too robustly downright for Italy. She is from Cagliari—and can't do much with the cabbage soup: and tells the waiter so, in her deep, hail-fellow-well-met voice. In the doorway hovers a little cloud of alpaca jackets grinning faintly with malignant anticipation of food, hoping, like blow-flies, we shall be too ill to eat. Away goes the soup and appears a massive yellow omelette, like some log of bilious wood. It is hard, and heavy, and cooked in the usual rank-tasting olive oil. The young woman doesn't have much truck with it: neither do we. To the triumph of the blow-flies, who see the yellow monster borne to their altar. After which a long long slab of the inevitable meat cut into innumerable slices, tasting of dead nothingness and having a thick sauce of brown neutrality: sufficient for twelve people at least. This, with masses of strong-tasting greenish cauliflower liberally weighted with oil, on a ship that was already heaving its heart out, made up the dinner. Accumulating malevolent triumph among the blow-flies in the passage. So on to a dessert of oranges, pears with wooden hearts and thick yellowish wash-leather flesh, and apples. Then coffee.

And we had sat through it, which is something. The alpaca blue-bottles buzzed over the masses of food that went back on the dishes to the tin altar. Surely it had been made deliberately so that we should not eat it! The Cagliarese young woman talked to us. Yes, she broke into that awful language which the Italians—the quite ordinary ones—call French, and which they insist on speaking for their own glorification: yea, when they get to heaven's gate they will ask St. Peter for:

"OOn bigliay pour ung—trozzième classe."

Fortunately or unfortunately her inquisitiveness got the better of her, and she fell into her native Italian. What were we, where did we come from, where were we going, *why* were we going, had we any children, did we want any, etc. After every answer she nodded her head and said Ahu! and watched us with energetic dark eyes. Then she ruminated over our nationalities and said, to the unseeing witnesses: Una bella coppia, a fine couple. As at the moment we felt neither beautiful nor coupled, we only looked greener. The grim man-at-arms coming up to ask us again if we weren't going to have a little wine, she lapsed into her ten-pounder French, which was most difficult to follow. And she said that on a sea-voyage one must eat, one must eat, if only a little. But—and she lapsed into Italian—one must by no means drink wine—no—no! One didn't want to, said I sadly. Whereupon the grim man-at-arms, whom, of course, we had cheated out of the bottle we refused to have opened for us, said with a lost sarcasm that wine made a man of a man, etc., etc. I was too weary of that underground, however. All I knew was that he wanted wine, wine, wine, and we hadn't ordered any. He didn't care for food.

The Cagliarese told us she came now from Naples, and her husband was following in a few days. He was doing business in Naples. I nearly asked if he was a little dog-fish—this being the Italian for profiteer, but refrained in time. So the two ladies retired to lie down, I went and sat under my tarpaulin.

I felt very dim, and only a bit of myself. And I dozed blankly. The afternoon grew more sunny. The ship turned southwards, and with the wind and waves behind, it became much warmer, much smoother. The sun had the lovely strong winey warmth, golden over the dark-blue sea. The old oak-wood looked almost white, the afternoon was sweet upon the sea. And in the sunshine and the swishing of the sea, the speedier running of the empty ship, I slept a warm, sweet hour away, and awoke new. To see ahead pale, uplooming islands upon the right: the windy Egades: and on the right a mountain or high conical hill, with buildings on the summit: and in front against the sea, still rather far away, buildings rising upon a quay, within a harbor: and a mole, and a castle forward to sea, all small and far away, like a view. The buildings were square and fine. There was something impressive—magical under the far sunshine and the keen wind, the square and well-proportioned buildings waiting far off, waiting like a lost city in a story, a Rip van Winkle city. I knew it was Trapani, the western port of Sicily, under the western sun.

And the hill near us was Mount Eryx. I had never seen it before. So I had imagined a mountain in the sky. But it was only a hill, with undistinguishable cluster of a village on the summit, where even now cold wisps of vapour caught. They say it is 2,500 feet high. Still it looks only a hill.

But why in the name of heaven should my heart stand still as I watch that hill which rises above the sea? It is the Etna of the west: but only a town-crowned hill. To men it must have had a magic almost greater than Etna's. Watching Africa! Africa, showing her coast on clear days. Africa the dreaded. And the great watch-temple of the summit, world-sacred, world-mystic in the world that was. Venus of the aborigines, older than Greek Aphrodite. Venus of the aborigines, from her watch-temple looking at Africa, beyond the Egatian isles. The world-mystery, the smiling Astarte. This, one of the world centres, older than old! and the woman-goddess watching Africa! *Erycina ridens.* Laughing, the woman-goddess, at this centre of an ancient, quite-lost world.

I confess my heart stood still. But is mere historical fact so strong, that what one learns in bits from books can move one so? Or does the very word call an echo out of the dark blood? It seems so to me. It seems to me from the darkest recesses of my blood comes a terrible echo at the name of Mount Eryx: something quite unaccountable. The name of Athens hardly moves me. At Eryx—my darkness quivers. Eryx, looking west into Africa's sunset. *Erycina ridens.*

There is a tick-tocking in the little cabin against which I lean. The wireless operator is busy communicating with Trapani, no doubt. He is a fat young man with fairish curly hair and an important bearing. Give a man control of some machine, and at once his air of importance and more-than-human dignity develops. One of the unaccountable members of the crew lounges in the little doorway, like a chicken on one foot, having nothing to do. The girl from Cagliari comes up with two young men—also Sardinians by their thick-set, independent look, and the touch of pride in their dark eyes. She has no wraps at all: just her elegant fine-cloth dress, her bare head from which the wisps of hair blow across her brow, and the transparent "nigger" silk stockings. Yet she does not seem cold. She talks with great animation, sitting between the two young men. And she holds the hand of the one in the overcoat affectionately. She is always holding the hand of one or other of the two young men: and wiping wisps of wind-blown hair from her brow: and talking in her strong, nonchalant voice, rapidly, ceaselessly, with massive energy. Heaven knows if the two young men—they are third-class passengers—were previous acquaintances. But they hold her hand like brothers—quite simply and nicely, not at all sticky and libidinous. It all has an air of "Why not?"

She shouts at me as I pass, in her powerful, extraordinary French:

"Madame votre femme, elle est au lit?"

I say she is lying down.

"Ah!" she nods. "Elle a le mal de mer?"

No, she is not sea-sick, just lying down.

The two young men, between whom she is sitting as between two pillows, watch with the curious Sardinian dark eyes that seem alert and show the white all round. They are pleasant—a bit like seals. And they have a numb look for the moment, impressed by this strange language. She proceeds energetically to translate into Sardinian, as I pass on.

We do not seem to be going to Trapani. There lies the town on the left, under the hill, the square buildings that suggest to me the factories of the East India Company shining in the sun along the curious, closed-in harbour, beyond the running, dark blue sea. We seem to be making for the island bulk of Levanzo. Perhaps we shall steer away to Sardinia without putting in to Trapani.

On and on we run—and always as if we were going to steer between the pale blue, heaped-up islands, leaving Trapani behind us on our left. The town has been in sight for an hour or more: and still we run out to sea towards Levanzo. And the wireless-operator busily tick-tocks and throbs in his little cabin on this upper deck. Peeping in, one sees his bed and chair behind a curtain, screened off from his little office. And all so tidy and pleased-looking.

From the islands one of the Mediterranean sailing ships is beating her way, across our track, to Trapani. I don't know the name of ships but the carpenter says she is a schooner: he says it with that Italian misgiving which doesn't really know but which can't bear not to know. Anyhow on she comes, with her tall ladder of square sails white in the afternoon light, and her lovely prow, curved in with a perfect hollow, running like a wild animal on a scent across the waters. There—the scent leads her north again. She changes her tack from the harbour mouth, and goes coursing away, passing behind us. Lovely she is, nimble and quick and palpitating, with all her sails white and bright and eager.

We are changing our course. We have all the time been heading for the south of Levanzo. Now I see the island slowly edging back, as if clearing out of the way for us, like a man in the street. The island edges and turns aside: and walks away. And clearly we are making for the harbour mouth. We have all this time been running, out at sea, round the back of the harbour. Now I see the fortress-castle, an old thing, out forward to sea: and a little lighthouse and the way in. And beyond, the town-front with great palm trees and other curious dark trees, and behind these the large square buildings of the south rising imposingly, as if severe, big palaces upon the promenade. It all has a stately, southern, imposing appearance, withal remote from our modern centuries: standing back from the tides of our industrial life.

I remember the Crusaders, how they called here so often on their way to the East. And Trapani seems waiting for them still, with its palm trees and its silence, full in the afternoon sun. It has not much to do but wait, apparently.

The q-b emerges into the sun, crying out how lovely! And the sea is quieter: we are already in the lea of the harbour-curve. From the north the many-sailed ship from the islands is running down towards us, with the wind. And away on the south, on the sea-level, numerous short windmills are turning their sails briskly, windmill after windmill, rather stumpy, spinning gaily in the blue, silent afternoon, among the salt-lagoons stretching away towards Marsala. But there is a whole legion of windmills, and Don Quixote would have gone off his head. There they spin, hither and thither, upon the pale-blue sea-levels. And perhaps one catches a glitter of white salt-heaps. For these are the great salt-lagoons which make Trapani rich.

We are entering the harbour-basin, however, past the old castle out on the spit, past the little lighthouse, then through the entrance, slipping quietly on the now tranquil water. Oh, and how pleasant the fulness of the afternoon sun flooding this round, fast-sleeping harbour, along whose side the tall palms drowse, and whose waters are fast asleep. It seems quite a small, cosy harbour, with the great buildings warm-colored in the sun behind the dark tree-avenue of the marina. The same silent, sleeping, endlessly sun-warmed stateliness.

In the midst of this tranquillity we slowly turn round upon the shining water, and in a few moments are moored. There are other ships moored away to the right: all asleep, apparently, in the flooding of the afternoon sun. Beyond the harbour entrance runs the great sea and the wind. Here all is still and hot and forgotten.

"Vous descendez en terre?" shouts the young woman, in her energetic French—she leaves off holding the young men's hands for the moment. We are not quite sure: and we don't want her to come with us, anyhow, for her French is not our French.

The land sleeps on: nobody takes any notice of us: but just one boat paddles out the dozen yards to our side. We decide to set foot on shore.

One should not, and we knew it. One should never enter into these southern towns that look so nice, so lovely, from the outside. However, we thought we would buy some cakes. So we crossed the avenue which looks so beautiful from the sea, and which, when you get into it, is a cross between an outside place where you throw rubbish and a humpy unmade road in a raw suburb, with a few iron seats, and litter of old straw and rag. Indescribably dreary in itself: yet with noble trees, and lovely sunshine, and the sea and the islands gleaming magic beyond the harbour mouth, and the sun, the eternal sun full focussed. A few mangy, nothing-to-do people stand disconsolately about, in southern fashion, as if they had been left there, water-logged, by the last flood, and were waiting for the next flood to wash them further. Round the corner along the quay a Norwegian steamer dreams that she is being loaded, in the muddle of the small port.

We looked at the cakes—heavy and wan they appeared to our sea-rolled stomachs. So we strolled into a main street, dark and dank like a sewer. A tram bumped to a standstill, as if now at last was the end of the world. Children coming from school ecstatically ran at our heels, with bated breath, to hear the vocal horrors of our foreign speech. We turned down a dark side alley, about forty paces deep: and were on the northern bay, and on a black stench that seemed like the perpetual sewer, a bank of mud.

So we got to the end of the black main street, and turned in haste to the sun. Ah—in a moment we were in it. There rose the palms, there lay our ship in the shining, curving basin—and there focussed the sun, so that in a moment we were drunk or dazed by it. Dazed. We sat on an iron seat in the rubbish-desolate, sun-stricken avenue.

A ragged and dirty girl was nursing a fat and moist and immovable baby and tending to a grimy fat infant boy. She stood a yard away and gazed at us as one would gaze at a pig one was going to buy. She came nearer, and examined the q-b. I had my big hat down over my eyes. But no, she had taken her seat at my side, and poked her face right under my hat brim, so that her towzled hair touched me, and I thought she would kiss me. But again no. With her breath on my cheek she only gazed on my face as if it were a wax mystery. I got up hastily.

"Too much for me," said I to the q-b.

She laughed, and asked what the baby was called. The baby was called Beppina, as most babies are.

Driven forth, we wandered down the desolate avenue of shade and sun towards the ship, and turned once more into the town. We had not been on shore more than ten minutes. This time we went to the right, and found more shops. The streets were dark and sunless and cold. And Trapani seemed to me to sell only two commodities: cured rabbit skins and cat-skins, and great, hideous, modern bed-spread arrangements of heavy flowered silk and fabulous price. They seem to think nothing of thousands of liras, in Trapani.

But most remarkable was bunny and pussy. Bunny and pussy, flattened out like pressed leaves, dangling in clusters everywhere. Furs! white bunny, black bunny in great abundance, piebald bunny, grey bunny:—then pussy, tabby pussy, and tortoiseshell pussy, but mostly black pussy, in a ghastly semblance of life, all flat, of course. Just single furs. Clusters, bunches, heaps, and dangling arrays of plain-superficies puss and bun-bun! Puss and bun by the dozen and the twenty, like dried leaves, for your choice. If a cat from a ship should chance to find itself in Trapani streets, it would give a mortal yell, and go mad, I am sure.

We strolled for ten more minutes in this narrow, tortuous, unreal town, that seemed to have plenty of flourishing inhabitants, and a fair number of Socialists, if one was to judge by the great scrawlings on the walls: W. LENIN and ABASSO LA BORGHESIA. Don't imagine, by the way, that Lenin is another Wille on the list. The apparent initial stands for *Evviva*, the double V.

Cakes one dared not buy, after looking at them. But we found macaroon biscuits, and a sort of flat plaster-casts of the Infant Jesus under a dove, of which we bought two. The q-b ate her macaroon biscuits all through the streets, and we went towards the ship. The fat boatman hailed us to take us back. It was just about eight yards of water to row, the ship being moored on the quay: one could have jumped it. I gave the fat boatman two liras, two francs. He immediately put on the socialist-workman indignation, and thrust the note back at me. Sixty centimes more! The fee was thirteen sous each way! In Venice or Syracuse it would be two sous. I looked at him and gave him the money and said: "Per Dio, we are in Trapani!" He muttered back something about foreigners. But the hateful, unmanly insolence of these lords of toil, now they have their various "unions" behind them and their "rights" as working men, sends my blood black. They are ordinary men no more: the human, happy Italian is most marvellously vanished. New honors come upon them, etc. The dignity of human labour is on its hind legs, busy giving every poor innocent who isn't ready for it a kick in the mouth.

But, once more in parenthesis, let me remind myself that it is our own English fault. We have slobbered about the nobility of toil, till at last the nobles naturally insist on eating the cake. And more than that, we have set forth, politically, on such a high and Galahad quest of holy liberty, and been caught so shamelessly filling our pockets, that no wonder the naïve and idealistic south turns us down with a bang.

Well, we are back on the ship. And we want tea. On the list by the door it says we are to have coffee, milk and butter at 8.30: luncheon at 11.30: tea, coffee or chocolate at 3.00: and dinner at 6.30. And moreover: "The company will feed the passengers for the normal duration of the voyage only." Very well—very well. Then where is tea? Not any signs! and the alpaca jackets giving us a wide berth. But we find our man, and demand our rights: at least the q-b does.

The tickets from Palermo to Cagliari cost, together, 583 liras. Of this, 250 liras was for the ticket, and 40 liras each for the food. This, for two tickets, would make 580 liras. The odd three for usual stamps. The voyage was supposed to last about thirty or thirty-two hours: from eight of the morning of departure to two or four of the following afternoon. Surely we pay for our tea.

The other passengers have emerged: a large, pale, fat, "handsome" Palermitan who is going to be professor at Cagliari: his large, fat, but high-coloured wife: and three children, a boy of fourteen like a thin, frail, fatherly girl, a little boy in a rabbit-skin overcoat, coming rather unfluffed, and a girl-child on the mother's knee. The one-year-old girl-child being, of course, the only man in the party.

They have all been sick all day, and look washed out. We sympathise. They lament the cruelties of the journey—and *senza servizio! senza servizio!* without any maid servant. The mother asks for coffee, and a cup of milk for the children: then, seeing our tea with lemon, and knowing it by repute, she will have tea. But the rabbit-boy will have coffee—coffee and milk—and nothing else. And an orange. And the baby will have lemon, pieces of lemon. And the fatherly young "miss" of an adolescent brother laughs indulgently at all the whims of these two young ones: the father laughs and thinks it all adorable and expects us to adore. He is almost too washed-out to attend properly, to give the full body of his attention.

So the mother gets her cup of tea—and puts a piece of lemon in—and then milk on top of that. The rabbit boy sucks an orange, slobbers in the tea, insists on coffee and milk, tries a piece of lemon, and gets a biscuit. The baby, with weird faces, chews pieces of lemon: and drops them in the family cup: and fishes them out with a little sugar, and dribbles them across the table to her mouth, throws them away and reaches for a new sour piece. They all think it humorous and adorable. Arrives the milk, to be treated as another loving cup, mingled with orange, lemon, sugar, tea, biscuit, chocolate, and cake. Father, mother, and elder brother partake of nothing, they haven't the stomach. But they are charmed, of course, by the pretty pranks and messes of the infants. They have extraordinary amiable patience, and find the young ones a perpetual source of charming amusement. They look at one another, the elder ones, and laugh and comment, while the two young ones mix themselves and the table into a lemon-milk-orange-tea-sugar-biscuit-cake-chocolate mess. This inordinate Italian amiable patience with their young monkeys is astonishing. It makes the monkeys more monkey-like, and self-conscious incredibly, so that a baby has all the tricks of a Babylonian harlot, making eyes and trying new pranks. Till at last one sees the southern Holy Family as an unholy triad of imbecility.

Meanwhile I munched my Infant-Jesus-and-Dove arrangement, which was rather like eating thin glass, so hard and sharp. It was made of almond and white of egg presumably, and was not so bad if you could eat it at all. It was a Christmas relic.—And I watched the Holy Family across the narrow board, and tried not to look all I felt.

Going on deck as soon as possible, we watched the loading of barrels of wine into the hold—a mild and happy-go-lucky process. The ship seemed to be almost as empty of cargo as of passengers. Of the latter, we were apparently twelve adults, all told, and the three children. And as for cargo, there were the wooden chests of the officer, and these fourteen barrels of wine from Trapani. The last were at length settled more or less firm, the owner, or the responsible landsman seeing to it. No one on the ship seemed to be responsible for anything. And four of the innumerable crew were replacing the big planks over the hold. It was curious how forlorn the ship seemed to feel, now she was ready for sea again. Her innumerable crew did not succeed in making her alive. She ran her course like a lost soul across the Mid-Mediterranean.

Outside the harbour the sun was sinking, gorgeous gold and red the sky, and vast, beyond the darkening islands of the Egades group. Coming as we did from the east side of the island, where dawn beyond the Ionian sea is the day's great and familiar event: so decisive an event, that as the light appears along the sea's rim, so do my eyes invariably open and look at it, and know it is dawn, and as the

night-purple is fused back, and a little scarlet thrills towards the zenith, invariably, day by day, I feel I must get up: coming from the east, shut off hermetically
from the west by the steep spikes of the mountains at our back, we felt this sunset
in the African sea terrible and dramatic. It seemed much more magnificent and
tragic than our Ionian dawn, which has always a suggestion of a flower opening.
But this great red, trumpet-flaring sunset had something African, half-sinister,
upon the sea: and it seemed so far off, in an unknown land. Whereas our Ionian
dawn always seems near and familiar and happy.

A different goddess the Eryx Astarte, the woman Ashtaroth, *Erycina ridens*
must have been, in her prehstoric dark smiling, watching the fearful sunsets
beyond the Egades, from our gold-lighted Apollo of the Ionian east. She is a
strange goddess to me, this Erycina Venus, and the west is strange and unfamiliar and a little fearful, be it Africa or be it America.

Slowly at sunset we moved out of the harbour. And almost as we passed the
bar, away in front we saw, among the islands, the pricking of a quick pointed
light. Looking back, we saw the light at the harbour entrance twitching: and the
remote, lost town beginning to glimmer. And night was settling down upon the
sea, through the crimsoned purple of the last afterglow.

The islands loomed big as we drew nearer, dark in the thickening darkness.
Overhead a magnificent evening-star blazed above the open sea, giving me a
pang at the heart, for I was so used to see her hang just above the spikes of the
mountains, that I felt she might fall, having the space beneath.

Levanzo and the other large island were quite dark: absolutely dark, save
for one beam of a lighthouse low down in the distance. The wind was again
strong and cold: the ship had commenced her old slither and heave, slither and
heave, which mercifully we had forgotten. Overhead were innumerable great
stars active as if they were alive in the sky. I saw Orion high behind us, and the
dog-star glaring. And *swish!* went the sea as we took the waves, then after a
long trough, *swish!* This curious rhythmic swishing and hollow drumming of
a steamer at sea has a narcotic, almost maddening effect on the spirit, a long,
hissing burst of waters, then the hollow roll, and again the upheaval to a sudden
hiss-ss-ss!

A bell had clanged and we knew the crew were once more feeding. At every
moment of the day and presumably of the night, feeding was going on—or
coffee-drinking.

We were summoned to dinner. Our young woman was already seated: and a
fat uniformed mate or purser or official of some sort was finishing off in the
distance. The pale professor also appeared: and at a certain distance down the
table sat a little hard-headed grey man in a long grey alpaca travelling coat.
Appeared the beloved macaroni with tomato sauce: no food for the sea. I put

my hopes on the fish. Had I not seen the cook making whiting bite their own tails viciously?—The fish appeared. And what was it? Fried ink-pots. A *cala-maio* is an ink-pot: also it is a polyp, a little octopus which, alas, frequents the Mediterranean and squirts ink if offended. This polyp with its tentacles is cut up and fried, and reduced to the consistency of boiled celluloid. It is esteemed a delicacy: but is tougher than indiarubber, gristly through and through.

I have a peculiar aversion to these ink-pots. Once in Liguria we had a boat of our own and paddled with the peasant paddlers. Alessandro caught ink-pots: and like this. He tied up a female by a string in a cave—the string going through a convenient hole in her end. There she lived, like an Amphitrite's wire-haired terrier tied up, till Alessandro went a-fishing. Then he towed her, like a poodle behind. And thus, like a poodly-bitch, she attracted hangers-on in the briny seas. And these poor polyp inamorati were the victims. They were lifted as prey on board, where I looked with horror on their grey, translucent tentacles and large, cold, stony eyes. The she-polyp was towed behind again. But after a few days she died.

And I think, even for creatures so awful-looking, this method is indescribably base, and shows how much lower than an octopus even, is lordly man.

Well, we chewed a few ends of oil-fried ink-pots, and gave it up. The Cagliari girl gave up too: the professor had not even tried. Only the hard-headed grey man in the alpaca coat chewed animatedly, with bouncing jaws. Mountains of calamaio remained for the joyous blue-bottles.

Arrived the inevitable meat—this long piece of completely tasteless undercut in innumerable grey-brown slices. Oh, Italy! The professor fled.

Arrived the wash-leather pears, the apples, the oranges—we saved an apple for a happier hour.

Arrived coffee, and, as a magnificent treat, a few well-known pastries. They all taste wearily alike. The young woman shakes her head. I shake mine, but the q-b, like a child, is pleased. Most pleased of all, however, are the blue-bottles, who dart in a black-alpaca bunch to the tin altar, and there loudly buzz, wildly, above the sallow cakes.

The citron-cheeked, dry one, however, cares darkly nothing for cakes. He comes once more to twit us about wine. So much so that the Cagliari girl orders a glass of Marsala: and I must second her. So there we are, three little glasses of brown liquid. The Cagliari girl sips hers and suddenly flees. The q-b sips hers with infinite caution, and quietly retires. I finish the q-b's little glass, and my own, and the voracious blow-flies buzz derisively and excited. The yellow-cheeked one has disappeared with the bottle.

From the professorial cabin faint wails, sometimes almost fierce, as one or another is going to be ill. Only a thin door is between this state-room and them. The most down-trodden frayed ancient rag of a man goes discreetly with basins, trying not to let out glimpses of the awful within. I climb up to look at the vivid, drenching stars, to breathe the cold wind, to see the dark sea sliding. Then I too go to the cabin, and watch the sea run past the porthole for a minute, and insert myself like the meat in a sandwich into the tight lower bunk. Oh, infinitesimal cabin, where we sway like two matches in a match box! Oh strange, but even yet excellent gallop of a ship at sea.

I slept not so badly through the stifled, rolling night—in fact later on slept soundly. And the day was growing bright when I peered through the porthle, the sea was much smoother. It was a brilliant clear morning. I made haste and washed myself cursorily in the saucer that dribbled into a pail in a corner: there was not space even for one chair, this saucer was by my bunk-head. And I went on deck.

Ah the lovely morning! Away behind us the sun was just coming above the sea's horizon, and the sky all golden, all a joyous, fire-heated gold, and the sea was glassy bright, the wind gone still, the waves sunk into long, low undulations, the foam of the wake was pale ice-blue in the yellow air. Sweet, sweet wide morning on the sea, with the sun coming, swimming up, and a tall sailing bark, with her flat fore-ladder of sails delicately across the light, and a far-far steamer on the electric vivid morning horizon.

The lovely dawn: the lovely pure, wide morning in the mid-sea, so golden-aired and delighted, with the sea like sequins shaking, and the sky far, far, far above, unfathomably clear. How glad to be on a ship! What a golden hour for the heart of man! Ah if one could sail for ever, on a small quiet, lonely ship, from land to land and isle to isle, and saunter through the spaces of this lovely world, always through the spaces of this lovely world. Sweet it would be sometimes to come to the opaque earth, to block oneself against the stiff land, to annul the vibration of one's flight against the inertia of our *terra firma!* but life itself would be in the flight, the tremble of space. Ah the trembling of never-ended space, as one moves in flight! Space, and the frail vibration of space, the glad lonely wringing of the heart. Not to be clogged to the land any more. Not to be any more like a donkey with a log on its leg, fastened to weary earth that has no answer now. But to be off.

To find three masculine, world-lost souls, and world-lost saunter, and saunter on along with them, across the dithering space, as long as life lasts! Why come to anchor? There is nothing to anchor for. Land has no answer to the soul any more. It has gone inert. Give me a little ship, kind gods, and three world-lost comrades. Hear me! And let me wander aimless across this vivid outer world, the world empty of man, where space flies happily.

The lovely, celandine-yellow morning of the open sea, paling towards a rare, sweet blue! The sun stood above the horizon, like the great burning stigma of the sacred flower of day. Mediterranean sailing-ships, so mediaeval, hovered on the faint morning wind, as if uncertain which way to go, curious, odd-winged insects of the flower. The steamer, hull-down, was sinking towards Spain. Space rang clear about us: the level sea!

Appeared the Cagliari young woman and her two friends. She was looking handsome and restored now the sea was easy. Her two male friends stood touching her, one at either shoulder.

"Bonjour, Monsieur!" she barked across at me. "Vous avez pris le café?"

"Pas encore. Et vous?"

"Non! Madame votre femme...."

She roared like a mastiff dog: and then translated with unction to her two uninitiated friends. How it was they did not understand her French I do not know, it was so like travestied Italian.

I went below to find the q-b.

When we came up, the faint shape of land appeared ahead, more transparent than thin pearl. Already Sardinia. Magic are high lands seen from the sea, when they are far, far off, and ghostly translucent like ice-bergs. This was Sardinia, looming like fascinating shadows in mid-sea. And the sailing ships, as if cut out of frailest pearl translucency, were wafting away towards Naples. I wanted to count their sails—five square ones which I call the ladder, one above the other—but how many wing-blades? That remained yet to be seen.

Our friend the carpenter spied us out: at least, he was not my friend. He didn't find me *simpatico*, I am sure. But up he came, and proceeded to entertain us with weary banality. Again the young woman called, had we had coffee? We said we were just going down. And then she said that whatever we had today we had to pay for: our food ended with the one day. At which the q-b was angry, feeling swindled. But I had known before.

We went down and had our coffee notwithstanding. The young woman came down, and made eyes at one of the alpaca blue-bottles. After which we saw a cup of coffee and milk and two biscuits being taken to her into her cabin, discreetly. When Italians are being discreet and on the sly, the very air about them becomes tell-tale, and seems to shout with a thousand tongues. So with a thousand invisible tongues clamouring the fact, the young woman had her coffee secretly and *gratis*, in her cabin.

But the morning was lovely. The q-b and I crept round the bench at the very stern of the ship and sat out of the wind and out of sight, just above the foaming of the wake. Before us was the open morning—and the glisten of our ship's track, like a snail's path, trailing across the sea: straight for a little while, then giving a bend to the left, always a bend towards the left: and coming at us from the pure horizon, like a bright snail-path. Happy it was to sit there in the stillness, with nothing but the humanless sea to shine about us.

But no, we were found out. Arrived the carpenter.

"Ah, you have found a fine place—!"

"Molto bello!" This from the q-b. I could not bear the irruption.

He proceeded to talk—and as is inevitable, the war. Ah, the war—it was a terrible thing. He had become ill—very ill. Because, you see, not only do you go without proper food, without proper rest and warmth, but, you see, you are in an agony of fear for your life all the time. An agony of fear for your life. And that's what does it. Six months in hospital—! The q-b, of course, was sympathetic.

The Sicilians are quite simple about it. They just tell you they were frightened to death, and it made them ill. The q-b, woman-like, loves them for being so simple about it. I feel angry somewhere. For they *expect* a full-blown sympathy. And however the great god Mars may have shrunk and gone wizened in the world, it still annoys me to hear him *so* blasphemed.

Near us the automatic log was spinning, the thin rope trailing behind us in the sea. Erratically it jerked and spun, with spasmodic torsion. He explained that the little screw at the end of the line spun to the speed of travelling. We were going from ten to twelve Italian miles to the hour. Ah, yes, we *could* go twenty. But we went no faster than ten or twelve, to save the coal.

The coal—il carbone! I knew we were in for it. England—l'Inghilterra she has the coal. And what does she do? She sells it very dear. Particularly to Italy. Italy won the war and now can't even have coal. Because why! The price. The exchange! *Il cambio.* Now I am doubly in for it. Two countries had been able to keep their money high—England and America. The English sovereign—la sterlina—and the American dollar—sa, these were money. The English and the Americans flocked to Italy, with their *sterline* and their *dollari*, and they bought what they wanted for nothing, for nothing. Ecco! Whereas we poor Italians—we are in a state of ruination—proper ruination. The allies, etc., etc.

I am so used to it—I am so wearily used to it. I can't walk a stride without having this wretched *cambio*, the exchange, thrown at my head. And this with an injured petulant spitefulness which turns my blood. For I assure them, whatever I have in Italy I pay for: and I am not England. I am not the British Isles on two legs.

Germany—La Germania—she did wrong to make the war. But—there you are, that was war. Italy and Germany—l'Italia e la Germania—they had always been friends. In Palermo....

My God, I felt I could not stand it another second. To sit above the foam and have this miserable creature stuffing wads of chewed newspaper into my ear—no, I could not bear it. In Italy, there is no escape. Say two words, and the individual starts chewing old newspaper and stuffing it into you. No escape. You become—if you are English—*l'Inghilterra*, *il carbone*, and *il cambio*; and as England, coal and exchange you are treated. It is more than useless to try to be human about it. You are a State usury system, a coal fiend and an exchange thief. Every Englishman has disappeared into this triple abstraction, in the eyes of the Italian, of the proletariat particularly. Try and get them to be human, try and get them to see that you are simply an individual, if you can. After all, I am no more than a single human man wandering my lonely way across these years. But no—to an Italian I am a perfected abstraction, England—coal—exchange. The Germans were once devils for inhuman theoretic abstracting of living beings. But now the Italians beat them. I am a walking column of statistics, which adds up badly for Italy. Only this and nothing more. Which being so, I shut my mouth and walk away.

For the moment the carpenter is shaken off. But I am in a rage, fool that I am. It is like being pestered by their mosquitoes. The sailing ships are near—and I count fifteen sails. Beautiful they look! Yet if I were on board somebody would be chewing newspaper at me, and addressing me as England—coal—exchange.

The mosquito hovers—and hovers. But the stony blank of the side of my cheek keeps him away. Yet he hovers. And the q-b feels sympathetic towards him: quite sympathetic. Because of course he treats her—a *bel pezzo*—as if he would lick her boots, or anything else that she would let him lick.

Meanwhile we eat the apples from yesterday's dessert, and the remains of the q-b's Infant-Jesus-and-dove cake. The land is drawing nearer—we can see the shape of the end promontory and peninsula—and a white speck like a church. The bulk of the land is forlorn and rather shapeless, coming towards us: but attractive.

Looking ahead towards the land gives us away. The mosquito swoops on us. Yes—he is not sure—he thinks the white speck is a church—or a lighthouse. When you pass the cape on the right, and enter the wide bay between Cape Spartivento and Cape Carbonara, then you have two hours sail to Cagliari. We shall arrive between two and three o'clock. It is now eleven.

Yes, the sailing ships are probably going to Naples. There is not much wind for them now. When there is wind they go fast, faster than our steamer. Ah Naples—bella, bella, eh? A little dirty, say I. But what do you want? says he. A great city! Palermo of course is better.

Ah—the Neapolitan women—he says, à propos or not. They do their hair so fine, so neat and beautiful—but underneath—sotto—sotto—they are dirty. This being received in cold silence, he continues: *Noi giriamo il mondo! Noi, chi giriamo, conosciamo il mondo. We* travel about, and *we* know the world. Who *we* are, I do not know: his highness the Palermitan carpenter lout, no doubt. But *we*, who travel, know the world. He is preparing his shot. The Neapolitan women, and the English women, in this are equal: that they are dirty underneath. Underneath, they are dirty. The women of London—

But it is getting too much for me.

"You who look for dirty women," say I, "find dirty women everywhere."

He stops short and watches me.

"No! No! You have not understood me. No! I don't mean that. I mean that the Neapolitan women and the English women have dirty underclothing—"

To which he gets no answer but a cold look and a cold cheek. Whereupon he turns to the q-b, and proceeds to be *simpatica*. And after a few moments he turns again to me:

"Il signore is offended! He is offended with me."

But I turn the other way. And at last he clears out: in triumph, I must admit: like a mosquito that has bitten one in the neck. As a matter of fact one should *never* let these fellows get into conversation nowadays. They are no longer human beings. They hate one's Englishness, and leave out the individual.

We walk forward, towards the fore-deck, where the captain's lookout cabin is. The captain is an elderly man, silent and crushed: with the look of a gentleman. But he looks beaten down. Another, still another member of the tray-carrying department is just creeping up his ladder with a cup of black coffee. Returning, we peep down the sky-light into the kitchen. And there we see roast chicken and sausages—roast chicken and sausages! Ah, this is where the sides of kid and the chickens and the good things go: all down the throats of the crew. There is no more food for us, until we land.

We have passed the cape—and the white thing is a lighthouse. And the fattish, handsome professor has come up carrying the little girl-child, while the femalish elder brother leads the rabbit-fluffy small boy by the hand. So *en famille*: so terribly *en famille*. They deposit themselves near us, and it threatens another conversation. But not for anything, my dears!

The sailors—not sailors, some of the street-corner loafers, are hoisting the flag, the red-white-and-green Italian tricolor. It floats at the mast-head, and the femalish brother, in a fine burst of feeling, takes off his funny hat with a flourish and cries:

"Ecco la bandiera italiana!"

Ach, the hateful sentimentalism of these days.

The land passes slowly, very slowly. It is hilly, but barren looking, with few trees. And it is not spikey and rather splendid, like Sicily. Sicily has style. We keep along the east side of the bay—away in the west is Cape Spartivento. And still no sight of Cagliari.

"Two hours yet!" cries the Cagliari girl. "Two hours before we eat. Ah, when I get on land, what a good meal I shall eat."

The men haul in the automatic log. The sky is clouding over with that icy curd which comes after midday when the bitter north wind is blowing. It is no longer warm.

Slowly, slowly we creep along the formless shore. An hour passes. We see a little fort ahead, done in enormous black-and-white checks, like a fragment of gigantic chess-board. It stands at the end of a long spit of land—a long, barish peninsula that has no houses and looks as if it might be golf-links. But it is not golf-links.

And suddenly there is Cagliari: a naked town rising steep, steep, golden-look-ing, piled naked to the sky from the plain at the head of the formless hollow bay. It is strange and rather wonderful, not a bit like Italy. The city piles up lofty and almost miniature, and makes me think of Jerusalem: without trees, without cover, rising rather bare and proud, remote as if back in history, like a town in a monkish, illuminated missal. One wonders how it ever got there. And it seems like Spain—or Malta: not Italy. It is a steep and lonely city, treeless, as in some old illumination. Yet withal rather jewel-like: like a sudden rose-cut amber jewel naked at the depth of the vast indenture. The air is cold, blowing bleak and bitter, the sky is all curd. And that is Cagliari. It has that curious look, as if it could be seen, but not entered. It is like some vision, some memory, something that has passed away. Impossible that one can actually *walk* in that city: set foot there and eat and laugh there. Ah, no! Yet the ship drifts nearer, nearer, and we are looking for the actual harbour.

The usual sea-front with dark trees for a promenade and palatial buildings behind, but here not so pink and gay, more reticent, more sombre of yellow stone. The harbour itself a little basin of water, into which we are slipping carefully, while three salt-barges laden with salt as white as snow creep round from the left, drawn by an infinitesimal tug. There are only two other forlorn ships in the basin. It is cold on deck. The ship turns slowly round, and is being hauled to the quay side. I go down for the knapsack, and a fat blue-bottle pounces at me.

"You pay nine francs fifty."

I pay them, and we get off that ship.

III. CAGLIARI

There is a very little crowd waiting on the quay: mostly men with their hands in their pockets. But, thank Heaven, they have a certain aloofness and reserve. They are not like the tourist-parasites of these post-war days, who move to the attack with a terrifying cold vindictiveness the moment one emerges from any vehicle. And some of these men look really poor. There are no poor Italians any more: at least, loafers.

Strange the feeling round the harbour: as if everybody had gone away. Yet there are people about. It is "festa" however, Epiphany. But it is so different from Sicily: none of the suave Greek-Italian charms, none of the airs and graces, none of the glamour. Rather bare, rather stark, rather cold and yellow—somehow like Malta, without Malta's foreign liveliness. Thank Goodness no one wants to carry my knapsack. Thank Goodness no one has a fit at the sight of it. Thank Heaven no one takes any notice. They stand cold and aloof, and don't move.

We make our way through the Customs: then through the Dazio, the City Customs-house. Then we are free. We set off up a steep, new, broad road, with little trees on either side. But stone, arid, new, wide stone, yellowish under the cold sky—and abandoned-seeming. Though, of course, there are people about. The north wind blows bitingly.

We climb a broad flight of steps, always upwards, up the wide, precipitous, dreary boulevard with sprouts of trees. Looking for the Hotel, and dying with hunger.

At last we find it, the Scala di Ferro: through a courtyard with green plants. And at last a little man with lank, black hair, like an esquimo, comes smiling. He is one brand of Sardinian—esquimo looking. There is no room with two beds: only single rooms. And thus we are led off, if you please, to the "bagnio": the bathing-establishment wing, on the dank ground floor. Cubicles on either side a stone passage, and in every cubicle a dark stone bath, and a little bed. We can have each a little bath cubicle. If there's nothing else for it, there isn't: but it seems dank and cold and horrid, underground. And one thinks of all the unsavory "assignations" at these old bagnio places. True, at the end of the passage are seated two carabinieri. But whether to ensure respectibility or not, Heaven knows. We are in the baths, that's all.

The esquimo returns after five minutes, however. There *is* a bedroom in the house. He is pleased, because he didn't like putting us into the bagnio. Where he found the bedroom I don't know. But there it was, large, sombre, cold, and over the kitchen fumes of a small inner court like a well. But perfectly clean and all right. And the people seemed warm and good-natured, like human beings. One has got so used to the non-human ancient-souled Sicilians, who are suave and so completely callous.

After a really good meal we went out to see the town. It was after three o'clock and everywhere was shut up like an English Sunday. Cold, stony Cagliari: in summer you must be sizzling hot, Cagliari, like a kiln. The men stood about in groups, but without the intimate Italian watchfulness that never leaves a pass-er-by alone.

Strange, stony Cagliari. We climbed up a street like a corkscrew stairway. And we saw announcements of a children's fancy-dress ball. Cagliari is very steep. Half-way up there is a strange place called the bastions, a large, level space like a drill-ground with trees, curiously suspended over the town, and send-ing off a long shoot like a wide viaduct, across above the corkscrew street that comes climbing up. Above this bastion place the town still rises steeply to the Cathedral and the fort. What is so curious is that this terrace or bastion is so large, like some big recreation ground, that it is almost dreary, and one cannot understand its being suspended in mid-air. Down below is the little circle of the harbour. To the left a low, malarial-looking sea plain, with tufts of palm trees and Arab-looking houses. From this runs out the long spit of land towards that black-and-white watch-fort, the white road trailing forth. On the right, most curiously, a long strange spit of sand runs in a causeway far across the shallows of the bay, with the open sea on one hand, and vast, end-of-the-world lagoons on the other. There are peaky, dark mountains beyond this—just as across the vast bay are gloomy hills. It is a strange, strange landscape: as if here the world left off. The bay is vast in itself; and all these curious things happening at its head: this curious, craggy-studded town, like a great stud of house-covered rock jutting up out of the bay flats: around it on one side the weary, Arab-looking palm-deso-lated malarial plain, and on the other side great salt lagoons, dead beyond the sand-bar: these backed again by serried, clustered mountains, suddenly, while away beyond the plain, hills rise to sea again. Land and sea both seem to give out, exhausted, at the bay head: the world's end. And into this world's end starts up Cagliari, and on either side, sudden, serpent-crest hills.

But it still reminds me of Malta: lost between Europe and Africa and belong-ing to nowhere. Belonging to nowhere, never having belonged to anywhere. To Spain and the Arabs and the Phœnicians most. But as if it had never really had a fate. No fate. Left outside of time and history.

The spirit of the place is a strange thing. Our mechanical age tries to override it. But it does not succeed. In the end the strange, sinister spirit of the place, so diverse and adverse in differing places, will smash our mechanical oneness into smithereens, and all that we think the real thing will go off with a pop, and we shall be left staring.

On the great parapet above the Municipal Hall and above the corkscrew high-street a thick fringe of people is hanging, looking down. We go to look too: and behold, below there is the entrance to the ball. Yes, there is a china shepherdess in pale blue and powdered hair, crook, ribbons, Marie Antoinette satin dainti-ness and all, slowly and haughtily walking up the road, and gazing superbly round. She is not more than twelve years old, moreover. Two servants accom-pany her. She gazes supremely from right to left as she goes, mincingly, and I would give her the prize for haughtiness. She is perfect—a little too haughty for Watteau, but "marquise" to a T. The people watch in silence. There is no yelling and screaming and running. They watch in a suitable silence.

Comes a carriage with two fat bay horses slithering, almost swimming up the corkscrew high-street. That in itself is a "tour-de-force": for Cagliari doesn't have carriages. Imagine a street like a corkscrew stair, paved with slippery stone. And imagine two bay horses rowing their way up it: they did not walk a single stride. But they arrived. And there fluttered out three strangely exquisite chil-dren, two frail, white satin Pierrots and a white satin Pierrette. They were like fragile winter butterflies with black spots. They had a curious, indefinable remote elegance, something conventional and "fin-de-siècle". But not our century. The wonderful artificial delicacy of the eighteenth. The boys had big, perfect ruffs round their necks: and behind were slung old, cream-colored Spanish shawls, for warmth. They were frail as tobacco flowers, and with remote, cold elegance they fluttered by the carriage, from which emerged a large black-satin Mama. Fluttering their queer little butterfly feet on the pavement, hovering round the large Mama like three frail-tissued ghosts, they found their way past the solid, seated Carabinieri into the hall.

Arrived a primrose-brocade beau, with ruffles, and his hat under his arm: about twelve years old. Walking statelily, without a qualm up the steep twist of the street. Or perhaps so perfect in his self-consciousness that it became an elegant "aplomb" in him. He was a genuine eighteenth-century exquisite, rather stiffer than the French, maybe, but completely in the spirit. Curious, curious children! They had a certain stand-offish superbness, and not a single trace of misgiving. For them, their "noblesse" was indisputable. For the first time in my life I recognized the true cold superbness of the old "noblesse". They had not a single qualm about their own perfect representing of the higher order of being.

Followed another white satin "marquise", with a maid-servant. They are strong on the eighteenth century in Cagliari. Perhaps it is the last bright reality to them. The nineteenth hardly counts.

Curious the children in Cagliari. The poor seem thoroughly poor-bare-footed urchins, gay and wild in the narrow dark streets. But the more well-to-do children are so fine: so extraordinarily elegantly dressed. It quite strikes one of a heap. Not so much the grown-ups. The children. All the "chic," all the fashion, all the originality is expended on the children. And with a great deal of success. Better than Kensington Gardens very often. And they promenade with Papa and Mama with such alert assurance, having quite brought it off, their fashionable get-up. Who would have expected it?

Oh narrow, dark, and humid streets going up to the Cathedral, like crevices. I narrowly miss a huge pail of slop-water which comes crashing down from heaven. A small boy who was playing in the street, and whose miss is not quite a clean miss, looks up with that naïve, impersonal wonder with which children stare at a star or a lamp-lighter.

The Cathedral must have been a fine old pagan stone fortress once. Now it has come, as it were, through the mincing machine of the ages, and oozed out baroque and sausagey, a bit like the horrible baldachins in St. Peter's at Rome. None the less it is homely and hole-and-cornery, with a rather ragged high mass trailing across the pavement towards the high altar, since it is almost sunset, and Epiphany. It feels as if one might squat in a corner and play marbles and eat bread and cheese and be at home: a comfortable old-time churchey feel.

There is some striking filet lace on the various altar-cloths. And St. Joseph must be a prime saint. He has an altar and a verse of invocation praying for the dying.

"Oh, St. Joseph, true potential father of Our Lord." What can it profit a man, I wonder, to be the potential father of anybody! For the rest I am not Baedeker.

The top of Cagliari is the fortress: the old gate, the old ramparts, of honey-combed, fine yellowish sandstone. Up in a great sweep goes the rampart wall, Spanish and splendid, dizzy. And the road creeping down again at the foot, down the back of the hill. There lies the country: that dead plain with its bunch of palms and a fainting sea, and inland again, hills. Cagliari must be on a single, loose, lost bluff of rock.

From the terrace just below the fortress, above the town, not behind it, we stand and look at the sunset. It is all terrible, taking place beyond the knotted, serpent-crested hills that lie, bluey and velvety, beyond the waste lagoons. Dark, sultry, heavy crimson the west is, hanging sinisterly, with those gloomy blue cloud-bars and cloud-banks drawn across. All behind the blue-gloomy peaks stretches the curtain of sinister, smouldering red, and away to the sea. Deep below lie the sea-meres. They seem miles and miles, and utterly waste. But the sand-bar crosses like a bridge, and has a road. All the air is dark, a sombre bluish tone. The great west burns inwardly, sullenly, and gives no glow, yet a deep red. It is cold.

We go down the steep streets, smelly, dark, dank, and very cold. No wheeled vehicle can scramble up them, presumably. People live in one room. Men are combing their hair or fastening their collars in the doorways. Evening is here, and it is a feast day.

At the bottom of the street we come to a little bunch of masked youths, one in a long yellow frock and a frilled bonnet, another like an old woman, another in red twill. They are arm in arm and are accosting the passers-by. The q-b gives a cry, and looks for escape. She has a terror of maskers, a terror that comes from childhood. To say the truth, so have I. We hasten invisibly down the far side of the street, and come out under the bastions. Then we go down our own familiar wide, short, cold boulevard to the sea.

At the bottom, again, is a carriage with more maskers. Carnival is beginning. A man dressed as a peasant woman in native costume is clambering with his great wide skirts and wide strides on to the box, and, flourishing his ribboned whip, is addressing a little crowd of listeners. He opens his mouth wide and goes on with a long yelling harangue of taking a drive with his mother—another man in old-woman's gaudy finery and wig who sits already bobbing on the box. The would-be daughter flourishes, yells, and prances up there on the box of the carriage. The crowd listens attentively and mildly smiles. It all seems real to them. The q-b hovers in the distance, half-fascinated, and watches. With a great flourish of whip and legs—showing his frilled drawers—the masker pulls round to drive along the boulevard by the sea—the only place where one can drive.

The big street by the sea is the Via Roma. It has the cafés on one side and across the road the thick tufts of trees intervening between the sea and us. Among these thick tufts of sea-front trees the little steam tram, like a little train, bumps to rest, after having wound round the back of the town.

The Via Roma is all social Cagliari. Including the cafés with their outdoor tables on the one side of the road, and the avenue strand on the other, it is very wide, and at evening it contains the whole town. Here, and here alone carriages can spank along, very slowly, officers can ride, and the people can promenade "en masse."

We were amazed at the sudden crowd we found ourselves amongst—like a short, dense river of people streaming slowly in a mass. There is practically no vehicular traffic—only the steady dense streams of human beings of all sorts, all on a human footing. It must have been something like this in the streets of imperial Rome, where no chariots might drive and humanity was all on foot.

Little bunches of maskers, and single maskers danced and strutted along in the thick flow under the trees. If you are a mask you don't walk like a human being: you dance and prance along extraordinarily like the life-size marionettes, conducted by wires from above. That is how you go: with that odd jauntiness as if lifted and propelled by wires from the shoulders. In front of me went a charming coloured harlequin, all in diamond-shaped colours, and beautiful as a piece of china. He tripped with the light, fantastic trip, quite alone in the thick crowd, and quite blithe. Came two little children hand in hand in brilliant scarlet and white costumes, sauntering calmly. They did not do the mask trip. After a while a sky-blue girl with a high hat and full skirts, very short, that went flip-flip-flip, as a ballet dancer's, whilst she strutted; after her a Spanish grandee capering like a monkey. They threaded among the slow stream of the crowd. Appeared Dante and Beatrice, in Paradise apparently, all in white sheet-robes, and with silver wreaths on their heads, arm in arm, and prancing very slowly and majestically, yet with the long lilt as if hitched along by wires from above. They were very good: all the well-known vision come to life, Dante incorporate, and white as a shroud, with his tow-haired, silver-crowned, immortal Beatrice on his arm, strutting the dark avenues. He had the nose and cheek-bones and banded cheek, and the stupid wooden look, and offered a modern criticism on the Inferno.

It had become quite dark, the lamps were lighted. We crossed the road to the Café Roma, and found a table on the pavement among the crowd. In a moment we had our tea. The evening was cold, with ice in the wind. But the crowd surged on, back and forth, back and forth, slowly. At the tables were seated mostly men, taking coffee or vermouth or aqua vitae, all familiar and easy, without the modern self-consciousness. There was a certain pleasant, natural robustness of spirit, and something of a feudal free-and-easiness. Then arrived a family, with children, and nurse in her native costume. They all sat at table together, perfectly easy with one another, though the marvellous nurse seemed to be seated below the salt. She was bright as a poppy, in a rose-scarlet dress of fine cloth, with a curious little waistcoat of emerald green and purple, and a bodice of soft, homespun linen with great full sleeves. On her head she had a rose-scarlet and white head-dress, and she wore great studs of gold filigree, and similar ear-rings. The feudal-bourgeois family drank its syrup-drinks and watched the crowd. Most remarkable is the complete absence of self-consciousness. They all have a perfect natural "sang-froid," the nurse in her marvellous native costume is as thoroughly at her ease as if she were in her own village street. She moves and speaks and calls to a passer-by without the slightest constraint, and much more, without the slightest presumption. She is below the invisible salt, the invisible but insuperable salt. And it strikes me the salt-barrier is a fine thing for both parties: they both remain natural and human on either side of it, instead of becoming devilish, scrambling and pushing at the barricade.

The crowd is across the road, under the trees near the sea. On this side stroll occasional pedestrians. And I see my first peasant in costume. He is an elderly, upright, handsome man, beautiful in the black-and-white costume. He wears the full-sleeved white shirt and the close black bodice of thick, native frieze, cut low. From this sticks out a short kilt or frill, of the same black frieze, a band of which goes between the legs, between the full loose drawers of coarse linen. The drawers are banded below the knee into tight black frieze gaiters. On his head he has the long black stocking cap, hanging down behind. How handsome he is, and so beautifully male! He walks with his hands loose behind his back, slowly, upright, and aloof. The lovely unapproachableness, indomitable. And the flash of the black and white, the slow stride of the full white drawers, the black gaiters and black cuirass with the bolero, then the great white sleeves and white breast again, and once more the black cap—what marvellous massing of the contrast, marvellous, and superb, as on a magpie.—How beautiful maleness is, if it finds its right expression.—And how perfectly ridiculous it is made in modern clothes.

There is another peasant too, a young one with a swift eye and hard cheek and hard, dangerous thighs. He has folded his stocking cap, so that it comes forward to his brow like a phrygian cap. He wears close knee breeches and close sleeved waistcoat of thick brownish stuff that looks like leather. Over the waistcoat a sort of cuirass of black, rusty sheepskin, the curly wool outside. So he strides, talking to a comrade. How fascinating it is, after the soft Italians, to see these limbs in their close knee-breeches, so definite, so manly, with the old fierceness in them still. One realises, with horror, that the race of men is almost extinct in Europe. Only Christ-like heroes and woman-worshipping Don Juans, and rabid equality-mongrels. The old, hardy, indomitable male is gone. His fierce single-ness is quenched. The last sparks are dying out in Sardinia and Spain. Nothing left but the herd-proletariat and the herd-equality mongrelism, and the wistful poisonous self-sacrificial cultured soul. How detestable.

But that curious, flashing, black-and-white costume! I seem to have known it before: to have worn it even: to have dreamed it. To have dreamed it: to have had actual contact with it. It belongs in some way to something in me—to my past, perhaps. I don't know. But the uneasy sense of blood-familiarity haunts me. I *know* I have known it before. It is something of the same uneasiness I feel before Mount Eryx: but without the awe this time.

In the morning the sun was shining from a blue, blue sky, but the shadows were deadly cold, and the wind like a flat blade of ice. We went out running to the sun. The hotel could not give us coffee and milk: only a little black coffee. So we descended to the sea-front again, to the Via Roma, and to our café. It was Friday: people seemed to be bustling in from the country with huge baskets.

The Café Roma had coffee and milk, but no butter. We sat and watched the movement outside. Tiny Sardinian donkeys, the tiniest things ever seen, trotted their infinitesimal little paws along the road, drawing little wagons like hand-carts. Their proportion is so small, that they make a boy walking at their side look like a tall man, while a natural man looks like a Cyclops stalking hugely and cruelly. It is ridiculous for a grown man to have one of these little creatures, hardly bigger than a fly, hauling his load for him. One is pulling a chest of drawers on a cart, and it seems to have a whole house behind it. Nevertheless it plods bravely, away beneath the load, a wee thing.

They tell me there used to be flocks of these donkeys, feeding half wild on the wild, moor-like hills of Sardinia. But the war—and also the imbecile wantonness of the war-masters—consumed these flocks too, so that few are left. The same with the cattle. Sardinia, home of cattle, hilly little Argentine of the Mediterranean, is now almost deserted. It is war, say the Italiana.—And also the wanton, imbecile, foul lavishness of the war-masters. It was not alone the war which exhausted the world. It was the deliberate evil wastefulness of the war-makers in their own countries. Italy ruined Italy.

Two peasants in black-and-white are strolling in the sun, flashing. And my dream of last evening was not a dream. And my nostalgia for something I know not what was not an illusion. I feel it again, at once, at the sight of the men in frieze and linen, a heart yearning for something I have known, and which I want back again.

It is market day. We turn up the Largo Carlo-Felice, the second wide gap of a street, a vast but very short boulevard, like the end of something. Cagliari is like that: all bits and bobs. And by the side of the pavement are many stalls, stalls selling combs and collar-studs, cheap mirrors, handkerchiefs, shoddy Manchester goods, bed-ticking, boot-paste, poor crockery, and so on. But we see also Madame of Cagliari going marketing, with a servant accompanying her, carrying a huge grass-woven basket: or returning from marketing, followed by a small boy supporting one of these huge grass-woven baskets—like huge dishes—on his head, piled with bread, eggs, vegetables, a chicken, and so forth. Therefore we follow Madame going marketing, and find ourselves in the vast market house, and it fairly glows with eggs: eggs in these great round dish-baskets of golden grass: but eggs in piles, in mounds, in heaps, a Sierra Nevada of eggs, glowing warm white. How they glow! I have never noticed it before. But they give off a warm, pearly effulgence into the air, almost a warmth. A pearly-gold heat seems to come out of them. Myriads of eggs, glowing avenues of eggs.

And they are marked—60 centimes, 65 centimes. Ah, cries the q-b, I must live in Cagliari—For in Sicily the eggs cost 1.50 each.

This is the meat and poultry and bread market. There are stalls of new, various-shaped bread, brown and bright: there are tiny stalls of marvellous native cakes, which I want to taste, there is a great deal of meat and kid: and there are stalls of cheese, all cheeses, all shapes, all whitenesses, all the cream-colours, on into daffodil yellow. Goat cheese, sheeps cheese, Swiss cheese, Parmegiano, stracchino, caciocavallo, torolone, how many cheeses I don't know the names of! But they cost about the same as in Sicily, eighteen francs, twenty francs, twenty-five francs the kilo. And there is lovely ham—thirty and thirty-five francs the kilo. There is a little fresh butter too—thirty or thirty-two francs the kilo. Most of the butter, however, is tinned in Milan. It costs the same as the fresh. There are splendid piles of salted black olives, and huge bowls of green salted olives. There are chickens and ducks and wild-fowl: at eleven and twelve and fourteen francs a kilo. There is mortadella, the enormous Bologna sausage, thick as a church pillar: 16 francs: and there are various sorts of smaller sausage, salami, to be eaten in slices. A wonderful abundance of food, glowing and shining. We are rather late for fish, especially on Friday. But a barefooted man offers us two weird objects from the Mediterranean, which teems with marine monsters.

The peasant women sit behind their wares, their home-woven linen skirts, hugely full, and of various colours, ballooning round them. The yellow baskets give off a glow of light. There is a sense of profusion once more. But alas no sense of cheapness: save the eggs. Every month, up goes the price of everything.

"I must come and live in Cagliari, to do my shopping here," says the q-b. "I must have one of those big grass baskets."

We went down to the little street—but saw more baskets emerging from a broad flight of stone stairs, enclosed. So up we went-and found ourselves in the vegetable market. Here the q-b was happier still. Peasant women, sometimes barefoot, sat in their tight little bodices and voluminous, coloured skirts behind the piles of vegetables, and never have I seen a lovelier show. The intense deep green of spinach seemed to predominate, and out of that came the monuments of curd-white and black-purple cauliflowers: but marvellous cauliflowers, like a flower-show, the purple ones intense as great bunches of violets. From this green, white, and purple massing struck out the vivid rose-scarlet and blue crimson of radishes, large radishes like little turnips, in piles. Then the long, slim, grey-purple buds of artichokes, and dangling clusters of dates, and piles of sugar-dusty white figs and sombre-looking black figs, and bright burnt figs: basketfuls and basketfuls of figs. A few baskets of almonds, and many huge walnuts. Basket-pans of native raisins. Scarlet peppers like trumpets: magnificent fennels, so white and big and succulent: baskets of new potatoes: scaly kohlrabi: wild asparagus in bunches, yellow-budding sparacelli: big, clean-fleshed carrots: feathery salads with white hearts: long, brown-purple onions and then, of course pyramids of big oranges, pyramids of pale apples, and baskets of brilliant shiny mandarini, the little tangerine orange with their green-black leaves. The green and vivid-coloured world of fruit-gleams I have never seen in such splendour as under the market roof at Cagliari: so raw and gorgeous. And all quite cheap, the one remaining cheapness, except potatoes. Potatoes of any sort are 1.40 or 1.50 the kilo.

"Oh!" cried the q-b, "If I don't live at Cagliari and come and do my shopping here, I shall die with one of my wishes unfulfilled."

But out of the sun it was cold, nevertheless. We went into the streets to try and get warm. The sun was powerful. But alas, as in southern towns generally, the streets are sunless as wells.

So the q-b and I creep slowly along the sunny bits, and then perforce are swallowed by shadow. We look at the shops. But there is not much to see. Little, frowsy provincial shops, on the whole.

But a fair number of peasants in the streets, and peasant women in rather ordinary costume: tight-bodiced, volume-skirted dresses of hand-woven linen or thickish cotton. The prettiest is of dark-blue-and-red, stripes-and-lines, intermingled, so made that the dark-blue gathers round the waist into one colour, the myriad pleats hiding all the rosy red. But when she walks, the full-petticoated peasant woman, then the red goes flash-flash-flash, like a bird showing its colours. Pretty that looks in the sombre street. She has a plain, light bodice with a peak: sometimes a little vest, and great full white sleeves, and usually a handkerchief or shawl loose knotted. It is charming the way they walk, with quick, short steps. When all is said and done, the most attractive costume for women in my eye, is the tight little bodice and the many-pleated skirt, full and vibrating with movement. It has a charm which modern elegance lacks completely—a bird-like play in movement.

They are amusing, these peasant girls and women: so brisk and defiant. They have straight backs, like little walls, and decided, well-drawn brows. And they are amusingly on the alert. There is no eastern creeping. Like sharp, brisk birds they dart along the streets, and you feel they would fetch you a bang over the head as leave as look at you. Tenderness, thank heaven, does not seem to be a Sardinian quality. Italy is so tender—like cooked macaroni—yards and yards of soft tenderness ravelled round everything. Here men don't idealise women, by the looks of things. Here they don't make these great leering eyes, the inevitable yours-to-command look of Italian males. When the men from the country look at these women, then it is Mind-yourself, my lady. I should think the grovelling Madonna-worship is not much of a Sardinian feature. These women have to look out for themselves, keep their own back-bone stiff and their knuckles hard.

Man is going to be male Lord if he can. And woman isn't going to give him too much of his own way, either. So there you have it, the fine old martial split between the sexes. It is tonic and splendid, really, after so much sticky intermingling and backboneless Madonna-worship. The Sardinian isn't looking for the "noble woman nobly planned." No, thank you. He wants that young madam over there, a young stiff-necked generation that she is. Far better sport than with the nobly-planned sort: hollow frauds that they are. Better sport too than with a Carmen, who gives herself away too much, In these women there is something shy and defiant and un-get-atable. The defiant, splendid split between the sexes, each absolutely determined to defend his side, her side, from assault. So the meeting has a certain wild, salty savour, each the deadly unknown to the other. And at the same time, each his own, her own native pride and courage, taking the dangerous leap and scrambling back.

Give me the old, salty way of love. How I am nauseated with sentiment and nobility, the macaroni slithery-slobbery mess of modern adorations.

One sees a few fascinating faces in Cagliari: those great dark unlighted eyes. There are fascinating dark eyes in Sicily, bright, big, with an impudent point of light, and a curious roll, and long lashes: the eyes of old Greece, surely. But here one sees eyes of soft, blank darkness, all velvet, with no imp looking out of them. And they strike a stranger, older note: before the soul became self-conscious: before the mentality of Greece appeared in the world. Remote, always remote, as if the intelligence lay deep within the cave, and never came forward. One searches into the gloom for one second, while the glance lasts. But without being able to penetrate to the reality. It recedes, like some unknown creature deeper into its lair. There is a creature, dark and potent. But what?

Sometimes Velasquez, and sometimes Goya gives us a suggestion of these large, dark, unlighted eyes. And they go with fine, fleecy black hair—almost as fine as fur. I have not seen them north of Cagliari.

The q-b spies some of the blue-and-red stripe-and-line cotton stuff of which the peasants make their dress: a large roll in the doorway of a dark shop. In we go, and begin to feel it. It is just soft, thickish cotton stuff—twelve francs a metre. Like most peasant patterns, it is much more complicated and subtle than appears: the curious placing of the stripes, the subtle proportion, and a white thread left down one side only of each broad blue block. The stripes, moreover, run *across* the cloth, not lengthwise with it. But the width would be just long enough for a skirt—though the peasant skirts have almost all a band at the bottom with the stripes running round-ways.

The man—he is the esquimo type, simple, frank and aimiable—says the stuff is made in France, and this the first roll since the war. It is the old, old pattern, quite correct—but the material not *quite* so good. The q-b takes enough for a dress.

He shows us also cashmeres, orange, scarlet, sky-blue, royal blue: good, pure-wool cashmeres that were being sent to India, and were captured from a German mercantile sub-marine. So he says. Fifty francs a metre—very, very wide. But they are too much trouble to carry in a knapsack, though their brilliance fascinates.

So we stroll and look at the shops, at the filigree gold jewelling of the peasants, at a good bookshop. But there is little to see and therefore the question is, shall we go on? Shall we go forward?

There are two ways of leaving Cagliari for the north: the State railway that runs up the west side of the island, and the narrow-gauge secondary railway that pierces the centre. But we are too late for the big trains. So we will go by the secondary railway, wherever it goes.

There is a train at 2.30, and we can get as far as Mandas, some fifty miles in the interior. When we tell the queer little waiter at the hotel, he says he comes from Mandas, and there are two inns. So after lunch—a strictly fish menu—we pay our bill. It comes to sixty odd francs—for three good meals each, with wine, and the night's lodging, this is cheap, as prices now are in Italy.

Pleased with the simple and friendly Scala di Ferre, I shoulder my sack and we walk off to the second station. The sun is shining hot this afternoon—burning hot, by the sea. The road and the buildings look dry and desiccated, the harbour rather weary and end of the world.

There is a great crowd of peasants at the little station. And almost every man has a pair of woven saddle-bags—a great flat strip of coarse-woven wool, with flat pockets at either end, stuffed with purchases. These are almost the only carrying bags. The men sling them over their shoulder, so that one great pocket hangs in front, one behind.

These saddle bags are most fascinating. They are coarsely woven in bands of raw black-rusty wool, with varying bands of raw white wool or hemp or cotton—the bands and stripes of varying widths going cross-wise. And on the pale bands are woven sometimes flowers in most lovely colours, rose-red and blue and green, peasant patterns—and sometimes fantastic animals, beasts, in dark wool again. So that these striped zebra bags, some wonderful gay with flowery colours on their stripes, some weird with fantastic, griffin-like animals, are a whole landscape in themselves.

The train has only first and third class. It costs about thirty francs for the two of us, third class to Mandas, which is some sixty miles. In we crowd with the joyful saddle-bags, into the wooden carriage with its many seats.

And, wonder of wonders, punctually to the second, off we go, out of Cagliari. En route again.

IV. MANDAS

The coach was fairly full of people, returning from market. On these railways the third class coaches are not divided into compartments. They are left open, so that one sees everybody, as down a room. The attractive saddle-bags, *bercole*, were disposed anywhere, and the bulk of the people settled down to a lively *conversazione*. It is much nicest, on the whole, to travel third class on the railway. There is space, there is air, and it is like being in a lively inn, everybody in good spirits.

At our end was plenty of room. Just across the gangway was an elderly couple, like two children, coming home very happily. He was fat, fat all over, with a white moustache and a little not-unamiable frown. She was a tall lean, brown woman, in a brown full-skirted dress and black apron, with huge pocket. She wore no head covering, and her iron grey hair was parted smoothly. They were rather pleased and excited being in the train. She took all her money out of her big pocket, and counted it and gave it to him: all the ten Lira notes, and the five Lira and the two and the one, peering at the dirty scraps of pink-backed one-lira notes to see if they were good. Then she gave him her half-pennies. And he stowed them away in the trouser pocket, standing up to push them down his fat leg. And then one saw, to one's amazement, that the whole of his shirt-tail was left out behind, like a sort of apron worn backwards. Why—a mystery. He was one of those fat, good-natured, unheeding men with a little masterful frown, such as usually have tall, lean, hard-faced, obedient wives.

They were very happy. With amazement he watched us taking hot tea from the Thermos flask. I think he too had suspected it might be a bomb. He had blue eyes and standing-up white eyebrows.

"Beautiful hot—!" he said, seeing the tea steam. It is the inevitable exclamation. "Does it do you good?"

"Yes," said the q-b. "Much good." And they both nodded complacently. They were going home.

The train was running over the malarial-looking sea-plain—past the down-at-heel palm trees, past the mosque-looking buildings. At a level crossing the woman crossing-keeper darted out vigorously with her red flag. And we rambled into the first village. It was built of sun-dried brick-adobe houses, thick adobe garden-walls, with tile ridges to keep off the rain. In the enclosures were dark orange trees. But the clay-coloured villages, clay-dry, looked foreign: the next thing to mere earth they seem, like fox-holes or coyote colonies.

Looking back, one sees Cagliari bluff on her rock, rather fine, with the thin edge of the sea's blade curving round. It is rather hard to believe in the real sea, on this sort of clay-pale plain.

But soon we begin to climb to the hills. And soon the cultivation begins to be intermittent. Extraordinary how the heathy, moor-like hills come near the sea: extraordinary how scrubby and uninhabited the great spaces of Sardinia are. It is wild, with heath and arbutus scrub and a sort of myrtle, breast-high. Sometimes one sees a few head of cattle. And then again come the greyish arable-patches, where the corn is grown. It is like Cornwall, like the Land's End region. Here and there, in the distance, are peasants working on the lonely landscape. Sometimes it is one man alone in the distance, showing so vividly in his black-and-white costume, small and far-off like a solitary magpie, and curiously distinct. All the strange magic of Sardinia is in this sight. Among the low, moor-like hills, away in a hollow of the wide landscape one solitary figure, small but vivid black-and-white, working alone, as if eternally. There are patches and hollows of grey arable land, good for corn. Sardinia was once a great granary.

Usually, however, the peasants of the South have left off the costume. Usually it is the invisible soldiers' grey-green cloth, the Italian khaki. Wherever you go, wherever you be, you see this khaki, this grey-green war-clothing. How many millions of yards of the thick, excellent, but hateful material the Italian government must have provided I don't know: but enough to cover Italy with a felt carpet, I should think. It is everywhere. It cases the tiny children in stiff and neutral frocks and coats, it covers their extinguished fathers, and sometimes it even encloses the women in its warmth. It is symbolic of the universal grey mist that has come over men, the extinguishing of all bright individuality, the blotting out of all wild singleness. Oh democracy! Oh khaki democracy!

This is very different from Italian landscape. Italy is almost always dramatic, and perhaps invariably romantic. There is drama in the plains of Lombardy, and romance in the Venetian lagoons, and sheer scenic excitement in nearly all the hilly parts of the peninsula. Perhaps it is the natural floridity of lime-stone formations. But Italian landscape is really eighteenth-century landscape, to be represented in that romantic-classic manner which makes everything rather marvelous and very topical: aqueducts, and ruins upon sugar-loaf mountains, and craggy ravines and Wilhelm Meister water-falls: all up and down.

Sardinia is another thing. Much wider, much more ordinary, not up-and-down at all, but running away into the distance. Unremarkable ridges of moor-like hills running away, perhaps to a bunch of dramatic peaks on the southwest. This gives a sense of space, which is so lacking in Italy. Lovely space about one, and traveling distances—nothing finished, nothing final. It is like liberty itself, after the peaky confinement of Sicily. Room—give me room—give me room for my spirit: and you can have all the toppling crags of romance.

So we ran on through the gold of the afternoon, across a wide, almost Celtic landscape of hills, our little train winding and puffing away very nimbly. Only the heath and scrub, breast-high, man-high, is too big and brigand-like for a Celtic land. The horns of black, wild-looking cattle show sometimes.

After a long pull, we come to a station after a stretch of loneliness. Each time, it looks as if there were nothing beyond—no more habitations. And each time we come to a station.

Most of the people have left the train. And as with men driving in a gig, who get down at every public-house, so the passengers usually alight for an airing at each station. Our old fat friend stands up and tucks his shirt-tail comfortably in his trousers, which trousers all the time make one hold one's breath, for they seem at each very moment to be just dropping right down: and he clambers out, followed by the long, brown stalk of a wife.

So the train sits comfortably for five or ten minutes, in the way the trains have. At last we hear whistles and horns, and our old fat friend running and clinging like a fat crab to the very end of the train as it sets off. At the same instant a loud shriek and a bunch of shouts from outside. We all jump up. There, down the line, is the long brown stork of a wife. She had just walked back to a house some hundred yards off, for a few words, and has now seen the train moving.

Now behold her with her hands thrown to heaven, and hear the wild shriek "Madonna!" through all the hubbub. But she picks up her two skirt-knees, and with her thin legs in grey stockings starts with a mad rush after the train. In vain. The train inexorably pursues its course. Prancing, she reaches one end of the platform as we leave the other end. Then she realizes it is not going to stop for her. And then, oh horror, her long arms thrown out in wild supplication after the retreating train: then flung aloft to God: then brought down in absolute despair on her head. And this is the last sight we have of her, clutching her poor head in agony and doubling forward. She is left—she is abandoned.

The poor fat husband has been all the time on the little outside platform at the end of the carriage, holding out his hand to her and shouting frenzied scolding to her and frenzied yells for the train to stop. And the train has not stopped. And she is left—left on that God-forsaken station in the waning light.

So, his face all bright, his eyes round and bright as two stars, absolutely trans-figured by dismay, chagrin, anger and distress, he comes and sits in his seat, ablaze, stiff, speechless. His face is almost beautiful in its blaze of conflicting emotions. For some time he is as if unconscious in the midst of his feelings. Then anger and resentment crop out of his consternation. He turns with a flash to the long-nosed, insidious, Phœnician-looking guard. Why couldn't they stop the train for her! And immediately, as if someone had set fire to him, off flares the guard. Heh!—the train can't stop for every person's convenience! The train is a train—the time-table is a time-table. What did the old woman want to take her trips down the line for? Heh! She pays the penalty for her own inconsiderateness. Had *she* paid for the train—heh? And the fat man all the time firing off his unheeding and unheeded answers. One minute—only one minute—if he, the conductor had told the driver! if he, the conductor, had shouted! A poor woman! Not another train! What was she going to do! Her ticket? And no money. A poor woman—

There was a train back to Cagliari that night, said the conductor, at which the fat man nearly burst out of his clothing like a bursting seed-pod. He bounced on his seat. What good was that? What good was a train back to Cagliari, when their home was in Snelli! Making matters worse—

So they bounced and jerked and argued at one another, to their hearts' content. Then the conductor retired, smiling subtly, in a way they have. Our fat friend looked at us with hot, angry, ashamed, grieved eyes and said it was a shame. Yes, we chimed, it *was* a shame. Whereupon a self-important miss who said she came from some Collegio at Cagliari advanced and asked a number of impertinent questions in a tone of pert sympathy. After which our fat friend, left alone, covered his clouded face with his hand, turned his back on the world, and gloomed.

It had all been so dramatic that in spite of ourselves we laughed, even while the q-b shed a few tears.

Well, the journey lasted hours. We came to a station, and the conductor said we must get out: these coaches went no further. Only two coaches would proceed to Mandas. So we climbed out with our traps, and our fat friend with his saddle-bag, the picture of misery.

The one coach into which we clambered was rather crowded. The only other coach was most of it first-class. And the rest of the train was freight. We were two insignificant passenger wagons at the end of a long string of freight-vans and trucks.

There was an empty seat, so we sat on it: only to realize after about five minutes, that a thin old woman with two children—her grandchildren—was chuntering her head off because it was *her* seat—why she had left it she didn't say. And under my legs was her bundle of bread. She nearly went off her head. And over my head, on the little rack, was her bercola, her saddle-bag. Fat soldiers laughed at her good-naturedly, but she fluttered and flipped like a tart, featherless old hen. Since she had another seat and was quite comfortable, we smiled and let her chunter. So she clawed her bread bundle from under my legs, and, clutching it and a fat child, sat tense.

It was getting quite dark. The conductor came and said that there was no more paraffin. If what there was in the lamps gave out, we should have to sit in the dark. There was no more paraffin all along the line.—So he climbed on the seats, and after a long struggle, with various boys striking matches for him, he managed to obtain a light as big as a pea. We sat in this *clair-obscur*, and looked at the sombre-shadowed faces round us: the fat soldier with a gun, the handsome soldier with huge saddle-bags, the weird, dark little man who kept exchanging a baby with a solid woman who had a white cloth tied round her head, a tall peasant-woman in costume, who darted out at a dark station and returned triumphant with a piece of chocolate: a young and interested young man, who told us every station. And the man who spat: there is always one.

Gradually the crowd thinned. At a station we saw our fat friend go by, bitterly, like a betrayed soul, his bulging saddle-bag hanging before and after, but no comfort in it now—no comfort. The pea of light from the paraffin lamp grew smaller. We sat in incredible dimness, and the smell of sheeps-wool and peasant, with only our fat and stoic young man to tell us where we were. The other dusky faces began to sink into a dead, gloomy silence. Some took to sleep. And the little train ran on and on, through unknown Sardinian darkness. In despair we drained the last drop of tea and ate the last crusts of bread. We knew we must arrive some time.

It was not much after seven when we came to Mandas. Mandas is a junction where these little trains sit and have a long happy chat after their arduous scramble over the downs. It had taken us somewhere about five hours to do our fifty miles. No wonder then that when the junction at last heaves in sight everybody bursts out of the train like seeds from an exploding pod, and rushes somewhere for something. To the station restaurant, of course. Hence there is a little station restaurant that does a brisk trade, and where one can have a bed.

A quite pleasant woman behind the little bar: a brown woman with brown parted hair and brownish eyes and brownish, tanned complexion and tight brown velveteen bodice. She led us up a narrow winding stone stair, as up a fortress, leading on with her candle, and ushered us into the bedroom. It smelled horrid and sourish, as shutup bedrooms do. We threw open the window. There were big frosty stars snapping ferociously in heaven.

The room contained a huge bed, big enough for eight people, and quite clean. And the table on which stood the candle actually had a cloth. But imagine that cloth! I think it had been originally white: now, however, it was such a web of time-eaten holes and mournful black inkstains and poor dead wine stains that it was like some 2000 B.C. mummy-cloth. I wonder if it could have been lifted from that table: or if it was mummified on to it! I for one made no attempt to try. But that table-cover impressed me, as showing degrees I had not imagined.—A table-cloth.

We went down the fortress-stair to the eating-room. Here was a long table with soup-plates upside down and a lamp burning an uncanny naked acetylene flame. We sat at the cold table, and the lamp immediately began to wane. The room—in fact the whole of Sardinia—was stone cold, stone, stone cold. Outside the earth was freezing. Inside there was no thought of any sort of warmth: dungeon stone floors, dungeon stone walls and a dead, corpse-like atmosphere, too heavy and icy to move.

The lamp went quite out, and the q-b gave a cry. The brown woman poked her head through a hole in the wall. Beyond her we saw the flames of the cooking, and two devil-figures stirring the pots. The brown woman came and shook the lamp—it was like a stodgy porcelain mantelpiece vase—shook it well and stirred up its innards, and started it going once more. Then she appeared with a bowl of smoking cabbage soup, in which were bits of macaroni: and would we have wine? I shuddered at the thought of death-cold red wine of the country, so asked what else there was. There was malvagia—malvoisie, the same old malmsey that did for the Duke of Clarence. So we had a pint of malvagia, and were comforted. At least we were being so, when the lamp went out again. The brown woman came and shook and smacked it, and started it off again. But as if to say "Shan't for you", it whipped out again.

Then came the host with a candle and a pin, a large, genial Sicilian with pendulous mustaches. And he thoroughly pricked the wretch with the pin, shook it, and turned little screws. So up flared the flame. We were a little nervous. He asked us where we came from, etc. And suddenly he asked us, with an excited gleam, were we Socialists. Aha, he was going to hail us as citizens and comrades. He thought we were a pair of Bolshevist agents: I could see it. And as such he was prepared to embrace us. But no, the q-b disclaimed the honor. I merely smiled and shook my head. It is a pity to rob people of their exciting illusions.

"Ah, there is too much socialism everywhere!" cried the q-b.

"Ma—perhaps, perhaps—" said the discreet Sicilian. She saw which way the land lay, and added:

"Si vuole un *pocchetino* di Socialismo: one wants a tiny bit of socialism in the world, a tiny bit. But not much. Not much. At present there is too much."

Our host, twinkling at this speech which treated of the sacred creed as if it were a pinch of salt in the broth, believing the q-b was throwing dust in his eyes, and thoroughly intrigued by us as a pair of deep ones, retired. No sooner had he gone than the lamp-flame stood up at its full length, and started to whistle.

The q-b drew back. Not satisfied by this, another flame suddenly began to whip round the bottom of the burner, like a lion lashing its tail. Unnerved, we made room: the q-b cried again: in came the host with a subtle smile and a pin and an air of benevolence, and tamed the brute.

What else was there to eat? There was a piece of fried pork for me, and boiled eggs for the q-b. As we were proceeding with these, in came the remainder of the night's entertainment: three station officials, two in scarlet peaked caps, one in a black-and-gold peaked cap. They sat down with a clamour, in their caps, as if there was a sort of invisible screen between us and them. They were young. The black cap had a lean and sardonic look: one of the red-caps was little and ruddy, very young, with a little mustache: we called him the *maialino*, the gay little black pig, he was so plump and food-nourished and frisky. The third was rather puffy and pale and had spectacles. They all seemed to present us the blank side of their cheek, and to intimate that no, they were not going to take their hats off, even if it were dinner-table and a strange *signora*. And they made rough quips with one another, still as if we were on the other side of the invisible screen.

Determined however, to remove this invisible screen, I said Good-evening, and it was very cold. They muttered Good-evening, and yes, it was fresh. An Italian never says it is cold: it is never more than *fresco*. But this hint that it was cold they took as a hint at their caps, and they became very silent, till the woman came in with the soup-bowl. Then they clamoured at her, particularly the *maialino*, what was there to eat. She told them—beef-steaks of pork. Whereat they pulled faces. Or bits of boiled pork. They sighed, looked gloomy, cheered up, and said beef-steaks, then.

And they fell on their soup. And never, from among the steam, have I heard a more joyful trio of soup-swilkering. They sucked it in from their spoons with long, gusto-rich sucks. The *maialino* was the treble—he trilled his soup into his mouth with a swift, sucking vibration, interrupted by bits of cabbage, which made the lamp start to dither again. Black-cap was the baritone; good, rolling spoon-sucks. And the one in spectacles was the bass: he gave sudden deep gulps. All was led by the long trilling of the *maialino*. Then suddenly, to vary matters, he cocked up his spoon in one hand, chewed a huge mouthful of bread, and swallowed it down with a smack-smack-smack! of his tongue against his palate. As children we used to call this "clapping".

"Mother, she's clapping!" I would yell with anger, against my sister. The German word is schmatzen.

So the *maialino* clapped like a pair of cymbals, while baritone and bass rolled on. Then in chimed the swift bright treble.

At this rate however, the soup did not last long. Arrived the beef-steaks of pork. And now the trio was a trio of castanet smacks and cymbal claps. Triumphantly the *maialino* looked around. He out-smacked all.

The bread of the country is rather coarse and brown, with a hard, hard crust. A large rock of this is perched on every damp serviette. The *maialino* tore his rock asunder, and grumbled at the black-cap, who had got a weird sort of three-cornered loaf-roll of pure white bread—starch white. He was a swell with this white bread.

Suddenly black-cap turned to me. Where had we come from, where were we going, what for? But in laconic, sardonic tone.

"I *like* Sardinia," cried the q-b.

"Why?" he asked sarcastically. And she tried to find out.

"Yes, the Sardinians please me more than the Sicilians," said I.

"Why?" he asked sarcastically.

"They are more open—more honest." He seemed to turn his nose down.

"The padrone is a Sicilian," said the *maialino*, stuffing a huge block of bread into his mouth, and rolling his insouciant eyes of a gay, well-fed little black pig towards the background. We weren't making much headway.

"You've seen Cagliari?" the black-cap said to me, like a threat.

"Yes! oh Cagliari pleases me—Cagliari is beautiful!" cried the q-b, who travels with a vial of melted butter ready for her parsnips.

"Yes—Cagliari is *so-so*—Cagliari is very fair," said the black cap. "*Cagliari è discreto.*" He was evidently proud of it.

"And is Mandas nice?" asked the q-b.

"In what way nice?" they asked, with immense sarcasm.

"Is there anything to see?"

"Hens," said the *maialino* briefly. They all bristled when one asked if Mandas was nice.

"What does one do here?" asked the q-b.

"*Niente!* At Mandas one does *nothing*. At Mandas one goes to bed when it's dark, like a chicken. At Mandas one walks down the road like a pig that is going nowhere. At Mandas a goat understands more than the inhabitants understand. At Mandas one needs socialism...."

They all cried out at once. Evidently Mandas was more than flesh and blood could bear for another minute to these three conspirators.

"Then you are very bored here?" say I.

"Yes."

And the quiet intensity of that naked yes spoke more than volumes.

"You would like to be in Cagliari?"

"Yes."

Silence, intense, sardonic silence had intervened. The three looked at one another and made a sour joke about Mandas. Then the black-cap turned to me.

"Can you understand Sardinian?" he said.

"Somewhat. More than Sicilian, anyhow."

"But Sardinian is more difficult than Sicilian. It is full of words utterly unknown to Italian—"

"Yes, but," say I, "it is spoken openly, in plain words, and Sicilian is spoken all stuck together, none of the words there at all."

He looks at me as if I were an imposter. Yet it is true. I find it quite easy to understand Sardinian. As a matter of fact, it is more a question of human approach than of sound. Sardinian seems open and manly and downright. Sicilian is gluey and evasive, as if the Sicilian didn't want to speak straight to you. As a matter of fact, he doesn't. He is an over-cultured, sensitive, ancient soul, and he has so many sides to his mind that he hasn't got any definite one mind at all. He's got a dozen minds, and uneasily he's aware of it, and to commit himself to anyone of them is merely playing a trick on himself and his interlocutor. The Sardinian, on the other hand, still seems to have one downright mind. I bump up against a downright, smack-out belief in Socialism, for example. The Sicilian is much too old in our culture to swallow Socialism whole: much too ancient and rusé not to be sophisticated about any and every belief. He'll go off like a squib: and then he'll smoulder acridly and sceptically even against his own fire. One sympathizes with him in retrospect. But in daily life it is unbearable.

"Where do you find such white bread?" say I to the black cap, because he is proud of it.

"It comes from my home." And then he asks about the bread of Sicily. Is it any whiter than *this*—the Mandas rock. Yes, it is a little whiter. At which they gloom again. For it is a very sore point, this bread. Bread means a great deal to an Italian: it is verily his staff of life. He practically lives on bread. And instead of going by taste, he now, like all the world, goes by eye. He has got it into his head that bread should be white, so that every time he fancies a darker shade in the loaf a shadow falls on his soul. Nor is he altogether wrong. For although, personally, I don't like white bread any more, yet I do like my brown bread to be made of pure, unmixed flour. The peasants in Sicily, who have kept their own wheat and make their own natural brown bread, ah, it is amazing how fresh and sweet and *clean* their loaf seems, so perfumed as home-bread used all to be before the war. Whereas the bread of the commune, the regulation supply, is hard, and rather coarse and rough, so rough and harsh on the palate. One gets tired to death of it. I suspect myself the maize meal mixed in. But I don't know. And finally the bread varies immensely from town to town, from commune to commune. The so-called just and equal distribution is all my-eye. One place has abundance of good sweet bread, another scrapes along, always stinted, on an allowance of harsh coarse stuff. And the poor suffer bitterly, really, from the bread-stinting, because they depend so on this one food. They say the inequality and the injustice of distribution comes from the Camorra—la grande Camorra—which is no more nowadays than a profiteering combine, which the poor hate. But for myself, I don't know. I only know that one town—Venice, for example—seems to have an endless supply of pure bread, of sugar, of tobacco, of salt—while Florence is in one continual ferment of irritation over the stinting of these supplies—which are all government monopoly, doled out accordingly.

We said Good-night to our three railway friends, and went up to bed. We had only been in the room a minute or two, when the brown woman tapped: and if you please, the black-cap had sent us one of his little white loaves. We were really touched. Such delicate little generosities have almost disappeared from the world.

It was a queer little bread—three-cornered, and almost as hard as ships biscuit, made of starch flour. Not strictly bread at all.

The night was cold, the blankets flat and heavy, but one slept quite well till dawn. At seven o'clock it was a clear, cold morning, the sun not yet up. Standing at the bedroom window looking out, I could hardly believe my eyes it was so like England, like Cornwall in the bleak parts, or Derbyshire uplands. There was a little paddock-garden at the back of the Station, rather tumble-down, with two sheep in it. There were several forlorn-looking out-buildings, very like Cornwall. And then the wide, forlorn country road stretched away between borders of grass and low, drystone walls, towards a grey stone farm with a tuft of trees, and a naked stone village in the distance. The sun came up yellow, the bleak country glimmered bluish and reluctant. The low, green hill-slopes were divided into fields, with low drystone walls and ditches. Here and there a stone barn rose alone, or with a few bare, windy trees attached. Two rough-coated winter horses pastured on the rough grass, a boy came along the naked, wide, grass-bordered high-road with a couple of milk cans, drifting in from nowhere: and it was all so like Cornwall, or a part of Ireland, that the old nostalgia for the Celtic regions began to spring up in me. Ah, those old, drystone walls dividing the fields—pale and granite-blenched! Ah, the dark, sombre grass, the naked sky! the forlorn horses in the wintry morning! Strange is a Celtic landscape, far more moving, disturbing than the lovely glamor of Italy and Greece. Before the curtains of history lifted, one feels the world was like this—this Celtic bareness and sombreness and *air*. But perhaps it is not Celtic at all: Iberian. Nothing is more unsatisfactory than our conception of what is Celtic and what is not Celtic. I believe there never were any Celts, as a race.—As for the Iberians—!

Wonderful to go out on a frozen road, to see the grass in shadow bluish with hoar-frost, to see the grass in the yellow winter-sunrise beams melting and going cold-twinkly. Wonderful the bluish, cold air, and things standing up in cold distance. After two southern winters, with roses blooming all the time, this bleakness and this touch of frost in the ringing morning goes to my soul like an intoxication. I am so glad, on this lonely naked road, I don't know what to do with myself. I walk down in the shallow grassy ditches under the loose stone walls, I walk on the little ridge of grass, the little bank on which the wall is built, I cross the road across the frozen cow-droppings: and it is all so familiar to my *feet*, my very feet in contact, that I am wild as if I had made a discovery. And I realize that I hate lime-stone, to live on lime-stone or marble or any of those limey rocks. I hate them. They are dead rocks, they have no life—thrills for the feet. Even sandstone is much better. But granite! Granite is my favorite. It is so live under the feet, it has a deep sparkle of its own. I like its roundnesses—and I hate the jaggy dryness of lime-stone, that burns in the sun, and withers.

After coming to a deep well in a grassy plot in a wide space of the road, I go back, across the sunny naked upland country, towards the pink station and its out-buildings. An engine is steaming its white clouds in the new light. Away to the left there is even a row of small houses, like a row of railway-mens' dwellings. Strange and familiar sight. And the station precincts are disorderly and rather dilapidated. I think of our Sicilian host.

The brown woman gives us coffee, and very strong, rich goats' milk, and bread. After which the q-b and I set off once more along the road to the village. She too is thrilled. She too breathes deep. She too feels *space* around her, and freedom to move the limbs: such as one does not feel in Italy and Sicily, where all is so classic and fixed.

The village itself is just a long, winding, darkish street, in shadow, of houses and shops and a smithy. It might almost be Cornwall: not quite. Something, I don't know what, suggests the stark burning glare of summer. And then, of course, there is none of the cosiness which climbing roses and lilac trees and cottage shops and haystacks would give to an English scene. This is harder, barer, starker, more dreary. An ancient man in the black-and-white costume comes out of a hovel of a cottage. The butcher carries a huge side of meat. The women peer at us—but more furtive and reticent than the howling stares of Italy.

So we go on, down the rough-cobbled street through the whole length of the village. And emerging on the other side, past the last cottage, we find ourselves again facing the open country, on the gentle down-slope of the rolling hill. The landscape continues the same: low, rolling upland hills, dim under the yellow sun of the January morning: stone fences, fields, grey-arable land: a man slowly, slowly ploughing with a pony and a dark-red cow: the road trailing empty across the distance: and then, the one violently unfamiliar note, the enclosed cemetery lying outside on the gentle hill-side, closed in all round, very compact, with high walls: and on the inside face of the enclosure wall the marble slabs, like shut drawers of the sepulchres, shining white, the wall being like a chest of drawers, or pigeon holes to hold the dead. Tufts of dark and plumy cypresses rise among the flat graves of the enclosure. In the south, cemeteries are walled off and isolated very tight. The dead, as it were, are kept fast in pound. There is no spreading of graves over the face of the country. They are penned in a tight fold, with cypresses to fatten on the bones. This is the one thoroughly strange note in the landscape. But all-pervading there is a strangeness, that strange feeling as if the *depths* were barren, which comes in the south and the east, sun-stricken. Sun-stricken, and the heart eaten out by the dryness.

"I like it! I like it!" cries the q-b.

"But could you live here?" She would like to say yes, but daren't.

We stray back. The q-b wants to buy one of those saddle-bag arrangements. I say what for? She says to keep things in. Ach! but peeping in the shops, we see one and go in and examine it. It is quite a sound one, properly made: but plain, quite plain. On the white cross-stripes there are no lovely colored flowers of rose and green and magenta: the three favorite Sardinian colors: nor are there any of the fantastic and griffin-like beasts. So it won't do. How much does it cost? Forty-five francs.

There is nothing to do in Mandas. So we will take the morning train and go to the terminus, to Sorgono. Thus, we shall cross the lower slopes of the great central knot of Sardinia, the mountain knot called Gennargentu. And Sorgono we feel will be lovely.

Back at the station we make tea on the spirit lamp, fill the thermos, pack the knapsack and the kitchenino, and come out into the sun of the platform. The q-b goes to thank the black-cap for the white bread, whilst I settle the bill and ask for food for the journey. The brown woman fishes out from a huge black pot in the background sundry hunks of coarse boiled pork, and gives me two of these, hot, with bread and salt. This is the luncheon. I pay the bill: which amounts to twenty-four francs, for everything. (One says francs or liras, irrespective, in Italy.) At that moment arrives the train from Cagliari, and men rush in, roaring for the soup—or rather, for the broth. "Ready, ready!" she cries, going to the black pot.

V. TO SORGONO

The various trains in the junction squatted side by side and had long, long talks before at last we were off. It was wonderful to be running in the bright morning towards the heart of Sardinia, in the little train that seemed so familiar. We were still going third class, rather to the disgust of the railway officials at Mandas.

At first the country was rather open: always the long spurs of hills, steep-sided, but not high. And from our little train we looked across the country, across hill and dale. In the distance was a little town, on a low slope. But for its compact, fortified look it might have been a town on the English downs. A man in the carriage leaned out of the window holding out a white cloth, as a signal to someone in the far off town that he was coming. The wind blew the white cloth, the town in the distance glimmered small and alone in its hollow. And the little train pelted along.

It was rather comical to see it. We were always climbing. And the line curved in great loops. So that as one looked out of the window, time and again one started, seeing a little train running in front of us, in a diverging direction, making big puffs of steam. But lo, it was our own little engine pelting off around a loop away ahead. We were quite a long train, but all trucks in front, only our two passenger coaches hitched on behind. And for this reason our own engine was always running fussily into sight, like some dog scampering in front and swerving about us, while we followed at the tail end of the thin string of trucks.

I was surprised how well the small engine took the continuous steep slopes, how bravely it emerged on the sky-line. It is a queer railway. I would like to know who made it. It pelts up hill and down dale and round sudden bends in the most unconcerned fashion, not as proper big railways do, grunting inside deep cuttings and stinking their way through tunnels, but running up the hill like a panting, small dog, and having a look round, and starting off in another direction, whisking us behind unconcernedly. This is much more fun than the tunnel-and-cutting system.

They told me that Sardinia mines her own coal: and quite enough for her own needs: but very soft, not fit for steam-purposes. I saw heaps of it: small, dull, dirty-looking stuff. Truck-loads of it too. And truck-loads of grain.

At every station we were left ignominiously planted, while the little engines—they had gay gold names on their black little bodies—strolled about along the side-lines, and snuffed at the various trucks. There we sat, at every station, while some truck was discarded and some other sorted out like a branded sheep, from the sidings and hitched on to us. It took a long time, this did.

All the stations so far had had wire netting over the windows. This means malaria-mosquitoes. The malaria climbs very high in Sardinia. The shallow upland valleys, moorland with their intense summer sun and the riverless, boggy behaviour of the water breed the pest inevitably. But not very terribly, as far as one can make out: August and September being the danger months. The natives don't like to admit there is any malaria: a tiny bit, they say, a tiny bit. As soon as you come to the *trees* there is no more. So they say. For many miles the landscape is moorland and down-like, with no trees. But wait for the trees. Ah, the woods and forests of Gennargentu: the woods and forests higher up: no malaria there!

The little engine whisks up and up, around its loopy curves as if it were going to bite its own tail: we being the tail: then suddenly dives over the sky-line out of sight. And the landscape changes. The famous woods begin to appear. At first it is only hazel-thickets, miles of hazel-thickets, all wild, with a few black cattle trying to peep at us out of the green myrtle and arbutus scrub which forms the undergrowth; and a couple of rare, wild peasants peering at the train. They wear the black sheepskin tunic, with the wool outside, and the long stocking caps. Like cattle they too peer out from between deep bushes. The myrtle scrub here rises man-high, and cattle and men are smothered in it. The big hazels rise bare above. It must be difficult getting about in these parts.

Sometimes, in the distance one sees a black-and-white peasant riding lonely across a more open place, a tiny vivid figure. I like so much the proud instinct which makes a living creature distinguish itself from its background. I hate the rabbity khaki protection-colouration. A black-and-white peasant on his pony, only a dot in the distance beyond the foliage, still flashes and dominates the landscape. Ha-ha! proud mankind! There you ride! But alas, most of the men are still khaki-muffled, rabbit-indistinguishable, ignominious. The Italians look curiously rabbity in the grey-green uniform: just as our sand-colored khaki men look doggy. They seem to scuffle rather abased, ignominious on the earth. Give us back the scarlet and gold, and devil take the hindmost.

The landscape really begins to change. The hillsides tilt sharper and sharper. A man is ploughing with two small red cattle on a craggy, tree-hanging slope as sharp as a roof-side. He stoops at the small wooden plough, and jerks the ploughlines. The oxen lift their noses to heaven, with a strange and beseeching snake-like movement, and taking tiny little steps with their frail feet, move slantingly across the slope-face, between rocks and tree-roots. Little, frail, jerky steps the bullocks take, and again they put their horns back and lift their muzzles snakily to heaven, as the man pulls the line. And he skids his wooden plough round another scoop of earth. It is marvellous how they hang upon that steep, craggy slope. An English labourer's eyes would bolt out of his head at the sight.

There is a stream: actually a long tress of a water-fall pouring into a little gorge, and a stream-bed that opens a little, and shows a marvellous cluster of naked poplars away below. They are like ghosts. They have a ghostly, almost phosphorescent luminousness in the shadow of the valley, by the stream of water. If not phosphorescent, then incandescent: a grey, goldish-pale incandescence of naked limbs and myriad cold-glowing twigs, gleaming strangely. If I were a painter I would paint them: for they seem to have living, sentient flesh. And the shadow envelopes them.

Another naked tree I would paint is the gleaming mauve-silver fig, which burns its cold incandescence, tangled, like some sensitive creature emerged from the rock. A fig tree come forth in its nudity gleaming over the dark winter-earth is a sight to behold. Like some white, tangled sea anemone. Ah, if it could but answer! or if we had tree-speech!

Yes, the steep valley sides become almost gorges, and there are trees. Not forests such as I had imagined, but scattered, grey, smallish oaks, and some lithe chestnuts. Chestnuts with their long whips, and oaks with their stubby boughs, scattered on steep hillsides where rocks crop out. The train perilously winding round, half way up. Then suddenly bolting over a bridge and into a completely unexpected station. What is more, men crowd in—the station is connected with the main railway by a post motor-omnibus.

An unexpected irruption of men—they may be miners or navvies or land-workers. They all have huge sacks: some lovely saddle-bags with rose-coloured flowers across the darkness. One old man is in full black-and-white costume, but very dirty and coming to pieces. The others wear the tight madder-brown breeches and sleeved waistcoats. Some have the sheepskin tunic, and all wear the long stocking cap. And how they smell! of sheep-wool and of men and goat. A rank scent fills the carriage.

They talk and are very lively. And they have mediaeval faces, rusé, never really abandoning their defences for a moment, as a badger or a pole-cat never abandons its defences. There is none of the brotherliness and civilised simplicity. Each man knows he must guard himself and his own: each man knows the devil is behind the next bush. They have never known the post-Renaissance Jesus. Which is rather an eye-opener.

Not that they are suspicious or uneasy. On the contrary, noisy, assertive, vigorous presences. But with none of that implicit belief that everybody will be and ought to be good to them, which is the mark of our era. They don't expect people to be good to them: they don't want it. They remind me of half-wild dogs that will love and obey, but which won't be handled. They won't have their heads touched. And they won't be fondled. One can almost hear the half-savage growl.

The long stocking caps they wear as a sort of crest, as a lizard wears his crest at mating time. They are always moving them, settling them on their heads. One fat fellow, young, with sly brown eyes and a young beard round his face folds his stocking-foot in three, so that it rises over his brow martial and handsome. The old boy brings his stocking-foot over the left ear. A handsome fellow with a jaw of massive teeth pushes his cap back and lets it hang a long way down his back. Then he shifts it forward over his nose, and makes it have two sticking-out points, like fox-ears, above his temples. It is marvellous how much expression these caps can take on. They say that only those born to them can wear them. They seem to be just long bags, nearly a yard long, of black stockinette stuff.

The conductor comes to issue them their tickets. And they all take out rolls of paper money. Even a little mothy rat of a man who sits opposite me has quite a pad of ten-franc notes. Nobody seems short of a hundred francs nowadays: nobody.

They shout and expostulate with the conductor. Full of coarse life they are: but so coarse! The handsome fellow has his sleeved waistcoat open, and his shirt-breast has come unbuttoned. Not looking, it seems as if he wears a black undervest. Then suddenly, one sees it is his own hair. He is quite black inside his shirt, like a black goat.

But there is a gulf between oneself and them. They have no inkling of our crucifixion, our universal consciousness. Each of them is pivoted and limited to himself, as the wild animals are. They look out, and they see other objects, objects to ridicule or mistrust or to sniff curiously at. But "thou shalt love thy neighbour as thyself" has never entered their souls at all, not even the thin end of it. They might love their neighbour, with a hot, dark, unquestioning love. But the love would probably leave off abruptly. The fascination of what is beyond them has not seized on them. Their neighbour is a mere external. Their life is centripetal, pivoted inside itself, and does not run out towards others and mankind. One feels for the first time the real old mediaeval life, which is enclosed in itself and has no interest in the world outside.

And so they lie about on the seats, play a game, shout, and sleep, and settle their long stocking-caps: and spit. It is wonderful in them that at this time of day they still wear the long stocking-caps as part of their inevitable selves. It is a sign of obstinate and powerful tenacity. They are not going to be broken in upon by world-consciousness. They are not going into the world's common clothes. Coarse, vigorous, determined, they will stick to their own coarse dark stupidity and let the big world find its own way to its own enlightened hell. Their hell is their own hell, they prefer it unenlightened.

And one cannot help wondering whether Sardinia will resist right through. Will the last waves of enlightenment and world-unity break over them and wash away the stocking-caps? Or is the tide of enlightenment and world-unity already receding fast enough?

Certainly a reaction is setting in, away from the old universality, back, away from cosmopolitanism and internationalism. Russia, with her Third International, is at the same time reacting most violently away from all other contact, back, recoiling on herself, into a fierce, unapproachable Russianism. Which motion will conquer? The workman's International, or the centripetal movement into national isolation? Are we going to merge into one grey proletarian homogeneity?—or are we going to swing back into more-or-less isolated, separate, defiant communities?

Probably both. The workman's International movement will finally break the flow towards cosmopolitanism and world-assimilation, and suddenly in a crash the world will fly back into intense separations. The moment has come when America, that extremist in world-assimilation and world-oneness, is reacting into violent egocentricity, a truly Amerindian egocentricity. As sure as fate we are on the brink of American empire.

For myself, I am glad. I am glad that the era of love and oneness is over: hateful homogeneous world-oneness. I am glad that Russia flies back into savage Russianism, Scythism, savagely self-pivoting. I am glad that America is doing the same. I shall be glad when men hate their common, world-alike clothes, when they tear them up and clothe themselves fiercely for distinction, savage distinction, savage distinction against the rest of the creeping world: when America kicks the billy-cock and the collar-and-tie into limbo, and takes to her own national costume: when men fiercely react against looking all alike and being all alike, and betake themselves into vivid clan or nation-distinctions.

The era of love and oneness is over. The era of world-alike should be at an end. The other tide has set in. Men will set their bonnets at one another now, and fight themselves into separation and sharp distinction. The day of peace and oneness is over, the day of the great fight into multifariousness is at hand. Hasten the day, and save us from proletarian homogeneity and khaki all-alikeness.

I love my indomitable coarse men from mountain Sardinia, for their stocking-caps and their splendid, animal-bright stupidity. If only the last wave of all-alikeness won't wash those superb crests, those caps, away.

We are struggling now among the Gennargentu spurs. There is no single peak—no Etna of Sardinia. The train, like the plough, balances on the steep, steep sides of the hill-spurs, and winds around and around. Above and below the steep slopes are all bosky. These are the woods of Gennargentu. But they aren't woods in my sense of the word. They are thin sprinkles of oaks and chestnuts and cork-trees over steep hill-slopes. And cork-trees! I see curious slim oaky-looking trees that are stripped quite naked below the boughs, standing brown-ruddy, curiously distinct among the bluey grey pallor of the others. They remind me, again and again, of glowing, coffee-brown, naked aborigines of the South Seas. They have the naked suavity, skin-bare, and an intense coffee-red colour of unclothed savages. And these are the stripped cork-trees. Some are much stripped, some little. Some have the whole trunk and part of the lower limbs ruddy naked, some only a small part of the trunk.

It is well on in the afternoon. A peasant in black and white, and his young, handsome woman in rose-red costume, with gorgeous apron bordered deep with grass-green, and a little, dark-purple waistcoat over her white, full bodice, are sitting behind me talking. The workmen peasants are subsiding into sleep. It is well on in the afternoon, we have long ago eaten the meat. Now we finish the white loaf, the gift, and the tea. Suddenly looking out of the window, we see Gennargentu's mass behind us, a thick snow-deep knot-summit, beautiful beyond the long, steep spurs among which we are engaged. We lose the white mountain mass for half an hour: when suddenly it emerges unexpectedly almost in front, the great, snow-heaved shoulder.

How different it is from Etna, that lonely, self-conscious wonder of Sicily! This is much more human and knowable, with a deep breast and massive limbs, a powerful mountain-body. It is like the peasants.

The stations are far between—an hour from one to another. Ah, how weary one gets of these journeys, they last so long. We look across a valley—a stone's throw. But alas, the little train has no wings, and can't jump. So back turns the line, back and back towards Gennargentu, a long rocky way, till it comes at length to the poor valley-head. This it skirts fussily, and sets off to pelt down on its traces again, gaily. And a man who was looking at us doing our round-about has climbed down and crossed the valley in five minutes.

The peasants nearly all wear costumes now, even the women in the fields: the little fields in the half-populated valleys. These Gennargentu valleys are all half-populated, more than the moors further south.

It is past three o'clock, and cold where there is no sun. At last only one more station before the terminus. And here the peasants wake up, sling the bulging sacks over their shoulders, and get down. We see Tonara away above. We see our old grimy black-and-white peasant greeted by his two women who have come to meet him with the pony—daughters handsome in vivid rose and green costume. Peasants, men in black and white, men in madder-brown, with the close breeches on their compact thighs, women in rose-and-white, ponies with saddle-bags, all begin to trail up the hill-road in silhouette, very handsome, towards the far-off, perched, sun-bright village of Tonara, a big village, shining like a New Jerusalem.

The train as usual leaves us standing, and shuffles with trucks—water sounds in the valley: there are stacks of cork on the station, and coal. An idiot girl in a great full skirt entirely made of coloured patches mops and mows. Her little waistcoat thing is also incredibly old, and shows faint signs of having once been a lovely purple and black brocade. The valley and steep slopes are open about us. An old shepherd has a lovely flock of delicate merino sheep.

And at last we move. In one hour we shall be there. As we travel among the tree slopes, many brown cork-trees, we come upon a flock of sheep. Two peasants in our carriage looking out, give the most weird, unnatural, high-pitched shrieks, entirely unproduceable by any ordinary being. The sheep know, however, and scatter. And after ten minutes the shrieks start again, for three young cattle. Whether the peasants do it for love, I don't know. But it is the wildest and weirdest inhuman shepherd noise I have ever heard.

It is Saturday afternoon and four o'clock. The country is wild and uninhabited, the train almost empty, yet there is the leaving-off-work feeling in the atmosphere. Oh twisty, wooded, steep slopes, oh glimpses of Gennargentu, oh nigger-stripped cork-trees, oh smell of peasants, oh wooden, wearisome railway carriage, we are so sick of you! Nearly seven hours of this journey already: and a distance of sixty miles.

But we are almost there—look, look, Sorgono, nestling beautifully among the wooded slopes in front. Oh magic little town. Ah, you terminus and ganglion of the inland roads, we hope in you for a pleasant inn and happy company. Perhaps we will stay a day or two at Sorgono.

The train gives a last sigh, and draws to a last standstill in the tiny terminus station. An old fellow fluttering with rags as a hen in the wind flutters, asked me if I wanted the *Albergo*, the inn. I said yes, and let him take my knapsack. Pretty Sorgono! As we went down the brief muddy lane between hedges, to the village high-road, we seemed almost to have come to some little town in the English west-country, or in Hardy's country. There were glades of stripling oaks, and big slopes with oak trees, and on the right a saw-mill buzzing, and on the left the town, white and close, nestling round a baroque church-tower. And the little lane was muddy.

Three minutes brought us to the high-road, and a great, pink-washed building blank on the road facing the station lane, and labelled in huge letters: RISTORANTE RISVEGLIO: the letter N being printed backwards. *Risveglio* if you please: which means waking up or rousing, like the word *reveille*. Into the doorway of the Risveglio bolted the flutterer. "Half a minute," said I. "Where is the Albergo d'Italia?" I was relying on Baedeker.

"Non c'è più," replied my rag-feather. "There isn't it any more." This answer, being very frequent nowadays, is always most disconcerting.

"Well then, what other hotel?"

"There is no other."

Risveglio or nothing. In we go. We pass into a big, dreary bar, where are innumerable bottles behind a tin counter. Flutter-jack yells: and at length appears mine host, a youngish fellow of the Esquimo type, but rather bigger, in a dreary black suit and a cutaway waistcoat suggesting a dinner-waistcoat, and innumerable wine-stains on his shirt front. I instantly hated him for the filthy appearance he made. He wore a battered hat and his face was long unwashed.

Was there a bedroom?

Yes.

And he led the way down the passage, just as dirty as the road outside, up the hollow, wooden stairs also just as clean as the passage, along a hollow, drum-rearing dirty corridor, and into a bedroom. Well, it contained a large bed, thin and flat with a grey-white counterpane, like a large, poor, marble-slabbed tomb in the room's sordid emptiness; one dilapidated chair on which stood the miserablest weed of a candle I have ever seen: a broken wash-saucer in a wire ring: and for the rest, an expanse of wooden floor as dirty-grey-black as it could be, and an expanse of wall charted with the bloody deaths of mosquitoes. The window was about two feet above the level of a sort of stable-yard outside, with a fowl-house just by the sash. There, at the window flew lousy feathers and dirty straw, the ground was thick with chicken-droppings. An ass and two oxen comfortably chewed hay in an open shed just across, and plump in the middle of the yard lay a bristly black pig taking the last of the sun. Smells of course were varied.

The knapsack and the kitchenino were dropped on the repulsive floor, which I hated to touch with my boots even. I turned back the sheets and looked at other people's stains.

"There is nothing else?"

"Niente," said he of the lank, low forehead and beastly shirt-breast. And he sullenly departed. I gave the flutterer his tip and he too ducked and fled. Then the queen-bee and I took a few mere sniffs.

"Dirty, disgusting swine!" said I, and I was in a rage.

I could have forgiven him anything, I think, except his horrible shirt-breast, his personal shamelessness.

We strolled round—saw various other bedrooms, some worse, one really better. But this showed signs of being occupied. All the doors were open: the place was quite deserted, and open to the road. The one thing that seemed definite was honesty. It must be a very honest place, for every footed beast, man or animal, could walk in at random and nobody to take the slightest regard.

So we went downstairs. The only other apartment was the open public bar, which seemed like part of the road. A muleteer, leaving his mules at the corner of the Risveglio, was drinking at the counter.

This famous inn was at the end of the village. We strolled along the road between the houses, down-hill. A dreary hole! a cold, hopeless, lifeless, Saturday afternoon-weary village, rather sordid, with nothing to say for itself. No real shops at all. A weary-looking church, and a clutch of disconsolate houses. We walked right through the village. In the middle was a sort of open space where stood a great, grey motor-omnibus. And a bus-driver looking rather weary.

Where did the bus go?

It went to join the main railway.

When?

At half-past seven in the morning.

Only then?

Only then.

"Thank God we can get out, anyhow," said I.

We passed on, and emerged beyond the village, still on the descending great high-road that was mended with loose stones pitched on it. This wasn't good enough. Besides, we were out of the sun, and the place being at a considerable elevation, it was very cold. So we turned back, to climb quickly uphill into the sun.

We went up a little side-turning past a bunch of poor houses towards a steep little lane between banks. And before we knew where we were, we were in the thick of the public lavatory. In these villages, as I knew, there are no sanitary arrangements of any sort whatever. Every villager and villageress just betook himself at need to one of the side-roads. It is the immemorial Italian custom. Why bother about privacy? The most socially-constituted people on earth, they even like to relieve themselves in company.

We found ourselves in the full thick of one of these meeting-places. To get out at any price! So we scrambled up the steep earthen banks to a stubble field above. And by this time I was in a greater rage.

Evening was falling, the sun declining. Below us clustered the Sodom-apple of this vile village. Around were fair, tree-clad hills and dales, already bluish with the frost-shadows. The air bit cold and strong. In a very little time the sun would be down. We were at an elevation of about 2,500 feet above the sea.

No denying it was beautiful, with the oak-slopes and the wistfulness and the far-off feeling of loneliness and evening. But I was in too great a temper to admit it. We clambered frenziedly to get warm. And the sun immediately went right down, and the ice-heavy blue shadow fell over us all. The village began to send forth blue wood-smoke, and it seemed more than ever like the twilit West Country.

But thank you—we had to get back. And run the gauntlet of that stinking, stinking lane? Never. Towering with fury—quite unreasonable, but there you are—I marched the q-b down a declivity through a wood, over a ploughed field, along a cart-track, and so to the great high-road above the village and above the inn.

It was cold, and evening was falling into dusk. Down the high-road came wild half-ragged men on ponies, in all degrees of costume and not-costume: came four wide-eyed cows stepping down-hill round the corner, and three delicate, beautiful merino sheep which stared at us with their prominent, gold-curious eyes: came an ancient, ancient man with a stick: came a stout-chested peasant carrying a long wood-pole: came a straggle of alert and triumphant goats, long-horned, long-haired, jingling their bells. Everybody greeted us hesitatingly. And everything came to a halt at the Risveglio corner, while the men had a nip.

I attacked the spotty-breast again.

Could I have milk?

No. Perhaps in an hour there would be milk. Perhaps not.

Was there anything to eat?

No—at half past seven there would be something to eat.

Was there a fire?

No—the man hadn't made the fire.

Nothing to do but to go to that foul bedroom or walk the high-road. We turned up the high-road again. Animals stood about the road in the frost-heavy air, with heads sunk passively, waiting for the men to finish their drinks in the beastly bar—we walked slowly up the hill. In a field on the right a flock of merino sheep moved mistily, uneasily, climbing at the gaps in the broken road bank, and sounding their innumerable small fine bells with a frosty ripple of sound. A figure which in the dusk I had really thought was something inanimate broke into movement in the field. It was an old shepherd, very old, in very ragged dirty black-and-white, who had been standing like a stone there in the open field-end for heaven knows how long, utterly motionless, leaning on his stick. Now he broke into a dream-motion and hobbled after the wistful, feminine, inquisitive sheep. The red was fading from the far-off west. At the corner, climbing slowly and wearily, we almost ran into a grey and lonely bull, who came stepping down-hill in his measured fashion like some god. He swerved his head and went round us.

We reached a place which we couldn't make out: then saw it was a cork-shed. There were stacks and stacks of cork-bark in the dusk, like crumpled hides.

"Now I'm going back," said the q-b flatly, and she swung round. The last red was smouldering beyond the lost, thin-wooded hills of this interior. A fleece of blue, half-luminous smoke floated over the obscure village. The high-way wound down-hill at our feet, pale and blue.

And the q-b was angry with me for my fury.

"Why are you so indignant! Anyone would think your moral self had been outraged! Why take it morally? You petrify that man at the inn by the very way you speak to him, *such* condemnation! Why don't you take it as it comes? It's all life."

But no, my rage is black, black, black. Why, heaven knows. But I think it was because Sorgono had seemed so fascinating to me, when I imagined it beforehand. Oh so fascinating! If I had expected nothing I should not have been so hit. Blessed is he that expecteth nothing, for he shall not be disappointed.

I cursed the degenerate aborigines, the dirty-breasted host who *dared* to keep such an inn, the sordid villagers who had the baseness to squat their beastly human nastiness in this upland valley. All my praise of the long stocking-cap— you remember?—vanished from my mouth. I cursed them all, and the q-b for an interfering female....

In the bar a wretched candle was weeping light—uneasy, gloomy men were drinking their Saturday-evening-home-coming dram. Cattle lay down in the road, in the cold air as if hopeless.

Had the milk come?

No.

When would it come.

He didn't know.

Well, what were we to do? Was there no room? Was there nowhere where we could sit?

Yes, there was the *stanza* now.

Now! Taking the only weed of a candle, and leaving the drinkers in the dark, he led us down a dark and stumbly earthen passage, over loose stones and an odd plank, as it would seem underground, to the stanza: the room.

The stanza! It was pitch dark—But suddenly I saw a big fire of oak-root, a brilliant, flamy, rich fire, and my rage in that second disappeared.

The host, and the candle, forsook us at the door. The stanza would have been in complete darkness, save for that rushing bouquet of new flames in the chimney, like fresh flowers. By this firelight we saw the room. It was like a dungeon, absolutely empty, with an uneven, earthen floor, quite dry, and high bare walls, gloomy, with a handbreadth of window high up. There was no furniture at all, save a little wooden bench, a foot high, before the fire, and several home-made-looking rush mats rolled up and leaning against the walls. Furthermore a chair before the fire on which hung wet table-napkins. Apart from this, it was a high, dark, naked prison-dungeon.

But it was quite dry, it had an open chimney, and a gorgeous new fire rushing like a water-fall upwards among the craggy stubs of a pile of dry oak roots. I hastily put the chair and the wet corpse-cloths to one side. We sat on the low bench side by side in the dark, in front of this rippling rich fire, in front of the cavern of the open chimney, and we did not care any more about the dungeon and the darkness. Man can live without food, but he can't live without fire. It is an Italian proverb. We had found the fire, like new gold. And we sat in front of it, a little way back, side by side on the low form, our feet on the uneven earthen floor, and felt the flame-light rippling upwards over our faces, as if we were bathing in some gorgeous stream of fieriness. I forgave the dirty-breasted host everything and was as glad as if I had come into a kingdom.

So we sat alone for half an hour, smiling into the flames, bathing our faces in the glow. From time to time I was aware of steps in the tunnel-like passage outside, and of presences peering. But no one came. I was aware too of the faint steaming of the beastly table-napkins, the only other occupants of the room.

In dithers a candle, and an elderly, bearded man in gold-coloured corduroys, and an amazing object on a long, long spear. He put the candle on the mantel-ledge, and crouched at the side of the fire, arranging the oak-roots. He peered strangely and fixedly in the fire. And he held up the speared object before our faces.

It was a kid that he had come to roast. But it was a kid opened out, made quite flat, and speared like a flat fan on a long iron stalk. It was a really curious sight. And it must have taken some doing. The whole of the skinned kid was there, the head curled in against a shoulder, the stubby cut ears, the eyes, the teeth, the few hairs of the nostrils: and the feet curled curiously round, like an animal that puts its fore-paw over its ducked head: and the hind-legs twisted indescribably up: and all skewered flat-wise upon the long iron rod, so that it was a complete flat pattern. It reminded me intensely of those distorted, slim-limbed, dog-like animals which figure on the old Lombard ornaments, distorted and curiously infolded upon themselves. Celtic illuminations also have these distorted, invo-luted creatures.

The old man flourished the flat kid like a bannerette, whilst he arranged the fire. Then, in one side of the fire-place wall he poked the point of the rod. He himself crouched on the hearth-end, in the half-shadow at the other side of the fire-place, holding the further end of the long iron rod. The kid was thus extended before the fire, like a hand-screen. And he could spin it round at will.

But the hole in the masonry of the chimney-piece was not satisfactory. The point of the rod kept slipping, and the kid came down against the fire. He mut-tered and muttered to himself, and tried again. Then at length he reared up the kid-banner whilst he got large stones from a dark corner. He arranged these stones so that the iron point rested on them. He himself sat away on the opposite side of the fire-place, on the shadowy hearth-end, and with queer, spell-bound black eyes and completely immovable face, he watched the flames and the kid, and held the handle end of the rod.

We asked him if the kid was for the evening meal—and he said it was. It would be good! And he said yes, and looked with chagrin at the bit of ash on the meat, where it had slipped. It is a point of honour that it should never touch the ash. Did they do all their meat this way? He said they did. And wasn't it difficult to put the kid thus on the iron rod? He said it was not easy, and he eyed the joint closely, and felt one of the forelegs, and muttered that was not fixed properly.

He spoke with a very soft mutter, hard to catch, and sideways, never to us direct. But his manner was gentle, soft, muttering, reticent, sensitive. He asked us where we came from, and where we were going: always in his soft mutter. And what nation were we, were we French? Then he went on to say there was a war— but he thought it was finished. There was a war because the Austrians wanted to come into Italy again. But the French and the English came to help Italy. A lot of Sardinians had gone to it. But let us hope it is all finished. He thought it was—young men of Sorgono had been killed. He hoped it was finished.

Then he reached for the candle and peered at the kid. It was evident he was the born roaster. He held the candle and looked for a long time at the sizzling side of the meat, as if he would read portents. Then he held his spit to the fire again. And it was as if time immemorial were roasting itself another meal. I sat holding the candle.

A young woman appeared, hearing voices. Her head was swathed in a shawl, one side of which was brought across, right over the mouth, so that only her two eyes and her nose showed. The q-b thought she must have toothache—but she laughed and said no. As a matter of fact that is the way a head-dress is worn in Sardinia, even by both sexes. It is something like the folding of the Arab's burnoose. The point seems to be that the mouth and chin are thickly covered, also the ears and brow, leaving only the nose and eyes exposed. They say it keeps off the malaria. The men swathe shawls round their heads in the same way. It seems to me they want to keep their heads warm, dark and hidden: they feel secure inside.

She wore the workaday costume: a full, dark-brown skirt, the full white bodice, and a little waistcoat or corset. This little waistcoat in her case had become no more than a shaped belt, sending up graceful, stiffened points under the breasts, like long leaves standing up. It was pretty—but all dirty. She too was pretty, but with an impudent, not quite pleasant manner. She fiddled with the wet napkins, asked us various questions, and addressed herself rather jerkily to the old man, who answered hardly at all—Then she departed again. The women are self-conscious in a rather smirky way, bouncy.

When she was gone I asked the old man if she was his daughter. He said very brusquely, in his soft mutter, No. She came from a village some miles away. He did not belong to the inn. He was, as far as I understood, the postman. But I may have been mistaken about the word.

But he seemed laconic, unwilling to speak about the inn and its keepers. There seemed to be something queer. And again he asked where we were going. He told me there were now two motor-buses: a new one which ran over the mountains to Nuoro. Much better go to Nuoro than to Abbasanta. Nuoro was evidently the town towards which these villages looked, as a sort of capital.

The kid-roasting proceeded very slowly, the meat never being very near the fire. From time to time the roaster arranged the cavern of red-hot roots. Then he threw on more roots. It was very hot. And he turned the long spit, and still I held the candle.

Other people came strolling in, to look at us. But they hovered behind us in the dark, so I could not make out at all clearly. They strolled in the gloom of the dungeon-like room, and watched us. One came forward—a fat, fat young soldier in uniform. I made place for him on the bench—but he put out his hand and disclaimed the attention. Then he went away again.

The old man propped up the roast, and then he too disappeared for a time. The thin candle guttered, the fire was no longer flamy but red. The roaster reappeared with a new, shorter spear, thinner, and a great lump of raw hog-fat spitted on it. This he thrust into the red fire. It sizzled and smoked and spit fat, and I wondered. He told me he wanted it to catch fire. It refused. He groped in the hearth for the bits of twigs with which the fire had been started. These twig-stumps he stuck in the fat, like an orange stuck with cloves, then he held it in the fire again. Now at last it caught, and it was a flaming torch running downwards with a thin shower of flaming fat. And now he was satisfied. He held the fat-torch with its yellow flares over the browning kid, which he turned horizontal for the occasion. All over the roast fell the flaming drops, till the meat was all shiny and browny. He put it to the fire again, holding the diminishing fat, still burning bluish, over it all the time in the upper air.

While this was in process a man entered with a loud *Good evening*. We replied Good-evening—and evidently he caught a strange note. He came and bent down and peered under my hat-brim, then under the q-b's hat-brim, we still wore hats and overcoats, as did everybody. Then he stood up suddenly and touched his cap and said *Scusi*—excuse me. I said *Niente*, which one always says, and he addressed a few jovial words to the crouching roaster: who again would hardly answer him. The omnibus was arrived from Oristano, I made out—with few passengers.

This man brought with him a new breezy atmosphere, which the roaster did not like. However, I made place on the low bench, and the attention this time was accepted. Sitting down at the extreme end, he came into the light, and I saw a burly man in the prime of life, dressed in dark brown velvet, with a blond little moustache and twinkling blue eyes and a tipsy look. I thought he might be some local tradesman or farmer. He asked a few questions, in a boisterous familiar fashion, then went out again. He appeared with a small iron spit, a slim rod, in one hand, and in the other hand two joints of kid and a handful of sausages. He stuck his joints on his rod. But our roaster still held the interminable flat kid before the now red, flameless fire. The fat-torch was burnt out, the cinder pushed in the fire. A moment's spurt of flame, then red, intense redness again, and our kid before it like a big, dark hand.

"Eh," said the newcomer, whom I will call the girovago, "it's done. The kid's done. It's done."

The roaster slowly shook his head, but did not answer. He sat like time and eternity at the hearth-end, his face flame-flushed, his dark eyes still fire-abstract, still sacredly intent on the roast.

"Na-na-na!" said the girovago. "Let another body see the fire." And with his pieces of meat awkwardly skewered on his iron stick he tried to poke under the authorised kid and get at the fire. In his soft mutter, the old man bade him wait for the fire till the fire was ready for him. But the girovago poked impudently and good humouredly, and said testily that the authorised kid was done.

"Yes, surely it is done," said I, for it was already a quarter to eight.

The old roasting priest muttered, and took out his knife from his pocket. He pressed the blade slowly, slowly deep into the meat: as far as a knife will go in a piece of kid. He seemed to be feeling the meat inwardly. And he said it was not done. He shook his head, and remained there like time and eternity at the end of the rod.

The girovago said *Sangue di Dio*, but couldn't roast his meat! And he tried to poke his skewer near the coals. So doing his pieces fell off into the ashes, and the invisible onlookers behind raised a shout of laughter. However, he raked it out and wiped it with his hand and said No matter, nothing lost.

Then he turned to me and asked the usual whence and whither questions. These answered, he said wasn't I German. I said No, I was English. He looked at me many times, shrewdly, as if he wanted to make out something. Then he asked, where were we domiciled—and I said Sicily. And then, very pertinently, why had we come to Sardinia. I said for pleasure, and to see the island.

"Ah, per divertimento!" he repeated, half-musingly, not believing me in the least.

Various men had now come into the room, though they all remained indistinct in the background. The girovago talked and jested abroad in the company, and the half-visible men laughed in a rather hostile manner.

At last the old roaster decided the kid was done. He lifted it from the fire and scrutinised it thoroughly, holding the candle to it, as if it were some wonderful epistle from the flames. To be sure it looked marvellous, and smelled so good: brown, and crisp, and hot, and savoury, not burnt in any place whatever. It was eight o'clock.

"It's done! It's done! Go away with it! Go," said the girovago, pushing the old roaster with his hand. And at last the old man consented to depart, holding the kid like a banner.

"It looks so *good!*" cried the q-b. "And I am so hungry."

"Ha-ha! It makes one hungry to see good meat, Signora. Now it is my turn. Heh—Gino—" the girovago flourished his arm. And a handsome, unwashed man with a black moustache came forward rather sheepishly. He was dressed in soldier's clothes, neutral grey, and was a big, robust, handsome fellow with dark eyes and Mediterranean sheepishness. "Here, take it thou," said the girovago, pressing the long spit into his hand. "It is thy business, cook the supper, thou art the woman.—But I'll keep the sausages and do them."

The so-called woman sat at the end of the hearth, where the old roaster had sat, and with his brown, nervous hand piled the remaining coals together. The fire was no longer flamy: and it was sinking. The dark-browed man arranged it so that he could cook the meat. He held the spit negligently over the red mass. A joint fell off. The men laughed. "It's lost nothing," said the dark-browed man, as the girovago had said before, and he skewered it on again and thrust it to the fire. But meanwhile he was looking up from under his dark lashes at the girovago and at us.

The girovago talked continually. He turned to me, holding the handful of sausages.

"This makes the tasty bit," he said.

"Oh yes—good salsiccia," said I.

"You are eating the kid? You are eating at the inn?" he said. I replied that I was.

"No," he said. "You stay and eat with me. You eat with me. The sausage is good, the kid will soon be done, the fire is grateful."

I laughed, not quite understanding him. He was certainly a bit tipsy.

"Signora," he said, turning to the q-b. She did not like him, he was impudent, and she shut a deaf ear to him as far as she could. "Signora," he said, "do you understand me what I say?"

She replied that she did.

"Signora," he said, "I sell things to the women. I sell them things."

"What do you sell?" she asked in astonishment.

"Saints," he said.

"Saints!" she cried in more astonishment.

"Yes, saints," he said with tipsy gravity.

She turned in confusion to the company in the background. The fat soldier came forward, he was the chief of the carabinieri.

"Also combs and bits of soap and little mirrors," he explained sarcastically.

"Saints!" said the girovago once more. "And also *ragazzini*—also youngsters— Wherever I go there is a little one comes running calling Babbo! Babbo! Daddy! Daddy! Wherever I go—youngsters. And I'm the babbo."

All this was received with a kind of silent sneer from the invisible assembly in the background. The candle was burning low, the fire was sinking too. In vain the dark-browed man tried to build it up. The q-b became impatient for the food. She got up wrathfully and stumbled into the dark passage, exclaiming—"Don't we eat yet?"

"Eh—Patience! Patience, Signora. It takes time in this house," said the man in the background.

The dark-browed man looked up at the girovago and said:

"Are you going to cook the sausages with your fingers?"

He too was trying to be assertive and jesting, but he was the kind of person no one takes any notice of. The girovago rattled on in dialect, poking fun at us and at our being there in this inn. I did not quite follow.

"Signora!" said the girovago. "Do you understand Sardinian?"

"I understand Italian—and some Sardinian," she replied rather hotly. "And I know that you are trying to laugh at us—to make fun of us."

He laughed fatly and comfortably.

"Ah Signora," he said. "We have a language that you wouldn't understand— not one word. Nobody here would understand it but me and him—" he pointed to the black-browed one. "Everybody would want an interpreter—everybody."

But he did not say interpreter—he said *intreprete*, with the accent on the penultimate, as if it were some sort of priest.

"A what?" said I.

He repeated with tipsy unction, and I saw what he meant.

"Why?" said I. "Is it a dialect? What is your dialect?"

"My dialect," he said, "is Sassari. I come from Sassari. If I spoke my dialect they would understand something. But if I speak this language they would want an interpreter."

"What language is it then?"

He leaned up to me, laughing.

"It is the language we use when the women are buying things and we don't want them to know what we say: me and him—"

"Oh," said I. "I know. We have that language in England. It is called thieves Latin—*Latino dei furbi*."

The men at the back suddenly laughed, glad to turn the joke against the forward girovago. He looked down his nose at me. But seeing I was laughing without malice, he leaned to me and said softly, secretly:

"What is your affair then? What affair is it, yours?"

"How? What?" I exclaimed, not understanding.

"*Che genere di affari?* What sort of business?"

"How—*affari?*" said I, still not grasping.

"What do you *sell?*" he said, flatly and rather spitefully. "What goods?"

"I don't sell anything," replied I, laughing to think he took us for some sort of strolling quacks or commercial travellers.

"Cloth—or something," he said cajolingly, slyly, as if to worm my secret out of me.

"But nothing at all. Nothing at all," said I. "We have come to Sardinia to see the peasant costumes—" I thought that might sound satisfactory.

"Ah, the costumes!" he said, evidently thinking I was a deep one. And he turned bandying words with his dark-browed mate, who was still poking the meat at the embers and crouching on the hearth. The room was almost quite dark. The mate answered him back, and tried to seem witty too. But the girovago was the commanding personality! rather too much so: too impudent for the q-b, though rather after my own secret heart. The mate was one of those handsome, passive, stupid men.

"Him!" said the girovago, turning suddenly to me and pointing at the mate. "He's my wife."

"Your wife!" said I.

"Yes. He's my wife, because we're always together."

There had become a sudden dead silence in the background. In spite of it the mate looked up under his black lashes and said, with a half smile:

"Don't talk, or I shall give thee a good *bacio* to-night."

There was an instant's fatal pause, then the girovago continued:

"Tomorrow is festa of Sant 'Antonio at Tonara. Tomorrow we are going to Tonara. Where are you going?"

"To Abbasanta," said I.

"Ah Abbasanta! You should come to Tonara. At Tonara there is a brisk trade—and there are costumes. You should come to Tonara. Come with him and me to Tonara tomorrow, and we will do business together."

I laughed, but did not answer.

"Come," said he. "You will like Tonara! Ah, Tonara is a fine place. There is an inn: you can eat well, sleep well. I tell you, because to you ten francs don't matter. Isn't that so? Ten francs don't matter to you. Well, then come to Tonara. What?

What do you say?"

I shook my head and laughed, but did not answer.

To tell the truth I should have liked to go to Tonara with him and his mate and do the brisk trade: if only I knew what trade it would be.

"You are sleeping upstairs?" he said to me.

I nodded.

"This is my bed," he said, taking one of the home-made rush mats from against the wall. I did not take him seriously at any point.

"Do they make those in Sorgono?" I said.

"Yes, in Sorgono—they are the beds, you see! And you roll up this end a bit—so! and that is the pillow."

He laid his cheek sideways.

"Not really," said I.

He came and sat down again next to me, and my attention wandered. The q-b was raging for her dinner. It must be quite half-past eight. The kid, the perfect kid would be cold and ruined. Both fire and candle were burning low. Someone had been out for a new candle, but there was evidently no means of replenishing the fire. The mate still crouched on the hearth, the dull red fire-glow on his handsome face, patiently trying to roast the kid and poking it against the embers. He had heavy, strong limbs in his khaki clothes, but his hand that held the spit was brown and tender and sensitive, a real Mediterranean hand. The girovago, blond, round-faced, mature and aggressive with all his liveliness, was more like a northerner. In the background were four or five other men, of whom I had distinguished none but a stout soldier, probably chief carabiniere.

Just as the q-b was working up to the rage I had at last calmed down from, appeared the shawl-swathed girl announcing "Pronto!"

"Pronto! Pronto!" said everybody.

"High time, too," said the q-b, springing from the low bench before the fire. "Where do we eat? Is there another room?"

"There is another room, Signora," said the carabiniere.

So we trooped out of the fire-warmed dungeon, leaving the girovago and his mate and two other men, muleteers from the road, behind us. I could see that it irked my girovago to be left behind. He was by far the strongest personality in the place, and he had the keenest intelligence. So he hated having to fall into the background, when he had been dragging all the lime-light on to himself all the evening. To me, too, he was something of a kindred soul that night. But there we are: fate, in the guise of that mysterious division between a respectable life and a scamp's life divided us. There was a gulf between me and him, between my way and his. He was a kindred spirit—but with a hopeless difference. There was something a bit sordid about him—and he knew it. That is why he was always tipsy. Yet I like the lone wolf souls best—better than the sheep. If only they didn't feel mongrel inside themselves. Presumably a scamp is bound to be mongrel. It is a pity the untamable, lone-wolf souls should always become pariahs, almost of choice: mere scamps.

Top and bottom of it is, I regretted my girovago, though I knew it was no good thinking of him. His way was *not* my way. Yet I regretted him, I did.

We found ourselves in a dining room with a long white table and inverted soup-plates, tomb-cold, lighted by an acetylene flare. Three men had accompanied us: the carabiniere, a little dark youth with a small black moustache, in a soldier's short, wool-lined great-coat: and a young man who looked tired round his blue eyes, and who wore a dark-blue overcoat, quite smart. The be-shawled damsel came in with the inevitable bowl of minestrone, soup with cabbage and cauliflower and other things. We helped ourselves, and the fat carabiniere started the conversation with the usual questions—and where were we going tomorrow?

I asked about buses. Then the responsible-looking, tired-eyed youth told me he was the bus-driver. He had come from Oristano, on the main line, that day. It is a distance of some forty miles. Next morning he was going on over the mountains to Nuoro—about the same distance again. The youth with the little black moustache and the Greek, large eyes, was his mate, the conductor. This was their run, from Oristano to Nuoro—a course of ninety miles or more. And every day on, on, on. No wonder he looked nerve-tired. Yet he had that kind of dignity, the wistful seriousness and pride of a man in machine control: the only god-like ones today, those who pull the iron levers and are the gods in the machine.

They repeated what the old roaster said: much nicer for us to go to Nuoro than to Abbasanta. So to Nuoro we decided to go, leaving at half-past nine in the morning.

Every other night the driver and his mate spent in this benighted Risveglio inn. It must have been their bedroom we saw, clean and tidy. I said was the food always so late, was everything always as bad as today. Always—if not worse, they said, making light of it, with sarcastic humor against the Risveglio. You spent your whole life at the Risveglio sitting, waiting, and going block-cold: unless you were content to drink *aqua vitae*, like those in there. The driver jerked his head towards the dungeon.

"Who were those in there?" said I.

The one who did all the talking was a mercante, a mercante girovago, a wandering peddler. This was my girovago: a wandering peddler selling saints and youngsters! The other was his mate, who helped carry the pack. They went about together. Oh, my girovago was a known figure all over the country.—And where would they sleep? There, in the room where the fire was dying.

They would unroll the mats and lie with their feet to the hearth. For this they paid threepence, or at most fourpence. And they had the privilege of cooking their own food. The Risveglio supplied them with nothing but the fire, the roof, and the rush mat.—And, of course, the drink. Oh, we need have no sympathy with the girovago and his sort. *They* lacked for nothing. They had everything they wanted: everything: and money in abundance. *They* lived for the *aqua vitae* they drank. That was all they wanted: their continual allowance of *aqua vitae*. And they got it. Ah, they were not cold. If the room became cold during the night: if they had no coverings at all: pah, they waited for morning, and as soon as it was light they drank a large glass of *aqua vitae*. That was their fire, their hearth and their home: drink. *Aqua vitae*, was hearth and home to them.

I was surprised at the contempt, tolerant and yet profound, with which these three men in the dining-room spoke of the others in the *stanza*. How contemptuous, almost bitter, the driver was against alcohol. It was evident he hated it. And though we all had our bottles of dead-cold dark wine, and though we all drank: still, the feeling of the three youths against actual intoxication was deep and hostile, with a certain burning *moral* dislike that is more northern than Italian. And they curled their lip with real dislike of the girovago: his forwardness, his impudent aggressiveness.

As for the inn, yes, it was very bad. It had been quite good under the previous proprietors. But now—they shrugged their shoulders. The dirty-breast and the shawled girl were not the owners. They were merely conductors of the hotel: here a sarcastic curl of the lip. The owner was a man in the village—a young man. A week or two back, at Christmas time, there had been a roomful of men sitting drinking and roistering at this very table. When in had come the proprietor, mad-drunk, swinging a litre bottle round his head and yelling: "Out! Out! Out, all of you! Out every one of you! I am proprietor here. And when I want to clear my house I clear my house. Every man obeys—who doesn't obey has his brains knocked out with this bottle. Out, out, I say—Out, everyone!" And the men all cleared out. "But," said the bus-driver, "I told him that when I had paid for my bed I was going to sleep in it. I was not going to be turned out by him or anybody. And so he came down."

There was a little silence from everybody after this story. Evidently there was more to it, that we were not to be told. Especially the carabiniere was silent. He was a fat, not very brave fellow, though quite nice.

Ah, but—said the little dark bus-conductor, with his small-featured swarthy Greek face—you must not be angry with them. True the inn was very bad. Very bad—but you must pity them, for they are only ignorant. Poor things, they are *ignoranti*! Why be angry?

The other two men nodded their heads in agreement and repeated *ignoranti*. They are *ignoranti*. It is true. Why be angry?

And here the modern Italian spirit came out: the endless pity for the ignorant. It is only slackness. The pity makes the ignorant more ignorant, and makes the Risveglio daily more impossible. If somebody let a bottle buzz round the ears of the dirty-breast, and whipped the shawl from the head of the pert young madam and sent her flying down the tunnel with a flea in her ear, we might get some attention and they might find a little self-respect. But no: pity them, poor *ignoranti*, while they pull life down and devour it like vermin. Pity them! What they need is not pity but prods: they and all their myriad of likes.

The be-shawled appeared with a dish of kid. Needless to say, the *ignoranti* had kept all the best portions for themselves. What arrived was five pieces of cold roast, one for each of us. Mine was a sort of large comb of ribs with a thin web of meat: perhaps an ounce. That was all we got, after watching the whole process. There was moreover a dish of strong boiled cauliflower, which one ate, with the coarse bread, out of sheer hunger. After this a bilious orange. Simply one is not *fed* nowadays. In the good hotels and in the bad, one is given paltry portions of unnourishing food, and one goes unfed.

The bus-driver, the only one with an earnest soul, was talking of the Sardinians. Ah, the Sardinians! They were hopeless. Why—because they did not know how to strike. They, too, were *ignoranti*. But this form of ignorance he found more annoying. They simply did not know what a strike was. If you offered them one day ten francs a stint—he was speaking now of the miners of the Iglesias region.—No, no, no, they would not take it, they wanted twelve francs. Go to them the next day and offer them four francs for half a stint, and yes, yes, yes, they would take it. And there they were: ignorant: ignorant Sardinians. They absolutely did not know how to strike. He was quite sarcastically hot about it. The whole tone of these three young men was the tone of sceptical irony common to the young people of our day the world over. Only they had—or at least the driver had—some little fervour for his strikes and his socialism. But it was a pathetic fervour: a *pis-aller* fervour.

We talked about the land. The war has practically gutted Sardinia of her cattle: so they said. And now the land is being deserted, the arable land is going back to fallow. Why? Why, says the driver, because the owners of the land won't spend any capital. They have got the capital locked up, and the land is dead. They find it cheaper to let all the arable go back to fallow, and raise a few head of cattle, rather than to pay high wages, grow corn, and get small returns.

Yes, and also, chimes in the carabiniere, the peasants don't want to work the land. They hate the land. They'll do anything to get off the land. They want regular wages, short hours, and devil take the rest. So they will go into France as navvies, by the hundred. They flock to Rome, they besiege the Labor bureaus, they will do the artificial Government navvy-work at a miserable five francs a day—a railway shunter having at least eighteen francs a day—anything, anything rather than work the land.

Yes, and what does the Government do! replies the bus-driver. They pull the roads to pieces in order to find work for the unemployed, remaking them, across the campagna. But in Sardinia, where roads and bridges are absolutely wanting, will they do anything? No!

There it is, however. The bus-driver, with dark shadows under his eyes, represents the intelligent portion of the conversation. The carabiniere is soft and will go any way, though always with some interest. The little Greek-looking conductor just does not care.

Enters another belated traveller, and takes a seat at the end of the table. The be-shawled brings him soup and a skinny bit of kid. He eyes this last with contempt, and fetches out of his bag a large hunk of roast pork, and bread, and black olives, thus proceeding to make a proper meal.

We being without cigarettes, the bus-driver and his companion press them on us: their beloved Macedonia cigarettes. The driver says they are *squisitissimi*—most, most exquisite—so exquisite that all foreigners want them. In truth I believe they are exported to Germany now. And they are quite good, when they really have tobacco in them. Usually they are hollow tubes of paper which just flare away under one's nose and are done.

We decide to have a round drink: they choose the precious *aqua vitae*: the white sort I think. At last it arrives—when the little dark-eyed one has fetched it. And it tastes rather like sweetened petroleum, with a dash of aniseed: filthy. Most Italian liquors are now sweet and filthy.

At length we rise to go to bed. We shall all meet in the morning. And this room is dead cold, with frost outside. Going out, we glance into the famous stanza. One figure alone lies stretched on the floor in the almost complete darkness. A few embers still glow. The other men no doubt are in the bar.

Ah, the filthy bedroom. The q-b ties up her head in a large, clean white kerchief, to avoid contact with the unsavory pillow. It is a cold, hard, flat bed, with two cold, hard, flat blankets. But we are very tired. Just as we are going to sleep, however, weird, high-pitched singing starts below, very uncanny—with a refrain that is a yelp-yelp-yelp! almost like a dog in angry pain. Weird, almost gruesome this singing goes on, first one voice and then another and then a tangle of voices. Again we are roused by the pounding of heavy feet on the corridor outside, which is as hollow and resonant as a drum. And then in the infernal crew-yard outside a cock crows. Throughout the night—yea, through all the black and frosty hours this demoniac bird screams its demon griefs.

However, it is morning. I gingerly wash a bit of myself in the broken basin, and dry that bit on a muslin veil which masquerades upon the chair as a towel. The q-b contents herself with a dry wipe. And we go downstairs in hopes of the last-night's milk.

There is no one to be seen. It is a cold, frost-strong, clear morning. There is no one in the bar. We stumble down the dark tunnel passage. The stanza is as if no man had ever set foot in it: very dark, the mats against the wall, the fire-place grey with a handful of long dead ash. Just like a dungeon. The dining-room has the same long table and eternal table-cloth—and our serviettes, still wet, lying where we shovelled them aside. So back again to the bar.

And this time a man is drinking *aqua vitae*, and the dirty-shirt is officiating. He has no hat on: and extraordinary, he has no brow at all: just flat, straight black hair slanting to his eyebrows, no forehead at all.

Is there coffee?

No, there is no coffee.

Why?

Because they can't get sugar.

Ho! laughs the peasant drinking *aqua vitae*. You make coffee with sugar! Here, say I, they make it with nothing.—Is there milk?

No.

No milk at all?

No.

Why not?

Nobody brings it.

Yes, yes—there is milk if they like to get it, puts in the peasant. But they want you to drink *aqua vitae*.

I see myself drinking *aqua vitae*. My yesterday's rage towers up again suddenly, till it quite suffocates me. There is something in this unsavoury, black, wine-dabbled, thick, greasy young man that does for me.

"Why," say I, lapsing into the Italian rhetorical manner, "why do you keep an inn? Why do you write the word Ristorante so large, when you have nothing to offer people, and don't intend to have anything. Why do you have the impudence to take in travellers? What does it mean, that this is an inn? What, say, what does it mean? Say then—what does it mean? What does it mean, your Ristorante Risveglio, written so large?"

Getting all this out in one breath, my indignation now stifled me. Him of the shirt said nothing at all. The peasant laughed. I demanded the bill. It was twenty-five francs odd. I picked up every farthing of the change.

"Won't you leave any tip at all?" asks the q-b.

"Tip!" say I, speechless.

So we march upstairs and make tea to fill the thermos flask. Then, with sack over my shoulder, I make my way out of the Risveglio.

It is Sunday morning. The frozen village street is almost empty. We march down to the wider space where the bus stands: I hope they haven't the impudence to call it a Piazza.

"Is this the Nuoro bus?" I ask of a bunch of urchins.

And even they begin to jeer. But my sudden up-starting flare quenches them at once. One answers yes, and they edge away. I stow the sack and the kitchenino in the first-class part. The first-class is in front: we shall see better.

There are men standing about, with their hands in their pockets,—those who are not in costume. Some wear the black-and-white. All wear the stocking caps. And all have the wide shirt-breasts, white, their waistcoats being just like evening dress waistcoats. Imagine one of these soft white shirt fronts well slobbered, and you have mine host of the Risveglio. But these lounging, static, white-breasted men are snowily clean, this being Sunday morning. They smoke their pipes on the frosty air, and are none too friendly.

The bus starts at half-past nine. The campanile is clanging nine. Two or three girls go down the road in their Sunday costume of purplish brown. We go up the road, into the clear, ringing frosty air, to find the lane.

And again, from above, how beautiful it is in the sharp morning! The whole village lies in bluish shadow, the hills with their thin pale oak trees are in bluish shadow still, only in the distance the frost-glowing sun makes a wonderful, jewel-like radiance on the pleasant hills, wild and thinly-wooded, of this interior region. Real fresh wonder-beauty all around. And such humanity.

Returning to the village we find a little shop and get biscuits and cigarettes. And we find our friends the bus-men. They are shy this morning. They are ready for us when we are ready. So in we get, joyfully, to leave Sorgono.

One thing I say for it, it must be an honest place. For people leave their sacks about without a qualm.

Up we go, up the road. Only to stop, alas, at the Risveglio. The little conductor goes down the lane towards the station. The driver goes and has a little drink with a comrade. There is quite a crowd round the dreary entrances of the inn. And quite a little bunch of people to clamber up into the second class, behind us.

We wait and wait. Then in climbs an old peasant, in full black-and-white costume, smiling in the pleased, naïve way of the old. After him climbs a fresh-faced young man with a suit-case.

"Na!" said the young man. "Now you are in the automobile."

And the old man gazes round with the wondering, vacant, naïve smile.

"One is all right here, eh?" the young citizen persists, patronizing.

But the old man is too excited to answer. He gazes hither and thither. Then he suddenly remembers he had a parcel, and looks for it in fear. The bright-faced young man picks it from the floor and hands it him. Ah, it is all right.

I see the little conductor in his dashing, sheep-lined, short military overcoat striding briskly down the little lane with the post-bag. The driver climbs to his seat in front of me. He has a muffler round his neck and his hat pulled down to his ears. He pips at the horn, and our old peasant cranes forward to look how he does it.

And so, with a jerk and a spurt, we start uphill.

"Eh—what's that?" said the peasant, frightened.

"We're starting," explained the bright-faced young man.

"Starting! Didn't we start before?"

The bright face laughs pleasedly.

"No," he said. "Did you think we had been going ever since you got in?"

"Yes," says the old man, simply, "since the door was shut."

The young citizen looks at us for our joyful approval.

VI. TO NUORO

These automobiles in Italy are splendid. They take the steep, looping roads so easily, they seem to run so naturally. And this one was comfortable, too. The roads of Italy always impress me. They run undaunted over the most precipitous regions, and with curious ease. In England almost any such road, among the mountains at least, would be labelled three times dangerous and would be famous throughout the land as an impossible climb. Here it is nothing. Up and down they go, swinging about with complete sang-froid. There seems to have been no effort in their construction. They are so good, naturally, that one hardly notices what splendid gestures they represent. Of course, the surface is now often intolerably bad. And they are most of them roads which, with ten years' neglect, will become ruins. For they are cut through overhanging rock and scooped out of the sides of hills. But I think it is marvellous how the Italians have penetrated all their inaccessible regions, of which they have so many, with great high-roads: and how along these high-roads the omnibuses now keep up a perfect communication. The precipitous and craggily-involved land is threaded through and through with roads. There seems to be a passion for high-roads and for constant communication. In this the Italians have a real Roman instinct, *now*. For the roads are new.

The railways too go piercing through rock for miles and miles, and nobody thinks anything of it. The coast railway of Calabria, down to Reggio, would make us stand on our heads if we had it in England. Here it is a matter of course. In the same way I always have a profound admiration for their driving—whether of a great omnibus or of a motor-car. It all seems so easy, as if the man were part of the car. There is none of that beastly grinding, uneasy feeling one has in the north. A car behaves like a smooth, live thing, sensibly.

All the peasants have a passion for a high-road. They want their land opening out, opening out. They seem to hate the ancient Italian remoteness. They all want to be able to get out at a moment's notice, to get away—quick, quick. A village which is two miles off the high-road, even if it is perched like a hawk's nest on a peak, still chafes and chafes for the great road to come to it, chafes and chafes for the daily motor-bus connection with the railway. There is no placidity, no rest in the heart of the land. There is a fever of restless irritation all the time.

And yet the permanent way of almost every railway is falling into bad disrepair, the roads are shocking. And nothing seems to be done. Is our marvellous, mechanical era going to have so short a bloom? Is the marvellous openness, the opened-out wonder of the land going to collapse quite soon, and the remote places lapse back into inaccessibility again? Who knows! I rather hope so.

The automobile took us rushing and winding up the hill, sometimes through cold, solid-seeming shadow, sometimes across a patch of sun. There was thin, bright ice in the ruts, and deep grey hoar-frost on the grass. I cannot tell how the sight of the grass and bushes heavy with frost, and wild—in their own primitive wildness charmed me. The slopes of the steep wild hills came down shaggy and bushy, with a few berries lingering, and the long grass-stalks sere with the frost. Again the dark valley sank below like a ravine, but shaggy, bosky, unbroken. It came upon me how I loved the sight of the blue-shadowed, tawny-tangled winter with its frosty standstill. The young oaks keep their brown leaves. And doing so, surely they are best with a thin edge of rime.

One begins to realize how old the real Italy is, how man-gripped, and how withered. England is far more wild and savage and lonely, in her country parts. Here since endless centuries man has tamed the impossible mountain side into terraces, he has quarried the rock, he has fed his sheep among the thin woods, he has cut his boughs and burnt his charcoal, he has been half domesticated even among the wildest fastnesses. This is what is so attractive about the remote places, the Abruzzi, for example. Life is so primitive, so pagan, so strangely heathen and half-savage. And yet it is human life. And the wildest country is half humanized, half brought under. It is all conscious. Wherever one is in Italy, either one is conscious of the present, or of the mediaeval influences, or of the far, mysterious gods of the early Mediterranean. Wherever one is, the place has its conscious genus. Man has lived there and brought forth his consciousness there and in some way brought that place to consciousness, given it its expression, and, really, finished it. The expression may be Proserpine, or Pan, or even the strange "shrouded gods" of the Etruscans or the Sikels, none the less it is an expression. The land has been humanised, through and through: and we in our own tissued consciousness bear the results of this humanisation. So that for us to go to Italy and to *penetrate* into Italy is like a most fascinating act of self-discovery—back, back down the old ways of time. Strange and wonderful chords awake in us, and vibrate again after many hundreds of years of complete forgetfulness.

And then—and then—there is a final feeling of sterility. It is all worked out. It is all known: *connu, connu!*

This Sunday morning, seeing the frost among the tangled, still savage bushes of Sardinia, my soul thrilled again. This was not all known. This was not all worked out. Life was not only a process of rediscovering backwards. It is that, also: and it is that intensely. Italy has given me back I know not what of myself, but a very, very great deal. She has found for me so much that was lost: like a restored Osiris. But this morning in the omnibus I realize that, apart from the great rediscovery backwards, which one *must* make before one can be whole at all, there is a move forwards. There are unknown, unworked lands where the salt has not lost its savour. But one must have perfected oneself in the great past first.

If one travels one eats. We immediately began to munch biscuits, and the old peasant in his white, baggy breeches and black cuirass, his old face smiling wonderingly under his old stocking cap, although he was only going to Tonara, some seven or eight miles, began to peel himself a hard-boiled egg, which he got out of his parcel. With calm wastefulness he peeled away the biggest part of the white of the egg with the shell—because it came away so. The citizen of Nuoro, for such the bright-faced young man was, said to him—"But see how you waste it."—"Ha!" said the old peasant, with a reckless indifferent wave of the hand. What did he care how much he wasted, since he was *en voyage* and riding for the first time in his life in an automobile.

The citizen of Nuoro told us he had some sort of business in Sorgono, so he came back and forth constantly. The peasant did some work or other for him—or brought him something down from Tonara. He was a pleasant, bright-eyed young man, and he made nothing of eight hours in a motor-bus.

He told us there was still game among these hills: wild boars which were hunted in big hunts, and many hares. It was a curious and beautiful sight, he said, to see a hare at night fascinated by the flare of the lamps of the automobile, racing ahead with its ears back, always keeping in front, inside the beam, and flying like mad, on and on ahead, till at some hill it gathered speed and melted into the dark.

We descended into a deep, narrow valley to the road-junction and the canteen-house, then up again, up and up sharp to Tonara, our village we had seen in the sun yesterday. But we were approaching it from the back. As we swerved into the sunlight, the road took a long curve on to the open ridge between two valleys. And there in front we saw a glitter of scarlet and white. It was in slow motion. It was a far-off procession, scarlet figures of women, and a tall image moving away from us, slowly, in the Sunday morning. It was passing along the level sunlit ridge above a deep, hollow valley. A close procession of women glittering in scarlet, white and black, moving slowly in the distance beneath the grey-yellow buildings of the village on the crest, towards an isolated old church: and all along this narrow upland saddle as on a bridge of sunshine itself.

Were we not going to see any more? The bus turned again and rushed along the now level road and then veered. And there beyond, a little below, we saw the procession *coming*. The bus faded to a standstill, and we climbed out. Above us, old and mellowed among the smooth rocks and the bits of flat grass was the church, tanging its bell. Just in front, above, were old, half-broken houses of stone. The road came gently winding up to us, from what was evidently two villages ledged one above the other upon the steep summit of the south slope. Far below was the south valley, with a white puff of engine steam.

And slowly chanting in the near distance, curving slowly up to us on the white road between the grass came the procession. The high morning was still. We stood all on this ridge above the world, with the deeps of silence below on the right. And in a strange, brief, staccato monody chanted the men, and in quick, light rustle of women's voices came the responses. Again the men's voices! The white was mostly men, not women. The priest in his robes, his boys near him, was leading the chanting. Immediately behind him came a small cluster of bare-headed, tall, sunburnt men, all in golden-velveteen corduroy, mountain-peasants, bowing beneath a great life-size seated image of Saint Anthony of Padua. After these a number of men in the costume, but with the white linen breeches hanging wide and loose almost to the ankles, instead of being tucked into the black gaiters. So they seemed very white beneath the back kilt frill. The black frieze body-vest was cut low, like an evening suit, and the stocking caps were variously perched. The men chanted in low, hollow, melodic tones. Then came the rustling chime of the women. And the procession crept slowly, aimlessly forward in time with the chant. The great image rode rigid, and rather foolish.

After the men was a little gap—and then the brilliant wedge of the women. They were packed two by two, close on each other's heels, chanting inadvertently when their turn came, and all in brilliant, beautiful costume. In front were the little girl-children, two by two, immediately following the tall men in peasant black-and-white. Children, demure and conventional, in vermilion, white and green—little girl-children with long skirts of scarlet cloth down to their feet, green-banded near the bottom: with white aprons bordered with vivid green and mingled colour: having little scarlet, purple-bound, open boleros over the full white shirts: and black head-cloths folded across their little chins, just leaving the lips clear, the face framed in black. Wonderful little girl-children, perfect and demure in the stiffish, brilliant costume, with black head-dress! Stiff as Velasquez princesses! The bigger girls followed, and then the mature women, a close procession. The long vermilion skirts with their green bands at the bottom flashed a solid moving mass of colour, softly swinging, and the white aprons with their band of brilliant mingled green seemed to gleam. At the throat the full-bosomed white shirts were fastened with big studs of gold filigree, two linked filigree globes: and the great white sleeves billowed from the scarlet, purplish-and-green-edged boleros. The faces came nearer to us, framed all round in the dark cloths. All the lips still sang responses, but all the eyes watched us. So the softly-swaying coloured body of the procession came up to us. The poppy-scarlet smooth cloth rocked in fusion, the bands and bars of emerald green seemed to burn across the red and the showy white, the dark eyes peered and stared at us from under the black snood, gazed back at us with raging curiosity, while the lips moved automatically in chant. The bus had run into the inner side of the road, and the procession had to press round it, towards the sky-line, the great valley lying below.

The priest stared, hideous St. Anthony cockled a bit as he passed the butt end of the big grey automobile, the peasant men in gold-coloured corduroy, old, washed soft, were sweating under the load and still singing with opened lips, the loose white breeches of the men waggled as they walked on with their hands behind their backs, turning again, to look at us. The big, hard hands, folded behind black kilt-frill! The women, too, shuffled slowly past, rocking the scarlet and the bars of green, and all twisting as they sang, to look at us still more. And so the procession edged past the bus, and was trailing upwards, curved solid against the sky-line towards the old church. From behind, the geranium scarlet was intense, one saw the careful, curiously cut backs of the shapen boleros, poppy-red, edged with mauve-purple and green, and the white of the shirt just showing at the waist. The full sleeves billowed out, the black head-cloths hung down to a point. The pleated skirts swing slowly, the broad band of green accentuating the motion. Indeed that is what it must be for, this thick, rich band of jewel green, to throw the wonderful horizontal motion back and forth, back and forth, of the suave vermilion, and give that static, Demeta splendor to a peasant motion, so magnificent in colour, geranium and malachite.

All the costumes were not exactly alike. Some had more green, some had less. In some the sleeveless boleros were of a darker red, and some had poorer aprons, without such gorgeous bands at the bottom. And some were evidently old: probably thirty years old: still perfect and in keeping, reserved for Sunday and high holidays. A few were darker, ruddier than the true vermilion. This varying of the tone intensified the beauty of the shuffling woman-host.

When they had filed into the grey, forlorn little church on the ridge-top just above us, the bus started silently to run on to the rest-point below, whilst we climbed back up the little rock-track to the church. When we came to the side-door we found the church quite full. Level with us as we stood in the open side doorway, we saw kneeling on the bare stoneflags the little girl-children, and behind them all the women clustered kneeling upon their aprons, with hands negligently folded, filling the church to the further doorway, where the sun shone: the bigger west-end doorway. In the shadow of the whitewashed, bare church all these kneeling women with their colour and their black head-cloths looked like some thick bed of flowers, geranium, black hooded above. They all knelt on the naked, solid stone of the pavement.

There was a space in front of the geranium little girl-children, then the men in corduroys, gold-soft, with dark round heads, kneeling awkwardly in reverence; and then the queer, black cuirasses and full white sleeves of grey-headed peasant men, many bearded. Then just in front of them the priest in his white vestment, standing exposed, and just baldly beginning an address. At the side of the altar was seated large and important the modern, simpering, black-gowned Anthony of Padua, nursing a boy-child. He looked a sort of male Madonna.

"Now," the priest was saying, "blessed Saint Anthony shows you in what way you can be Christians. It is not enough that you are not Turks. Some think they are Christians because they are not Turks. It is true you are none of you Turks. But you have still to learn how to be good Christians. And this you can learn from our blessed Saint Anthony. Saint Anthony, etc., etc...."

The contrast between Turks and Christians is still forceful in the Mediterranean, where the Mohammedans have left such a mark. But how the word *cristiani*, *cristiani*, spoken with a peculiar priestly unction, gets on my nerves. The voice is barren in its homily. And the women are all intensely watching the q-b and me in the doorway, their folded hands are very negligently held together.

"Come away!" say I. "Come away, and let them listen."

We left the church crowded with its kneeling host, and dropped down past the broken houses towards the omnibus, which stood on a sort of level out-look place, a levelled terrace with a few trees, standing silent over the valley. It should be picketed with soldiers having arquebuses. And I should have welcomed a few thorough-paced infidels, as a leaven to this dreary Christianity of ours.

But it was a wonderful place. Usually, the life-level is reckoned as sea-level. But here, in the heart of Sardinia, the life-level is high as the golden-lit plateau, and the sea-level is somewhere far away, below, in the gloom, it does not signify. The life-level is high up, high and sun-sweetened and among rocks.

We stood and looked below, at the puff of steam, far down the wooded valley where we had come yesterday. There was an old, low house on this eagle-perching piazza. I would like to live there. The real village—or rather two villages, like an ear-ring and its pendant—lay still beyond, in front, ledging near the summit of the long, long, steep wooded slope, that never ended till it ran flush to the depths away below there in shadow.

And yesterday, up this slope the old peasant had come with his two brilliant daughters and the pack-pony.

And somewhere in those ledging, pearly villages in front must be my girovago and his "wife". I wish I could see their stall and drink aqua vitae with them.

"How beautiful the procession!" says the q-b to the driver.

"Ah yes—one of the most beautiful costumes of Sardinia, this of Tonara," he replied wistfully.

The bus sets off again—minus the old peasant. We retrace our road. A woman is leading a bay pony past the church, striding with long strides, so that her maroon skirt swings like a fan, and hauling the halter rope. Apparently the geranium red costume is Sunday only, the week-day is this maroon, or puce, or madder-brown.

Quickly and easily the bus slips down the hill into the valley. Wild, narrow valleys, with trees, and brown-legged cork trees. Across the other side a black and white peasant is working alone on a tiny terrace of the hill-side, a small, solitary figure, for all the world like a magpie in the distance. These people like being alone—solitary—one sees a single creature so often isolated among the wilds. This is different from Sicily and Italy, where the people simply cannot be alone. They *must* be in twos and threes.

But it is Sunday morning, and the worker is exceptional. Along the road we pass various pedestrians, men in their black sheepskins, boys in their soldiers' remains. They are trudging from one village to another, across the wild valleys. And there is a sense of Sunday morning freedom, of roving, as in an English countryside. Only the one old peasant works alone: and a goatherd watching his long-haired, white goats.

Beautiful the goats are: and so swift. They fly like white shadows along the road from us, then dart down-hill. I see one standing on a bough of an oak-tree, right in the tree, an enormous white tree-creature complacently munching up aloft, then rearing on her hind legs, so lengthy, and putting her slim paws far away on an upper, forward branch.

Whenever we come to a village we stop and get down, and our little conductor disappears into the post-office for the post-bag. This last is usually a limp affair, containing about three letters. The people crowd round—and many of them in very ragged costume. They look poor, and not attractive: perhaps a bit degenerate. It would seem as if the Italian instinct to get into rapid touch with the world were the healthy instinct after all. For in these isolated villages, which have been since time began far from any life-centre, there is an almost sordid look on the faces of the people. We must remember that the motor-bus is a great innovation. It has been running for five weeks only. I wonder for how many months it will continue.

For I am sure it cannot pay. Our first-class tickets cost, I believe, about twenty-seven francs each. The second class costs about three-quarters the first. Some parts of the journey we were very few passengers. The distance covered is so great, the population so thin, that even granted the passion for getting out of their own villages, which possesses all people now, still the bus cannot earn much more than an average of two hundred to three hundred francs a day. Which, with two men's wages, and petrol at its enormous price, and the cost of wear-and-tear, cannot possibly pay.

I asked the driver. He did not tell me what his wages were: I did not ask him. But he said the company paid for the keep and lodging for himself and mate at the stopping-places. This being Sunday, fewer people were travelling: a statement hard to believe. Once he had carried fifty people all the way from Tonara to Nuoro. Once! But it was in vain he protested. Ah well, he said, the bus carried the post, and the government paid a subsidy of so many thousands of lire a year: a goodly number. Apparently then the government was the loser, as usual. And there are hundreds, if not thousands of these omnibuses running the lonely districts of Italy and Sicily—Sardinia had a network of systems. They are splendid—and they are perhaps an absolute necessity for a nervous restless population which simply cannot keep still, and which finds some relief in being whirled about even on the *autovie*, as the bus-system is called.

The autovie are run by private companies, only subsidised by the government.

On we rush, through the morning—and at length see a large village, high on the summit beyond, stony on the high upland. But it has a magical look, as these tiny summit-cities have from the distance. They recall to me always my childish visions of Jerusalem, high against the air, and seeming to sparkle, and built in sharp cubes.

It is curious what a difference there is between the high, fresh, proud villages and the valley villages. Those that crown the world have a bright, flashing air, as Tonara had. Those that lie down below, infolded in the shadow, have a gloomy, sordid feeling and a repellent population, like Sorgono and other places at which we had halted. The judgment may be all wrong: but this was the impression I got.

We were now at the highest point of the journey. The men we saw on the road were in their sheepskins, and some were even walking with their faces shawl-muf-fled. Glancing back, we saw up the valley clefts the snow of Gennargentu once more, a white mantle on broad shoulders, the very core of Sardinia. The bus slid to a standstill in a high valley, beside a stream where the road from Fonni joined ours. There was waiting a youth with a bicycle. I would like to go to Fonni. They say it is the highest village in Sardinia.

In front, on the broad summit, reared the towers of Gavoi. This was the half-way halt, where the buses had their *coincidenza*, and where we would stay for an hour and eat. We wound up and up the looping road, and at last entered the village. Women came to the doors to look. They were wearing the dark madder-brown costume. Men were hastening, smoking their pipes, towards our stopping place.

We saw the other bus—a little crowd of people—and we drew up at last. We were tired and hungry. We were at the door of the inn, and we entered quickly. And in an instant, what a difference! At the clean little bar, men were drinking cheerfully. A side door led into the common room. And how charming it was. In a very wide chimney, white and stone-clean, with a lovely shallow curve above, was burning a fire of long, clean-split faggots, laid horizontally on the dogs. A clean, clear bright fire, with odd little chairs in front, very low, for us to sit on. The funny, low little chairs seem a specialty of this region.

The floor of this room was paved with round dark pebbles, beautifully clean. On the walls hung brilliant copper fans, glittering against the whitewash. And under the long, horizontal window that looked on the street was a stone slab with sockets for little charcoal fires. The curve of the chimney arch was wide and shallow, the curve above the window was still wider, and of a similar delicate shallowness, the white roof rose delicately vaulted. With the glitter of copper, the expanse of dark, rose-coloured, pebbled floor, the space, the few low, clean-gleaming faggots, it was really beautiful. We sat and warmed ourselves, welcomed by a plump hostess and a pleasant daughter, both in madder-brown dress and full white shirt. People strayed in and out, through the various doors. The houses are built without any plan at all, the rooms just happening, here or there. A bitch came from an inner darkness and stood looking at the fire, then looked up at me, smiling in her bitch-like, complacent fashion.

But we were dying with hunger. What was there to eat?—and was it nearly ready? There was *cinghiale*, the pleasant, hard-cheeked girl told us, and it was nearly ready. *Cinghiale* being wild boar, we sniffed the air. The girl kept tramping rather fecklessly back and forth, with a plate or a serviette: and at last it was served. We went through the dark inner place, which was apparently the windowless bit left over, inside, when the hap-hazard rooms were made round about, and from thence into a large, bare, darkish pebbled room with a white table and inverted soup-plates. It was deathly cold. The window looked north over the wintry landscape of the highlands, fields, stone walls, and rocks. Ah, the cold, motionless air of the room.

But we were quite a party: the second bus-driver and his mate, a bearded traveller on the second bus, with his daughter, ourselves, the bright-faced citizen from Nuoro, and our driver. Our little dark-eyed conductor did not come. It dawned on me later he could not afford to pay for this meal, which was not included in his wage.

The Nuoro citizen conferred with our driver—who looked tired round the eyes—and made the girl produce a tin of sardines. These were opened at table with a large pocket-knife belonging to the second conductor. He was a reckless, odd, hot-foot fellow whom I liked very much. But I was terrified at the way he carved the sardine-box with his jack-knife. However, we could eat and drink.

Then came the *brodo*, the broth, in a great bowl. This was boiling hot, and very, very strong. It was perfectly plain, strong meat-stock, without vegetables. But how good and invigorating it was, and what an abundance! We drank it down, and ate the good, cold bread.

Then came the boar itself. Alas, it was a bowl of hunks of dark, rather coarse boiled meat, from which the broth had been made. It was quite dry, without fat. I should have been very puzzled to know what meat it was, if I had not been told. Sad that the wild boar should have received so little culinary attention. However, we ate the hunks of hot, dry meat with bread, and were glad to get them. They were filling, at least. And there was a bowl of rather bitter green olives for a condiment.

The Nuoro citizen now produced a huge bottle of wine, which he said was *finissimo*, and refused to let us go on with the dark wine on the table, of which every guest was served with a bottle. So we drank up, and were replenished with the redder, lighter, finer Sorgono wine. It was very good.

The second bus-conductor also did not eat the inn meal. He produced a vast piece of bread, good, home-made bread, and at least half of a roast lamb, and a large paper of olives. This lamb he insisted on sending round the table, waving his knife and fork with dramatic gestures at every guest, insisting that every guest should take a hunk. So one by one we all helped ourselves to the extraordinarily good cold roast lamb, and to the olives. Then the bus-conductor fell to as well. There was a mass of meat still left to him.

It is extraordinary how generous and, from the inside, well-bred these men were. To be sure the second conductor waved his knife and fork and made bitter faces if one of us took only a little bit of the lamb. He wanted us to take more. But the *essential* courtesy in all of them was quite perfect, so manly and utterly simple. Just the same with the q-b. They treated her with a sensitive, manly simplicity, which one could not but be thankful for. They made none of the odious politenesses which are so detestable in well-brought-up people. They made no advances and did none of the hateful homage of the adulating male. They were quiet, and kind, and sensitive to the natural flow of life, and quite without airs. I liked them extremely. Men who can be quietly kind and simple to a woman, without wanting to show off or to make an impression, they are men still. They were neither humble nor conceited. They did not show off. And oh God, what a blessed relief, to be with people who don't bother to show off. We sat at that table quietly and naturally as if we were by ourselves, and talked or listened to their talk, just as it happened. When we did not want to talk, they took no notice of us. And that I call good manners. Middle-class, showing off people would have found them uncouth. I found them almost the only really well-bred people I have met. They did not show off in any way at all, not even a show of simplicity. They knew that in the beginning and in the end a man stands alone, his soul is alone in itself, and all attributes are nothing—and this curious final knowledge preserved them in simplicity.

When we had had coffee and were going out, I found our own conductor in a little chair by the fire. He was looking a bit pathetic. I had enough sense to give him a coffee, which brightened him. But it was not till afterwards, putting things together, that I realized he had wanted to be with us all at table, but that his conductor's wages probably did not allow him to spend the money. My bill for the dinner was about fifteen francs, for the two of us.

In the bus again, we were quite crowded. A peasant girl in Nuoro costume sat facing me, and a dark-bearded, middle-aged man in a brown velveteen suit was next me and glowering at her. He was evidently her husband. I did not like him: one of the jealous, carping sort. She, in her way, was handsome: but a bit of a devil as well, in all probability. There were two village women become fine, in town dress and black silk scarves over their heads, fancying themselves. Then there was a wild scuffle, and three bouncing village lasses were pushed in, laughing and wild with excitement. There were wild farewells, and the bus rolled out of Gavoi between the desolate mountain fields and the rocks, on a sort of table-land. We rolled on for a mile or so: then stopped, and the excited lasses got down. I gathered they had been given a little ride for a Sunday treat. Delighted they were. And they set off, with other bare-headed women in costume, along a bare path between flat, out-cropping rocks and cold fields.

The girl facing me was a study. She was not more than twenty years old I should say: or was she? Did the delicate and fine complication of lines against her eyes mean thirty-five? But anyhow she was the wife of the velveteen man. He was thick-set and had white hairs in his coarse black beard, and little, irritable brown eyes under his irritable brows. He watched her all the time. Perhaps, she was after all a young, new girl-wife. She sat with that expressionless look of one who is watched and who appears not to know it. She had her back to the engine.

She wore her black head-cloth from her brow and her hair was taken tight back from her rather hard, broad, well-shaped forehead. Her dark eyebrows were very finely drawn above her large, dark-grey, pellucid eyes, but they were drawn with a peculiar obstinate and irritating lift. Her nose was straight and small, her mouth well-shut. And her big, rather hostile eyes had a withheld look in them, obstinate. Yet, being newly wed and probably newly-awakened, her eyes looked sometimes at me with a provoking look, curious as to what I was in the husband line, challenging rather defiantly with her new secrets, obstinate in opposition to the male authority, and yet intrigued by the very fact that one was man. The velveteen husband—his velveteens too had gone soft and gold-faded, yet some-how they made him look ugly, common—he watched her with his irritable, yellow-brown eyes, and seemed to fume in his stiff beard.

She wore the costume: the full-gathered shirt fastened at the throat with the two gold filigree globes, a little dark, braided, stiff bolero just fastened at the waist, leaving a pretty pattern of white breast, and a dark maroon skirt. As the bus rushed along she turned somewhat pale, with the obstinate pinched look of a woman who is in opposition to her man. At length she flung him a few words which I did not catch—and her forehead seemed to go harder, as she drooped her lashes occasionally over her wide, alert, obstinate, rather treacherous eyes. She must have been a difficult piece of goods to deal with. And she sat with her knees touching mine, rocking against mine as the bus swayed.

We came to a village on the road: the landscape had now become wider, much more open. At the inn door the bus stopped, and the velveteen husband and the girl got down. It was cold—but in a minute I got down too. The bus conductor came to me and asked anxiously if the q-b were ill. The q-b said no, why? Because there was a signora whom the motion of the bus made ill. This was the girl.

There was a crowd and a great row at this inn. In the second dark room, which was bare of furniture, a man sat in a corner playing an accordion. Men in the close breeches were dancing together. Then they fell to wrestling wildly, crashing about among the others, with shouts and yells. Men in the black-and-white, but untidy, with the wide white drawers left hanging out over the black gaiters, surged here and there. All were rowdy with drink. This again was rather a squalid inn but roaring with violent, crude male life.

The Nuoro citizen said that here was very good wine, and we must try it. I did not want it, but he insisted. So we drank little glasses of merely moderate red wine. The sky had gone all grey with the afternoon curd-clouds. It was very cold and raw. Wine is no joy, cold, dead wine, in such an atmosphere.

The Nuoro citizen insisted on paying. He would let me pay, he said, when he came to England. In him, and in our bus men, the famous Sardinian hospitality and generosity still lingers.

When the bus ran on again the q-b told the peasant girl who again had the pinched look, to change places with me and sit with her face to the engine. This the young woman did, with that rather hard assurance common to these women. But at the next stop she got down, and made the conductor come with us into the compartment, whilst she sat in front between the driver and the citizen of Nuoro. That was what she wanted all the time. Now she was all right. She had her back to the velveteen husband, she sat close between two strange young men, who were condoling with her. And velveteens eyed her back, and his little eyes went littler and more pin-pointed, and his nose seemed to curl with irritation.

The costumes had changed again. There was again the scarlet, but no green.

The green had given place to mauve and rose. The women in one cold, stony, rather humbled broken place were most brilliant. They had the geranium skirts, but their sleeveless boleros were made to curl out strangely from the waist, and they were edged with a puckered rose-pink, a broad edge, with lines of mauve and lavender. As they went up between the houses that were dark and grisly under the blank, cold sky, it is amazing how these women of vermilion and rose-pink seemed to melt into an almost impossible blare of colour. What a risky blend of colours! Yet how superb it could look, that dangerous hard assurance of these women as they strode along so blaring. I would not like to tackle one of them.

Wider and colder the landscape grew. As we topped a hill at the end of a village, we saw a long string of wagons, each with a pair of oxen, and laden with large sacks, curving upwards in the cold, pallid Sunday afternoon. Seeing us, the procession came to a standstill at the curve of the road, and the pale oxen, the pale low wagons, the pale full sacks, all in the blenched light, each one headed by a tall man in shirt-sleeves, trailing a static procession on the hill-side, seemed like a vision: like a Doré drawing. The bus slid past, the man holding the wagon-pole, while some oxen stood like rock, some swayed their horns. The q-b asked the velveteener what they were carrying. For a long time he took no notice of the question. Then he volunteered, in a snappy voice, that it was the government grain being distributed to the communes for bread. On Sunday afternoon too.

Oh this government corn! What a problem those sacks represent!

The country became wider as we dropped lower. But it was bleak and treeless once more. Stones cropped up in the wide, hollow dales. Men on ponies passed forlorn across the distances. Men with bundles waited at the cross-roads to pick up the bus. We were drawing near to Nuoro. It was past three in the afternoon, cold with a blenched light. The landscape seemed bare and stony, wide, different from any before.

We came to the valley where the branch-line runs to Nuoro. I saw little pink railway-cabins at once, lonely along the valley bed. Turning sharp to the right, we ran in silence over the moor-land-seeming slopes, and saw the town beyond, clustered beyond, a little below, at the end of the long declivity, with sudden mountains rising around it. There it lay, as if at the end of the world, mountains rising sombre behind.

So, we stop at the Dazio, the town's customs hut, and velveteens has to pay for some meat and cheese he is bringing in. After which we slip into the cold high-street of Nuoro. I am thinking that this is the home of Grazia Deledda, the novelist, and I see a barber's shop. De Ledda. And thank heaven we are at the end of the journey. It is past four o'clock.

The bus has stopped quite close to the door of the inn: Star of Italy, was it? In we go at the open door. Nobody about, free access to anywhere and everywhere, as usual: testifying again to Sardinian honesty. We peer through a doorway to the left—through a rough little room: ah, there in a dark, biggish room beyond is a white-haired old woman with a long, ivory-coloured face standing at a large table ironing. One sees only the large whiteness of the table, and the long pallid face and the querulous pale-blue eye of the tall old woman as she looks up questioning from the gloom of the inner place.

"Is there a room, Signora?"

She looks at me with a pale, cold blue eye, and shouts into the dark for some-body. Then she advances into the passage and looks us up and down, the q-b and me.

"Are you husband and wife?" she demands, challenge.

"Yes, how shouldn't we be," say I.

A tiny maid, of about thirteen, but sturdy and brisk-looking, has appeared in answer to the shout.

"Take them to number seven," says the old dame, and she turns back to her gloom, and seizes the flat iron grimly.

We follow up two flights of cold stone stairs, disheartening narrow staircase with a cold iron rail, and corridors opening off gloomily and rather disorderly. These houses give the effect, inside, of never having been properly finished, as if, long, long ago, the inmates had crowded in, pig-sty fashion, without waiting for anything to be brought into order, and there it had been left, dreary and chaotic.

Thumbelina, the little maid, threw open the door of number seven with *eclat*. And we both exclaimed: "How fine!" It seemed to us palatial. Two good, thick white beds, a table, a chest of drawers, two mats on the tiled floor, and gor-geous oleographs on the wall—and two good wash-bowls side by side—and all perfectly clean and nice. What were we coming to! We felt we ought to be impressed.

We pulled open the latticed window doors, and looked down on the street: the only street. And it was a river of noisy life. A band was playing, rather terri-bly, round the corner at the end, and up and down the street jigged endless numbers of maskers in their Carnival costume, with girls and young women strolling arm-in-arm to participate. And how frisky they all were, how bubbly and unself-conscious!

The maskers were nearly all women—the street was full of women: so we thought at first. Then we saw, looking closer, that most of the women were young men, dressed up. All the maskers were young men, and most of these young men, *of course*, were masquerading as women. As a rule they did not wear face-masks, only little dominoes of black cloth or green cloth or white cloth coming down to the mouth. Which is much better. For the old modelled half-masks with the lace frill, the awful proboscis sticking forward white and ghastly like the beaks of corpse-birds—such as the old Venice masks—these I think are simply horrifying. And the more modern "faces" are usually only repulsive. While the simple little pink half-masks with the end of black or green or white cloth, these just form a human disguise.

It was quite a game, sorting out the real women from the false. Some were easy. They had stuffed their bosoms, and stuffed their bustles, and put on hats and very various robes, and they minced along with little jigging steps, like little dolls that dangle from elastic, and they put their heads on one side and dripped their hands, and danced up to flurry the actual young ladies, and sometimes they received a good clout on the head, when they broke into wild and violent gestures, whereat the *actual* young ladies scuffled wildly.

They were very lively and naïve.—But some were more difficult. Every conceivable sort of "woman" was there, broad shouldered and with rather large feet. The most usual was the semi-peasant, with a very full bosom and very full skirt and a very downright bearing. But one was a widow in weeds, drooping on the arm of a robust daughter. And one was an ancient crone in a crochet bedcover. And one was in an old skirt and blouse and apron, with a broom, wildly sweeping the street from end to end. He was an animated rascal. He swept with very sarcastic assiduity in front of two town-misses in fur coats, who minced very importantly along. He swept their way very humbly, facing them and going backwards, sweeping and bowing, whilst they advanced with their noses in the air. He made his great bow, and they minced past, daughters of dog-fish, pesce-carne, no doubt. Then he skipped with a bold, gambolling flurry behind them, and with a perfectly mad frenzy began to sweep after them, as if to sweep their tracks away. He swept so madly and so blindly with his besom that he swept on to their heels and their ankles. They shrieked and glowered round, but the blind sweeper saw them not. He swept and swept and pricked their thin silk ankles. And they, scarlet with indignation and rage, gave hot skips like cats on hot bricks, and fled discomfited forwards. He bowed once more after them, and started mildly and innocently to sweep the street. A pair of lovers of fifty years ago, she in a half crinoline and poke bonnet and veil, hanging on his arm came very coyly past, oh so simpering, and it took me a long time to be sure that the "girl" was a youth. An old woman in a long nightdress prowled up and down, holding out her candle and peering in the street as if for burglars. She would approach the *real* young women and put her candle in their faces and peer so hard, as if she suspected them of something. And they blushed and turned their faces away and protested confusedly. This old woman searched so fearfully in the face of one strapping lass in the pink and scarlet costume, who looked for all the world like a bunch of red and rose-pink geraniums, with a bit of white,—a *real* peasant lass—that the latter in a panic began to beat him with her fist, furiously, quite aroused. And he made off, running comically in his long white nightdress.

There were some really beautiful dresses of rich old brocade, and some gleaming old shawls, a shimmer of lavender and silver, or of dark, rich shot colours with deep borders of white silver and primrose gold, very lovely. I believe two of them were actual women—but the q-b says no. There was a Victorian gown of thick green silk, with a creamy blotched cross-over shawl. About her we both were doubtful. There were two wistful, drooping-lily sisters, all in white, with big feet. And there was a very successful tall miss in a narrow hobble-skirt of black satin and a toque with ospreys. The way she minced and wagged her posterior and went on her toes and peered over her shoulder and kept her elbows in was an admirable caricature. Especially the curious sagging heaving movement of "bustle" region, a movement very characteristic of modern feminism, was hit off with a bit of male exaggeration which rejoiced me. At first she even took me in.

We stood outside our window, and leaned on the little balcony rail looking down at this flow of life. Directly opposite was the chemist's house: facing our window the best bedroom of the chemist, with a huge white matrimonial bed and muslin curtains. In the balcony sat the chemist's daughters, very elegant in high-heeled shoes and black hair done in the fluffy fashion with a big sweep sideways. Oh very elegant! They eyed us a little and we eyed them. But without interest. The river of life was down below.

It was very cold and the day was declining. We too were cold. We decided to go into the street and look for the café. In a moment we were out of doors, walking as inconspicuously as possible near the wall. Of course there was no pavement. These maskers were very gentle and whimsical, no touch of brutality at all. Now we were level with them, how odd and funny they were. One youth wore a thin white blouse and a pair of his sister's wide, calico knickers with needlework frills near the ankle, and white stockings. He walked artlessly, and looked almost pretty. Only the q-b winced with pain: not because of the knickers, but because of that awful length, coming well below the knee. Another young man was wound into a sheet, and heavens knows if he could ever get out of it. Another was involved in a complicated entanglement of white crochet antimacassars, very troublesome to contemplate. I did not like him at all, like a fish in a net. But he strode robustly about.

We came to the end of the street, where there is a wide, desolate sort of gap. Here the little band stood braying away, there was a thick crowd of people, and on a slanting place just above, a little circle where youths and men, maskers and one or two girls were dancing, so crowded together and such a small ring that they looked like a jiggly set of upright rollers all turning rickettily against one another. They were doing a sort of intense jigging waltz. Why do they look so intense? Perhaps because they were so tight all together, like too many fish in a globe slipping through one another.

There was a café in this sort of piazza—not a piazza at all, a formless gap. But young men were drinking little drinks, and I knew it would be hopeless to ask for anything but cold drinks or black coffee: which we did not want. So we continued forwards, up the slope of the village street. These towns soon come to an end. Already we were wandering into the open. On a ledge above, a peasant family was making a huge bonfire, a tower of orange-coloured, rippling flame. Little, impish boys were throwing on more rubbish. Everybody else was in town. Why were these folk at the town-end making this fire alone?

We came to the end of the houses and looked over the road-wall at the hollow, deep, interesting valley below. Away on the other side rose a blue mountain, a steep but stumpy cone. High land reared up, dusky and dark-blue, all around. Somewhere far off the sun was setting with a bit of crimson. It was a wild, unusual landscape, of unusual shape. The hills seemed so untouched, dark-blue, virgin-wild, the hollow cradle of the valley was cultivated like a tapestry away below. And there seemed so little outlying life: nothing. No castles even. In Italy and Sicily castles perching everywhere. In Sardinia none—the remote, ungrappled hills rising darkly, standing outside of life.

As we went back it was growing dark, and the little band was about to leave off its brass noise. But the crowd still surged, the maskers still jigged and frisked unweariedly. Oh the good old energy of the bygone days, before men became so self-conscious. Here it was still on the hop.

We found no café that looked any good. Coming to the inn, we asked if there was a fire anywhere. There wasn't. We went up to our room. The chemist-daughters had lighted up opposite, one saw their bedroom as if it were one's own. In the dusk of the street the maskers were still jigging, all the youths still joyfully being women, but a little more roughly now. Away over the house-tops the purple-red of a dying sunset. And it was very cold.

There was nothing for it but just to lie in bed. The q-b made a little tea on the spirit-lamp, and we sat in bed and sipped it. Then we covered ourselves up and lay still, to get warm. Outside the noise of the street came unabated. It grew quite dark, the lights reflected into the room. There was the sound of an accordion across the hoarseness of the many voices and movements in the street: and then a solid, strong singing of men's voices, singing a soldier song.

"Quando torniamo in casa nostra—"

We got up to look. Under the small electric lights the narrow, cobbled street was still running with a river of people, but fewer maskers. Two maskers beating loudly at a heavy closed door. They beat and beat. At last the door opens a crack.

They rush to try to get in—but in vain. It had shut the moment it saw them, they are foiled, on they go down the street. The town is full of men, many peasants come in from the outlying parts, the black and white costume now showing in the streets.

We retire to bed again out of the cold. Comes a knock, and Thumbelina bursts in, in the darkness.

"Siamo qua!" says the q-b.

Thumbelina dashes at the window-doors and shuts them and shuts the casement. Then she dashes to my bedhead and turns on the light, looking down at me as if I were a rabbit in the grass. Then she flings a can of water against the wash-bowls—cold water, icy, alas. After which, small and explosive, she explodes her way out of the room again, and leaves us in the glaring light, having replied that it is now a little after six o'clock, and dinner is half past seven.

So we lie in bed, warm and in peace, but hungry, waiting for half past seven.

When the q-b can stand it no more she flounces up, though the clock from the Campanile has struck seven only a few minutes before. Dashing downstairs to reconnoitre, she is back in a breath to say that people are eating their heads off in the long dining room. In the next breath we are downstairs too.

The room was brightly lighted, and at many white tables sat diners, all men. It was quite city-like. Everyone was in convivial mood. The q-b spied men opposite having chicken and salad—and she had hopes. But they were brief. When the soup came, the girl announced that there was only bistecca: which meant a bit of fried cow. So it did: a quite, quite small bit of fried beef, a few potatoes and a bit of cauliflower. Really, it was not enough for a child of twelve. But that was the end of it. A few mandarini—tangerine oranges—rolled on a plate for dessert. And there's the long and short of these infernal dinners. Was there any cheese? No, there was no cheese. So we merely masticated bread.

There came in three peasants in the black and white costume, and sat at the middle table. They kept on their stocking caps. And queer they looked, coming in with slow, deliberate tread of these elderly men, and sitting rather remote, with a gap of solitude around them. The peculiar ancient loneliness of the Sardinian hills clings to them, and something stiff, static, pre-world.

All the men at our end of the room were citizens—employees of some sort—and they were all acquaintances. A large dog, very large indeed, with a great muzzle, padded slowly from table to table, and looked at us with big wistful topaz eyes. When the meal was almost over our bus-driver and conductor came in—looking faint with hunger and cold and fatigue. They were quartered at this house. They had eaten nothing since the boar-broth at Gavoi.

In a very short time they were through their portions: and was there nothing else? Nothing! But they were half starved. They ordered two eggs each, in padella. I ordered coffee—and asked them to come and take it with us, and a brandy. So they came when their eggs were finished.

A diversion was now created at the other side of the room. The red wine, which is good in Sardinia, had been drunk freely. Directly facing us sat a rather stout man with pleasant blue eyes and a nicely shaped head: dressed like any other town man on a Sunday. The dog had waddled up to him and sat down statuesque in front of him. And the fat man, being mellow, began to play with the big, gentle, brindled animal. He took a piece of bread and held it before the dog's nose—and the dog tried to take it. But the man, like a boy now he was ripe with wine, put the mastiff back with a restraining finger, and told him not to snatch. Then he proceeded with a little conversation with the animal. The dog again tried to snatch, gently, and again the man started, saved the bread, and startled the dog, which backed and gave a sharp, sad yelp, as if to say: "Why do you tease me!"

"Now," said the man, "you are not to snatch. Come here. Come here. Vieni qua!" And he held up the piece of bread. The animal came near. "Now," said the man, "I put this bread on your nose, and you don't move, un—Ha!!"

The dog had tried to snatch the bread, the man had shouted and jerked it away, the animal had recoiled and given another expostulating yelp.

The game continued. All the room was watching, smiling. The dog did not understand at all. It came forward again, troubled. The man held the bread near its nose, and held up a warning finger. The beast dropped its head mournfully, cocking up its eye at the bread with varied feelings.

"Now—!" said the man, "not until I say three—*Uno—due*—" the dog could bear it no longer, the man in jerking let go the bread and yelled at the top of his voice—"*e tre!*" The dog gulped the piece of bread with a resigned pleasure, and the man pretended it had all happened properly on the word "three."

So he started again. "Vieni qua! Vieni qua!" The dog, which had backed away with the bread, came hesitating, cringing forward, dropping its hind-quarters in doubt, as dogs do, advancing towards the new nugget of bread. The man preached it a little sermon.

"You sit there and look at this bread. I sit here and look at you, and I hold this bread. And you stop still, and I stop still, while I count three. Now then—uno—" the dog couldn't bear these numerals, with their awful slowness. He snatched desperately. The man yelled and lost the bread, the dog, gulping, turned to creep away.

Then it began again.

"Come here! Come here! Didn't I tell thee I would count three? Già! I said I would count three. Not one, but three. And to count three you need three numbers. Ha! Steady! Three numbers. Uno—due E TRE!" The last syllables were yelled so that the room rang again. The dog gave a mournful howl of excitement, missed the bread, groped for it, and fled.

The man was red with excitement, his eyes shining. He addressed the company at large. "I had a dog," he said, "ah, a dog! And I would put a piece of bread on his nose, and say a verse. And he looked at me so!" The man put his face sideways. "And he looked at me *so*!" He gazed up under his brows. "And he talked to me so—o: Zieu! Zieu!—But he never moved. No, he never moved. If he sat with that bread on his nose for half an hour, and if tears ran down his face, he never moved—not till I said *three*! Then—ah!" The man tossed up his face, snapped the air with his mouth, and gulped an imaginary crust. "AH, that dog was trained...." The man of forty shook his head.

"Vieni qua! Come here! Tweet! Come here!"

He patted his fat knee, and the dog crept forward. The man held another piece of bread.

"Now," he said to the dog, "listen! Listen. I am going to tell you something.

Il soldato va alla guerra—

No—no, Not yet. When I say *three*!

Il soldato va alla guerra
Mangia male, dorme in terra—

Listen. Be still. Quiet now. UNO—DUE—E—TRE!"

It came out in one simultaneous yell from the man, the dog in sheer bewilderment opened his jaws and let the bread go down his throat, and wagged his tail in agitated misery.

"Ah," said the man, "you are learning. Come! Come here! Come! Now then! Now you know. So! So! Look at me so!"

The stout, good-looking man of forty bent forward. His face was flushed, the veins in his neck stood out. He talked to the dog, and imitated the dog. And very well indeed he reproduced something of the big, gentle, wistful subservience of the animal. The dog was his totem—the affectionate, self-mistrustful, warmhearted hound.

So he started the rigmarole again. We put it into English.

"Listen now. Listen! Let me tell it you—

So the soldier goes to the war!
His food is rotten, he sleeps on the floor—

"Now! Now! No, you are not keeping quiet. Now! Now!

Il soldate va alla guerra
Mangia male, dorme in terra—"

The verses, known to every Italian, were sung out in a sing-song fashion. The audience listened as one man—or as one child—the rhyme chiming in every heart. They waited with excitement for the One—Two—and Three! The last two words were always ripped out with a tearing yell. I shall never forget the force of those syllables—E TRE! But the dog made a poor show—He only gobbled the bread and was uneasy.

This game lasted us a full hour: a full hour by the clock sat the whole room in intense silence, watching the man and the dog.

Our friends told us the man was the bus-inspector—their inspector. But they liked him. "Un brav' uomo! Un bravo uomo! Eh si!" Perhaps they were a little uneasy, seeing him in his cups and hearing him yell so nakedly: AND THREE!

We talked rather sadly, wistfully. Young people, especially nice ones like the driver, are too sad and serious these days. The little conductor made big brown eyes at us, wistful too, and sad we were going.

For in the morning they were driving back again to Sorgono, over the old road, and we were going on, to Terranova, the port. But we promised to come back in the summer, when it was warmer. Then we should all meet again.

"Perhaps you will find us on the same course still. Who knows!" said the driver sadly.

The morning was very clear and blue. We were up betimes. The old dame of the inn very friendly this morning. We were going already! Oh, but we hadn't stayed long in Nuoro. Didn't we like it?

Yes, we like it. We would come back in the summer when it was warmer.

Ah yes, she said, artists came in the summer. Yes, she agreed, Nuoro was a nice place—*simpatico, molto simpatico*. And really it is. And really she was an awfully nice, capable, human old woman: and I had thought her a beldame when I saw her ironing.

She gave us good coffee and milk and bread, and we went out into the town. There was the real Monday morning atmosphere of an old, same-as-ever provincial town: the vacant feeling of work resumed after Sunday, rather reluctantly; nobody buying anything, nobody quite at grips with anything. The doors of the old-fashioned shops stood open: in Nuoro they have hardly reached the stage of window-displays. One must go inside, into the dark caves, to see what the goods are. Near the doorways of the drapers' shops stood rolls of that fine scarlet cloth, for the women's costumes. In a large tailor's window four women sat sewing, tailoring, and looking out of the window with eyes still Sunday-emancipate and mischievous. Detached men, some in the black and white, stood at the street corners, as if obstinately avoiding the current of work. Having had a day off, the salt taste of liberty still lingering on their lips, they were not going to be dragged so easily back into harness. I always sympathise with these rather sulky, forlorn males who insist on making another day of it. It shows a spark of spirit, still holding out against our over-harnessed world.

There is nothing to see in Nuoro: which, to tell the truth, is always a relief. Sights are an irritating bore. Thank heaven there isn't a bit of Perugino or anything Pisan in the place: that I know of. Happy is the town that has nothing to show. What a lot of stunts and affectations it saves! Life is then life, not museum-stuffing. One could saunter along the rather inert, narrow, Monday-morning street, and see the women having a bit of a gossip, and see an old crone with a basket of bread on her head, and see the unwilling ones hanging back from work, and the whole current of industry disinclined to flow. Life is life and things are things. I am sick of gaping *things*, even Peruginos. I have had my thrills from Carpaccio and Botticelli. But now I've had enough. But I can always look at an old, grey-bearded peasant in his earthy white drawers and his black waist-frill, wearing no coat or over-garment, but just crooking along beside his little ox-wagon. I am sick of "things," even Perugino.

The sight of the woman with the basket of bread reminded us that we wanted some food. So we searched for bread. None, if you please. It was Monday morning, eaten out. There would be bread at the forno, the oven. Where was the oven? Up the road and down a passage. I thought we should smell it. But no. We wandered back. Our friends had told us to take tickets early, for perhaps the bus would be crowded. So we bought yesterday's pastry and little cakes, and slices of native sausage. And still no bread. I went and asked our old hostess.

"There is no fresh bread. It hasn't come in yet," she said.

"Never mind, give me stale."

So she went and rummaged in a drawer.

"Oh dear, Oh dear, the women have eaten it all! But perhaps over there—" she pointed down the street—"they can give you some."

They couldn't.

I paid the bill—about twenty-eight francs, I think—and went out to look for the bus. There it was. In a dark little hole they gave me the long ticket-strips, first-class to Terranova. They cost some seventy francs the two. The q-b was still vainly, aimlessly looking along the street for bread.

"Ready when you are," said our new driver rather snappily. He was a pale, cross-looking young man with brown eyes and fair "ginger" hair. So in we clambered, waved farewell to our old friends, whose bus was ready to roll away in the opposite direction. As we bumped past the "piazza" I saw Velveteens standing there, isolate, and still, apparently, scowling with unabated irritation.

I am sure he has money: why the first class, yesterday, otherwise. And I'm sure *she* married him because he is a townsman with property.

Out we rolled, on our last Sardinian drive. The morning was of a bell-like beauty, blue and very lovely. Below on the right stretched the concave valley, tapestried with cultivation. Up into the morning light rose the high, humanless hills, with wild, treeless moor-slopes.

But there was no glass in the left window of the *coupé*, and the wind came howling in, cold enough. I stretched myself on the front seat, the q-b screwed herself into a corner, and we watched the land flash by. How well this new man drove! the long-nosed, freckled one with his gloomy brown eyes. How cleverly he changed gear, so that the automobile mewed and purred comfortably, like a live thing enjoying itself. And how dead he was to the rest of the world, wrapped in his gloom like a young bus-driving Hamlet. His answers to his mate were monosyllabic—or just no answers at all. He was one of those responsible, capable, morose souls, who do their work with silent perfection and look as if they were driving along the brink of doom, say a word to them and they'll go over the edge. But gentle *au fond*, of course. Fiction used to be fond of them: a sort of ginger-haired, young, mechanic Mr. Rochester who has even lost the Jane illusion.

Perhaps it was not fair to watch him so closely from behind.

His mate was a bit of a bounder, with one of those rakish military caps whose soft tops cock sideways or backwards. He was in Italian khaki, riding-breeches and puttees. He smoked his cigarette bounderishly: but at the same time, with peculiar gentleness, he handed one to the ginger Hamlet. Hamlet accepted it, and his mate held him a light as the bus swung on. They were like man and wife. The mate was the alert and wide-eyed Jane Eyre whom the ginger Mr. Rochester was not going to spoil in a hurry.

The landscape was different from yesterday's. As we dropped down the shallow, winding road from Nuoro, quite quickly the moors seemed to spread on either side, treeless, bushy, rocky, desert. How hot they must be in summer! One knows from Grazia Deledda's books.

A pony with a low trap was prancing unhappily in the road-side. We slowed down and slid harmlessly past. Then again, on we whizzed down the looped road, which turned back on itself as sharply as a snake that has been wounded. Hamlet darted the bus at the curves; then softly padded round like an angel: then off again for the next parabola.

We came out into wide, rather desolate, moorland valley spaces, with low rocks away to the left, and steep slopes, rocky-bushy, on the right. Sometimes groups of black-and-white men were working in the forlorn distances. A woman in the madder costume led a panniered ass along the wastes. The sun shone magnificently, already it was hotter here. The landscape had quite changed. These slopes looked east and south to the sea, they were sun-wild and sea-wild.

The first stop was where a wild, rough lane came down the hill to our road. At the corner stood a lonely house—and in the road-side the most battered, life-weary old carriage I have ever seen. The jaunty mate sorted out the post— the boy with the tattered-battered brown carriage and brown pony signed the book as we all stood in the roadway. There was a little wait for a man who was fetching up another parcel. The post-bag and parcels from the tattered carriage were received and stowed and signed for. We walked up and down in the sun to get warm. The landscape was wild and open round about.

Pip! goes Mr. Rochester, peremptorily, at the horn. Amazing how obediently we scuffle in. Away goes the bus, rushing towards the sea. Already one felt that peculiar glare in the half-way heavens, that intensification of the light in the lower sky, which is caused by the sea to sunward.

Away in front three girls in brown costume are walking along the side of the white high-road, going with panniers towards a village up a slight incline. They hear us, turn round, and instantly go off their heads, exactly like chickens in the road. They fly towards us, crossing the road, and swifter than any rabbits they scuttle, one after another, into a deep side-track, like a deep ditch at right angles to the road. There, as we roll past, they are all crouched, peering out at us fearfully, like creatures from their hole. The bus mate salutes them with a shout, and we roll on towards the village on the low summit.

It is a small, stony, hen-scratched place of poor people. We roll on to a standstill. There is a group of poor people. The women wear the dark-brown costume, and again the bolero has changed shape. It is a rather fantastic low corset, curiously shapen; and originally, apparently, made of wonderful elaborate brocade. But look at it now.

There is an altercation because a man wants to get into the bus with two little black pigs, each of which is wrapped in a little sack, with its face and ears appearing like a flower from a wrapped bouquet. He is told that he must pay the fare for each pig as if it were a Christian. *Cristo del mondo!* A pig, a little pig, and paid for as if it were a Christian. He dangles the pig-bouquets, one from each hand, and the little pigs open their black mouths and squeal with self-conscious appreciation of the excitement they are causing. *Dio benedetto!* it is a chorus. But the bus mate is inexorable. Every animal, even if it were a mouse, must be paid for and have a ticket as if it were a Christian. The pig-master recoils stupified with indignation, a pig-bouquet under each arm. "How much do you charge for the fleas you carry?" asks a sarcastic youth.

A woman sitting sewing a soldier's tunic into a little jacket for her urchin, and thus beating the sword into a ploughshare, stitches unconcernedly in the sun. Round-cheeked but rather slatternly damsels giggle. The pig-master, speechless with fury, slings the pig-bouquets, like two bottles one on either side the saddle of the ass whose halter is held by a grinning but also malevolent girl: malevolent against pig-prices, that is. The pigs, looking abroad from their new situation, squeal the eternal pig-protest against an insufferable humanity.

"Andiamo! Andiamo!" says ginger Mr. Rochester in his quiet but intense voice. The bus-mate scrambles up and we charge once more into the strong light to seaward.

In we roll, into Orosei, a dilapidated, sun-smitten, god-forsaken little town not far from the sea. We descend in piazza. There is a great, false baroque façade to a church, up a wavering vast mass of steps: and at the side a wonderful jumble of roundnesses with a jumble of round tiled roofs, peaked in the centre. It must have been some sort of convent. But it is eminently what they call a "painter's bit"—that pallid, big baroque face, at the top of the slow incline, and the very curious dark building at the side of it, with its several dark-tiled round roofs, like pointed hats, at varying altitudes. The whole space has a strange Spanish look, neglected, arid, yet with a bigness and a dilapidated dignity and a stoniness which carry one back to the Middle Ages, when life was violent and Orosei was no doubt a port and a considerable place. Probably it had bishops.

The sun came hot into the wide piazza; with its pallid heavy façade up on the stony incline on one side, and arches and a dark great courtyard and outer stairways of some unknown building away on the other, the road entering downhill from the inland, and dropping out below to the sea-marshes, and with the impression that once some single power had had the place in grip, had given this centre an architectural unity and splendour, now lost and forgotten, Orosei was truly fascinating.

But the inhabitants were churlish. We went into a sort of bar-place, very primitive, and asked for bread.

"Bread alone?" said the churl.

"If you please."

"There isn't any," he answered.

"Oh—where can we get some then?"

"You can't get any."

"Really!"

And we couldn't. People stood about glum, not friendly.

There was a second great automobile, ready to set off for Tortolì, far to the south, on the east coast. Mandas is the railway junction both for Sorgono and Tortolì. The two buses stood near and communed. We prowled about the dead, almost extinct town—or call it village. Then Mr. Rochester began to pip his horn peremptorily, so we scuffled in.

The post was stowed away. A native in black broad-cloth came running and sweating, carrying an ox-blood suit-case, and said we must wait for his brother-in-law, who was a dozen yards away. Ginger Mr. Rochester sat on his driver's throne and glared in the direction whence the brother-in-law must come. His brow knitted irritably, his long, sharp nose did not promise much patience. He made the horn roar like a sea-cow. But no brother-in-law.

"I'm going to wait no longer," said he.

"Oh, a minute, a minute! That won't do us any harm," expostulated his mate. No answer from the long faced, long-nosed ginger Hamlet. He sat statuesque, but with black eyes looking daggers down the still void road.

"*Eh va bene*", he murmured through closed lips, and leaned forward grimly for the starting handle.

"Patience—patience—patience a moment—why—" cried the mate.

"Per l'amor' di Dio!" cried the black broad-cloth man, simply sizzling and dancing in anguish on the road, round the suit-case, which stood in the dust. "Don't go! God's love, don't start. He's got to catch the boat. He's got to be in Rome tomorrow. He won't be a second. He's here, he's here, he's here!"

This startled the fate-fixed, sharp-nosed driver. He released the handle and looked round, with dark and glowering eyes. No one in sight. The few glum natives stood round unmoved. Thunder came into the gloomy dark eyes of the Rochester. Absolutely nobody in sight. Click! went his face into a look of almost seraphic peace, as he pulled off the brakes. We were on an incline, and insidiously, oh most subtly the great bus started to lean forwards and steal into motion.

"Oh *ma che!*—what a will you've got!" cried the mate, clambering in to the side of the now seraphic-looking Rochester.

"Love of God—God!" yelled the broad-cloth, seeing the bus melt forwards and gather momentum. He put his hands up as if to arrest it, and yelled in a wild howl: "O Beppin'! Bepp*in*—O!"

But in vain. Already we had left the little groups of onlookers behind. We were rolling downwards out of the piazza. Broad-cloth had seized the bag and was running beside us in agony. Out of the piazza we rolled, Rochester had not put on the engines and we were just simply rolling down the gentle incline by the will of God. Into the dark outlet-street we melted, towards the still invisible sea.

Suddenly a yell—"OO—ahh!!"

"È qua! È qua! È qua! È qua!" gasped broad-cloth four times. "He's here!" And then: "Beppin'—she's going, she's going!"

Beppin' appeared, a middle-aged man also in black broad-cloth, with a very scrubby chin and a bundle, running *towards* us on fat legs. He was perspiring, but his face was expressionless and innocent-looking. With a sardonic flicker of a grin, half of spite, half of relief, Rochester put on the brakes again, and we stopped in the street. A woman tottered up panting and holding her breast. Now for farewells.

"Andiamo!" said Rochester curtly, looking over his shoulder and making his fine nose curl with malice. And instantly he took off the brakes again. The fat woman shoved Beppin' in, gasping farewells, the brother-in-law handed in the ox-blood-red suit-case, tottering behind, and the bus surged savagely out of Orosei.

Almost in a moment we had left the town on its slope, and there below us was a river winding through marshy flats to the sea, to where small white surf broke on a flat, isolated beach, a quarter of a mile away. The river ran rapidly between stones and then between belts of high sere reeds, high as a man. These tall reeds advanced almost into the slow, horizontal sea, from which stood up a white glare of light, massive light over the low Mediterranean.

Quickly we came down to the river-level, and rolled over a bridge. Before us, between us and the sea rose another hill, almost like a wall with a flat top, running horizontal, perfectly flat, parallel with the sea-edge, a sort of narrow long plateau. For a moment we were in the wide scoop of the river-bed. Orosei stood on the bluff behind us.

Away to the right the flat river-marshes with the thick dead reeds met the flat and shining sea, river and sea were one water, the waves rippled tiny and soft-foot into the stream. To the left there was great loveliness. The bed of the river curved upwards and inland, and there was cultivation: but particularly, there were noble almond trees in full blossom. How beautiful they were, their pure, silvery pink gleaming so nobly, like a transfiguration, tall and perfect in that strange cradled river-bed parallel with the sea. Almond trees were in flower beneath grey Orosei, almond trees came near the road, and we could see the hot eyes of the individual blossoms, almond trees stood on the upward slope before us. And they had flowered in such noble beauty there, in that trough where the sun fell magnificent and the sea-glare whitened all the air as with a sort of God-presence, they gleamed in their incandescent sky-rosiness. One could hardly see their iron trunks, in this weird valley.

But already we had crossed, and were charging up the great road that was cut straight, slant-wise along the side of the sea-hill, like a stairway outside the side of the house. So the bus turned southward to run up this stairway slant, to get to the top of the sea's long table-land. So, we emerged: and there was the Mediterranean rippling against the black rocks not so very far away below on our right. For, once on the long table-land the road turned due north, a long white dead-straight road running between strips of moorland, wild and bushy. The sea was in the near distance, blue, blue, and beating with light. It seemed more light than watery. And on the left was the wide trough of the valley, where almond trees like clouds in a wind seemed to poise sky-rosy upon the pale, sun-pale land, and beyond which Orosei clustered its lost grey houses on the bluff. Oh wonderful Orosei with your almonds and your reedy river, throbbing, throbbing with light and the sea's nearness, and all so lost, in a world long gone by, lingering as legends linger on. It is hard to believe that it is real. It seems so long since life left it and memory transfigured it into pure glamour, lost away like a lost pearl on the east Sardinian coast. Yet there it is, with a few grumpy inhabitants who won't even give you a crust of bread. And probably there is malaria—almost sure. And it would be hell to have to live there for a month. Yet for a moment, that January morning, how wonderful, oh, the timeless glamour of those Middle Ages when men were lordly and violent and shadowed with death.

"Timor mortis conturbat me."

The road ran along by the sea, above the sea, swinging gently up and down, and running on to a sea-encroaching hilly promontory in the distance. There were no high lands. The valley was left behind, and moors surrounded us, wild, desolate, uninhabited and uninhabitable moors sweeping up gently on the left, and finishing where the land dropped low and clifflike to the sea on the right. No life was now in sight: even no ship upon the pale blue sea. The great globe of the sky was unblemished and royal in its blueness and its ringing cerulean light. Over the moors a great hawk hovered. Rocks cropped out. It was a savage, dark-bushed, sky-exposed land, forsaken to the sea and the sun.

We were alone in the *coupé*. The bus-mate had made one or two sets at us, but he rather confused us. He was young—about twenty-two or three. He was quite good-looking, with his rakish military cap and his well-knitted figure in military clothes. But he had dark eyes that seemed to ask too much, and his manner of approach was abrupt, persistent, and disconcerting. Already he had asked us where we were going, where we lived, whence we came, of what nationality we were, and was I a painter. Already he knew so much. Further we rather fought shy of him. We ate those pale Nuoro pastries—they were just flaky pastry, good, but with nothing inside but a breath of air. And we gnawed slices of very highly-flavoured Nuoro sausage. And we drank the tea. And we were very hungry, for it was past noon, and we had eaten as good as nothing. The sun was magnificent in heaven, we rushed at a great, purring speed along that moorland road just above the sea.

And then the bus-mate climbed in to share the coupé with us. He put his dark, beseeching and yet persistent eyes on us, sat plumb in front of us, his knees squared, and began to shout awkward questions in a strong curious voice. Of course it was very difficult to hear, for the great rushing bus made much noise. We had to try to yell in our Italian—and he was as awkward as we were.

However, although it said "Smoking Forbidden" he offered us both cigarettes, and insisted we should smoke with him. Easiest to submit. He tried to point us out features in the landscape: but there were none to point, except that, where the hill ran to sea out of the moor, and formed a cape, he said there was a house away under the cliffs where coastguards lived. Nothing else.

Then, however, he launched. He asked once more was I English and was the q-b German. We said it was so. And then he started the old story. Nations popped up and down again like Punch and Judy. Italy—l'Italia—she had no quarrel with La Germania—never had had—no—no, good friends the two nations. But once the war was started, Italy had to come in. For why. Germany would beat France, occupy her lands, march down and invade Italy. Best then join the war whilst the enemy was only invading somebody else's territory.

They are perfectly naïve about it. That's what I like. He went on to say that he was a soldier: he had served eight years in the Italian cavalry. Yes, he was a cavalryman, and had been all through the war. But he had not therefore any quarrel with Germany. No—war was war, and it was over. So let it be over.

But France—*ma la Francia!* Here he sat forward on his seat, with his face near ours, and his pleading-dog's eyes suddenly took a look of quite irrational blazing rage. France! There wasn't a man in Italy who wasn't dying to get at the throat of France. France! Let there be war, and every Italian would leap to arms, even the old. Even the old—*anche i vecchi*. Yes, there must be war—with France. It was coming: it was bound to come. Every Italian was waiting for it. Waiting to fly at the French throat. For why? Why? He had served two years on the French front, and he knew why. Ah, the French! For arrogance, for insolence, Dio!—they were not to be borne. The French—they thought themselves lords of the world—*signori del mondo!* Lords of the world, and masters of the world. Yes. They thought themselves no less—and what are they? Monkeys! Monkeys! Not better than monkeys. But let there be war, and Italy would show them. Italy would give them *signori del mondo!* Italy was pining for war—all, all, pining for war. With no one, with no one but France. Ah, with no one—Italy loved everybody else—but France! France!

We let him shout it all out, till he was at the end of it. The passion and energy of him was amazing. He was like one possessed. I could only wonder. And wonder again. For it is curious what fearful passions these pleading, wistful souls fall into when they feel they have been insulted. It was evident he felt he had been insulted, and he went just beside himself. But dear chap, he shouldn't speak so loudly for all Italy—even the old. The bulk of Italian men are only too anxious to beat their bayonets into cigarette-holders, and smoke the cigarette of eternal and everlasting peace, to coincide at all with our friend. Yet there he was—raging at me in the bus as we dashed along the coast.

And then, after a space of silence, he became sad again, wistful, and looked at us once more with those pleading brown eyes, beseeching, beseeching—he knew not what: and I'm sure I didn't know. Perhaps what he really wants is to be back on a horse in a cavalry regiment: even at war.

But no, it comes out, what he thinks he wants.

When are we going to London? And are there many motor-cars in England?— many, many? In America too? Do they want men in America? I say no, they have unemployment out there: they are going to stop immigration in April: or at least cut it down. Why? he asks sharply. Because they have their own unemployment problem. And the q-b quotes how many millions of Europeans want to emigrate to the United States. His eye becomes gloomy. Are all nations of Europe going to be forbidden? he asks. Yes—and already the Italian Government will give no more passports for America—to emigrants. No passports? then you can't go? You can't go, say I.

By this time his hot-souled eagerness and his hot, beseeching eyes have touched the q-b. She asks him what he wants. And from his gloomy face it comes out in a rap. "*Andare fuori dell'Italia.*" To go out of Italy. To go out—away—to go away—to go away. It has become a craving, a neurasthenia with them.

Where is his home? His home is at a village a few miles ahead—here on this coast. We are coming to it soon. There is his home. And a few miles inland from the village he also has a property: he also has land. But he doesn't want to work it. He doesn't want it. In fact he won't bother with it. He hates the land, he detests looking after vines. He can't even bring himself to try any more.

What does he want then?

He wants to leave Italy, to go abroad—as a chauffeur. Again the long beseeching look, as of a distraught, pleading animal. He would prefer to be the chauffeur of a gentleman. But he would drive a bus, he would do anything—in England.

Now he has launched it. Yes, I say, but in England also we have more men than jobs. Still he looks at me with his beseeching eyes—so desperate too—and so young—and so full of energy—and so longing to *devote* himself—to devote himself: or else to go off in an unreasonable paroxysm against the French. To my horror I feel he is believing in my goodness of heart. And as for motor-cars, it is all I can do to own a pair of boots, so how am I to set about employing a *chauffeur*?

We have all gone quiet again. So at last he climbs back and takes his seat with the driver once more. The road is still straight, swinging on through the moorland strip by the sea. And he leans to the silent, nerve-tense Mr. Rochester, pleading again. And at length Mr. Rochester edges aside, and lets him take the driving wheel. And so now we are all in the hands of our friend the bus-mate. He drives—not very well. It is evident he is learning. The bus can't quite keep in the grooves of this wild bare road. And he shuts off when we slip down a hill—and there is a great muddle on the upslope when he tries to change gear. But Mr. Rochester sits squeezed and silently attentive in his corner. He puts out his hand and swings the levers. There is no fear that he will let anything go wrong. I would trust him to drive me down the bottomless pit and up the other side. But still the beseeching mate holds the steering wheel. And on we rush, rather uncertainly and hesitatingly now. And thus we come to the bottom of a hill where the road gives a sudden curve. My heart rises an inch in my breast. I know he can't do it. And he can't, oh Lord—but the quiet hand of the freckled Rochester takes the wheel, we swerve on. And the bus-mate gives up, and the nerve-silent driver resumes control.

But the bus-mate now feels at home with us. He clambers back into the coupé, and when it is too painfully noisy to talk, he simply sits and looks at us with brown, pleading eyes. Miles and miles and miles goes this coast road, and never a village. Once or twice a sort of lonely watch-house and soldiers lying about by the road. But never a halt. Everywhere moorland and desert, uninhabited.

And we are faint with fatigue and hunger and this relentless travelling. When, oh when shall we come to Siniscola, where we are due to eat our midday meal? Oh yes, says the mate. There is an inn at Siniscola where we can eat what we like. Siniscola—Siniscola! We feel we must get down, we must eat, it is past one o'clock and the glaring light and the rushing loneliness are still about us.

But it is behind the hill in front. We see the hill? Yes. Behind it is Siniscola. And down there on the beach are the Bagni di Siniscola, where many forestieri, strangers, come in the summer. Therefore we set high hopes on Siniscola. From the town to the sea, two miles, the bathers ride on asses. Sweet place. And it is coming near—really near. There are stone-fenced fields—even stretches of moor fenced off. There are vegetables in a little field with a stone wall—there is a strange white track through the moor to a forsaken sea-coast. We are near.

Over the brow of the low hill—and there it is, a grey huddle of a village with two towers. There it is, we are there. Over the cobbles we bump, and pull up at the side of the street. This is Siniscola, and here we eat.

We drop out of the weary bus. The mate asks a man to show us the inn—the man says he won't, muttering. So a boy is deputed—and he consents. This is the welcome.

And I can't say much for Siniscola. It is just a narrow, crude, stony place, hot in the sun, cold in the shade. In a minute or two we were at the inn, where a fat, young man was just dismounting from his brown pony and fastening it to a ring beside the door.

The inn did not look promising—the usual cold room opening gloomily on the gloomy street. The usual long table, with this time a foully blotched table-cloth. And two young peasant madams in charge, in the brown costume, rather sordid, and with folded white cloths on their heads. The younger was in attendance. She was a full-bosomed young hussy, and would be very queenly and cocky. She held her nose in the air, and seemed ready to jibe at any order. It takes one some time to get used to this cocky, assertive behaviour of the young damsels, the who'll-tread-on-the-tail-of-my-skirt bearing of the hussies. But it is partly a sort of crude defensiveness and shyness, partly it is barbaric *méfiance* or mistrust, and partly, without doubt, it is a tradition with Sardinian women that they must hold their own and be ready to hit first. This young sludge-queen was all hit. She flounced her posterior round the table, planking down the lumps of bread on the foul cloth with an air of take-it-as-a-condescension-that-I-wait-on-you, a subdued grin lurking somewhere on her face. It is not meant to be offensive: yet it is so. Truly, it is just uncouthness. But when one is tired and hungry....

We were not the only feeders. There was the man off the pony, and a sort of workman or porter or dazio official with him—and a smart young man: and later our Hamlet driver. Bit by bit the young damsel planked down bread, plates, spoons, glasses, bottles of black wine, whilst we sat at the dirty table in uncouth constraint and looked at the hideous portrait of His reigning Majesty of Italy. And at length came the inevitable soup. And with it the sucking chorus. The little *maialino* at Mandas had been a good one. But the smart young man in the country beat him. As water clutters and slavers down a choky gutter, so did his soup travel upwards into his mouth with one long sucking stream of noise, intensified as the bits of cabbage, etc., found their way through the orifice.

They did all the talking—the young men. They addressed the sludge-queen curtly and disrespectfully, as if to say: "What's she up to?" Her airs were finely thrown away. Still she showed off. What else was there to eat? There was the meat that had been boiled for the soup. We knew what that meant. I had as lief eat the foot of an old worsted stocking. Nothing else, you sludge queen? No, what do you want anything else for?—Beefsteak—what's the good of asking for beefsteak or any other steak on a Monday. Go to the butcher's and see for yourself.

The Hamlet, the pony rider, and the porter had the faded and tired chunks of boiled meat. The smart young man ordered eggs in padella—two eggs fried with a little butter. We asked for the same. The smart young man got his first—and of course they were warm and liquid. So he fell upon them with a fork, and once he had got hold of one end of the eggs he just sucked them up in a prolonged and violent suck, like a long, thin, ropy drink being sucked upwards from the little pan. It was a genuine exhibition. Then he fell upon the bread with loud chews.

What else was there? A miserable little common orange. So much for the dinner. Was there cheese? No. But the sludge-queen—they are quite good-natured really—held a conversation in dialect with the young men, which I did not try to follow. Our pensive driver translated that there *was* cheese, but it wasn't good, so they wouldn't offer it us. And the pony man interpolated that they didn't like to offer us anything that was not of the best. He said it in all sincerity—after such a meal. This roused my curiosity, so I asked for the cheese whether or not. And it wasn't so bad after all.

This meal cost fifteen francs, for the pair of us.

We made our way back to the bus, through the uncouth men who stood about. To tell the truth, strangers are not popular nowadays—not anywhere. Everybody has a grudge against them at first sight. This grudge may or may not wear off on acquaintance.

The afternoon had become hot—hot as an English June. And we had various other passengers—for one a dark-eyed, long-nosed priest who showed his teeth

On the paper he had written his name and his address, and if anyone would like him as chauffeur they have only to say so. On the back of the scrap of paper the inevitable goodwill: *Auguri infiniti e buon Viaggio.* Infinite good wishes and a good journey.

I folded the paper and put it in my waistcoat pocket, feeling a trifle disconcerted by my new responsibility. He was such a dear fellow and such bright trustful eyes.

This much achieved, there was a moment of silence. And the bus-mate turned to take a ticket of a fat, comfortable man who had got in at the last stop. There was a bit of flying conversation.

"Where are they from?" asked the good-looking stupid man next to me, inclining his head in our direction.

"Londra," said our friend, with stern satisfaction: and they have said so often to one another that London is the greatest city in the world, that now the very word Londra conveys it all. You should have seen the blank little-boy look come over the face of the big handsome fellow on hearing that we were citizens of the greatest city in the world.

"And they understand Italian?" he asked, rather nipped.

"Sicuro!" said our friend scornfully. "How shouldn't they?"

"Ah!" My large neighbour left his mouth open for a few moments. And then another sort of smile came on to his face. He began to peep at us sideways from his brown eyes, brightly, and was henceforth itching to get into conversation with the citizens of the world's mistress-city. His look of semi-impudence was quite gone, replaced by a look of ingratiating admiration.

Now I ask you, is this to be borne? Here I sit, and he talks half-impudently and patronisingly about me. And here I sit, and he is glegging at me as if he saw signs of an aureole under my grey hat. All in ten minutes. And just because, instead of *la Germania* I turn out to be *l'Inghilterra.* I might as well be a place on a map, or a piece of goods with a trade-mark. So little perception of the actual me! so much going by labels! I now could have kicked him harder. I would have liked to say I was ten times German, to see the fool change his smirk again.

The priest now chimed up, that he had been to America. He had been to America and hence he dreaded not the crossing from Terranuova di Sardegna to Cività Vecchia. For he had crossed the great Atlantic.

Apparently, however, the natives had all heard this song of the raven before, so he spat largely on the floor. Whereupon the new fat neighbour asked him was it true that the Catholic Church was now becoming the one Church in the United States? And the priest said there was no doubt about it.

The hot afternoon wore on. The coast was rather more inhabited, but we saw practically no villages. The view was rather desolate. From time to time we stopped at a sordid-looking canteen house. From time to time we passed natives riding on their ponies, and sometimes there was an equestrian exhibition as the rough, strong little beasts reared and travelled rapidly backwards, away from the horrors of our great automobile. But the male riders sat heavy and unshakeable, with Sardinian male force. Everybody in the bus laughed, and we passed, looking back to see the pony still corkscrewing, but in vain, in the middle of the lonely, grass-bordered high-road.

The bus-mate climbed in and out, coming in to sit near us. He was like a dove which has at last found an olive bough to nest in. And we were the olive bough in this world of waste waters. Alas, I felt a broken reed. But he sat so serenely near us, now, like a dog that has found a master.

The afternoon was declining, the bus pelted on at a great rate. Ahead we saw the big lump of the island of Tavolara, a magnificient mass of rock which fascinated me by its splendid, weighty form. It looks like a headland, for it apparently touches the land. There it rests at the sea's edge, in this lost afternoon world. Strange how this coast-country does not belong to our present-day world. As we rushed along we saw steamers, two steamers, steering south, and one sailing ship coming from Italy. And instantly, the steamers seemed like our own familiar world. But still this coast-country was forsaken, forgotten, not included. It just is not included.

How tired one gets of these long, long rides! It seemed we should never come up to Tavolara. But we did. We came right near to it, and saw the beach with the waves rippling undisturbed, saw the narrow waters between the rock-lump and the beach. For now the road was down at sea-level. And we were not very far from Terranova. Yet all seemed still forsaken, outside of the world's life.

The sun was going down, very red and strong, away inland. In the bus all were silent, subsiding into the pale travel-sleep. We charged along the flat road, down on a plain now. And dusk was gathering heavily over the land.

We saw the high-road curve flat upon the plain. It was the harbour head. We saw a magic, land-locked harbour, with masts and dark land encircling a glowing basin. We even saw a steamer lying at the end of a long, thin bank of land, in the shallow, shining, wide harbour, as if wrecked there. And this was our steamer. But no, it looked in the powerful glow of the sunset like some lonely steamer laid up in some land-locked bay away at Spitzbergen, towards the North Pole: a solemn, mysterious, blue-landed bay, lost, lost to mankind.

Our bus-mate came and told us we were to sit in the bus till the post-work was done, then we should be driven to the hotel where we could eat, and then he would accompany us on the town omnibus to the boat. We need not be on board till eight o'clock: and now it was something after five. So we sat still while the bus rushed and the road curved and the view of the weird, land-locked harbour changed, though the bare masts of ships in a bunch still pricked the upper glow, and the steamer lay away out, as if wrecked on a sand-bank, and dark, mysterious land with bunchy hills circled round, dark blue and wintry in a golden after-light, while the great, shallow-seeming bay of water shone like a mirror.

In we charged, past a railway, along the flat darkening road into a flat God-lost town of dark houses, on the marshy bay-head. It felt more like a settlement than a town. But it was Terranova-Pausanias. And after bumping and rattling down a sombre uncouth, barren-seeming street, we came up with a jerk at a doorway—which was the post-office. Urchins, mudlarks, were screaming for the luggage. Everybody got out and set off towards the sea, the urchins carrying luggage. We sat still.

Till I couldn't bear it. I did not want to stay in the automobile another moment, and I did not, I did not want to be accompanied by our new-found friend to the steamer. So I burst out, and the q-b followed. She too was relieved to escape the new attachment, though she had a great *tendre* for him. But in the end one runs away from one's *tendres* much harder and more precipitately than from one's *durs*.

The mudlarking urchins fell upon us. Had we any more luggage—were we going to the steamer? I asked how one went to the steamer—did one walk? I thought perhaps it would be necessary to row out. You go on foot, or in a car-riage, or in an aeroplane, said an impudent brat. How far? Ten minutes. Could one go on board at once? Yes, certainly.

So, in spite of the q-b's protests, I handed the sack to a wicked urchin, to be led. She wanted us to go alone—but I did not know the way, and am wary of stumbling into entanglements in these parts.

I told the bus-Hamlet, who was abstract with nerve fatigue, please to tell his comrade that I would not forget the commission: and I tapped my waist-coat pocket, where the paper lay over my heart. He briefly promised—and we escaped. We escaped any further friendship.

I bade the mud-lark lead me to the telegraph office: which of course was quite remote from the post-office. Shouldering the sack, and clamouring for the kitchenino which the q-b stuck to, he marched forward. By his height he was ten years old: by his face with its evil mud-lark pallor and good-looks, he was forty. He wore a cut-down soldier's tunic which came nearly to his knees, was barefoot, and sprightly with that alert mudlarking quickness which has its advantages.

So we went down a passage and climbed a stair and came to an office where one would expect to register births and deaths. But the urchin said it was the telegraph-office. No sign of life. Peering through the wicket I saw a fat individual seated writing in the distance. Feeble lights relieved the big, barren, official spaces—I wonder the fat official wasn't afraid to be up here alone.

He made no move. I banged the shutter and demanded a telegraph blank. His shoulders went up to his ears, and he plainly intimated his intention to let us wait. But I said loudly to the urchin: "Is *that* the telegraph official?" and the urchin said: "Si signore"—so the fat individual had to come.

After which considerable delay, we set off again. The bus, thank heaven, had gone, the savage dark street was empty of friends. We turned away to the harbour front. It was dark now. I saw a railway near at hand—a bunch of dark masts—the steamer showing a few lights, far down at the tip of a long spit of land, remote in mid-harbour. And so off we went, the barefoot urchin twinkling a few yards ahead, on the road that followed the spit of land. The spit was wide enough to carry this road, and the railway. On the right was a silent house apparently built on piles in the harbour. Away far down in front leaned our glimmering steamer, and a little train was shunting trucks among the low sheds beside it. Night had fallen, and the great stars flashed. Orion was in the air, and his dog-star after him. We followed on down the dark bar between the silent, lustrous water. The harbour was smooth as glass, and gleaming like a mirror. Hills came round encircling it entirely—dark land ridging up and lying away out, even to seaward. One was not sure which was exactly seaward. The dark encircling of the land seemed stealthy, the hills had a remoteness, guarding the waters in the silence. Perhaps the great mass away beyond was Tavolara again. It seemed like some lumpish berg guarding an arctic, locked-up bay where ships lay dead.

On and on we followed the urchin, till the town was left behind, until it also twinkled a few meagre lights out of its low, confused blackness at the bay-head, across the waters. We lad left the ship-masts and the settlement. The urchin padded on, only turning now and again and extending a thin, eager hand toward the kitchenino. Especially when some men were advancing down the railway he wanted it: the q-b's carrying it was a slur on his prowess. So the kitchenino was relinquished, and the lark strode on satisfied.

Till at last we came to the low sheds that squatted between the steamer and the railway-end. The lark led me into one, where a red-cap was writing. The cap let me wait some minutes before informing me that this was the goods office—the ticket office was further on. The lark flew at him and said "Then you've changed it, have you?" And he led me on to another shed, which was just going to shut up. Here they finally had the condescension to give me two tickets—a hundred and fifty francs the two. So we followed the lark who strode like Scipio Africanus up the gangway with the sack.

It was quite a small ship. The steward put me in number one cabin—the q-b in number seven. Each cabin had four berths. Consequently man and woman must separate rigorously on this ship. Here was a blow for the q-b, who knows what Italian female fellow-passengers can be. However, there we were. All the cabins were down below, and all, for some mysterious reason, inside—no portholes outside. It was hot and close down below already. I pitched the sack on my berth, and there stood the lark on the red carpet at the door.

I gave him three francs. He looked at it as if it were my death-warrant. He peered at the paper in the light of the lamp. Then he extended his arm with a gesture of superb insolence, flinging me back my gold without a word.

"How!" said I. "Three francs are quite enough."

"Three francs—two kilometers—and three pieces of luggage! No signore. No! Five francs. Cinque franchi!" And averting his pallid, old mudlarking face, and flinging his hand out at me, he stood the image of indignant repudiation. And truly, he was no taller than my upper waistcoat pocket. The brat! The brat! He was such an actor, and so impudent, that I wavered between wonder and amusement and a great inclination to kick him up the steps. I decided not to waste my energy being angry.

"What a beastly little boy! What a horrid little boy! What a *horrid* little boy! Really—a little thief. A little swindler!" I mused aloud.

"Swindler!" he quavered after me. And he was beaten. "Swindler" doubled him up: that and the quiet mildness of my tone of invocation. Now he would have gone with his three francs. And now, in final contempt, I gave him the other two.

He disappeared like a streak of lightning up the gangway, terrified lest the steward should come and catch him at his tricks. For later on I saw the steward send other larks flying for demanding more than one-fifty. The brat.

The question was now the cabin: for the q-b simply refused to entertain the idea of sharing a cabin with three Italian women, who would all be sick simply for the fuss of it, though the sea was smooth as glass. We hunted up the steward. He said all the first-class cabins had four berths—the second had three, but much smaller. How that was possible I don't know. However, if no one came, he would give us a cabin to ourselves.

The ship was clean and civilised, though very poky. And there we were.

We went on deck. Would we eat on board, asked another person. No, we wouldn't. We went out to a fourth little shed, which was a refreshment stall, and bought bread and sardines and chocolate and apples. Then we went on the upper deck to make our meal. In a sheltered place I lit the spirit lamp, and put on water to boil. The water we had taken from the cabin. Then we sat down alone in the darkness, on a seat which had its back against the deck cabins, now appropriated by the staff. A thin, cold wind was travelling. We wrapped the one plaid round us both and snugged together, waiting for the tea to boil. I could just see the point of the spirit-flame licking up, from where we sat.

The stars were marvellous in the soundless sky, so big, that one could see them hanging orb-like and alone in their own space, yet all the myriads. Particularly bright the evening-star. And he hung flashing in the lower night with a power that made me hold my breath. Grand and powerful he sent out his flashes, so sparkling that he seemed more intense than any sun or moon. And from the dark, uprising land he sent his way of light to us across the water, a marvellous star-road. So all above us the stars soared and pulsed, over that silent, night-dark, land-locked harbour.

After a long time the water boiled, and we drank our hot tea and ate our sardines and bread and bits of remaining Nuoro sausage, sitting there alone in the intense starry darkness of that upper deck. I said alone: but no, two ghoulish ship's cats came howling at us for the bits. And even when everything was eaten, and the sardine-tin thrown in the sea, still they circled and prowled and howled.

We sat on, resting under the magnificent deep heavens, wrapped together in the old shepherd's shawl for which I have blessed so often a Scottish friend, half sheltered from the cold night wind, and recovering somewhat from the sixty miles bus-ride we had done that day.

As yet there was nobody on the ship—we were the very first, at least in the first class. Above, all was silent and deserted. Below, all was lit-up and deserted. But it was a little ship, with accommodation for some thirty first-class and forty second-class passengers.

In the low deck forward stood two rows of cattle—eighteen cattle. They stood tied up side by side, and quite motionless, as if stupefied. Only two had lain down. The rest stood motionless, with tails dropped and heads dropped, as if drugged or gone insensible. These cattle on the ship fascinated the q-b. She insisted on going down to them, and examining them minutely. But there they were—stiff almost as Noah's Ark cows. What she could not understand was that they neither cried nor struggled. Motionless—terribly motionless. In her idea cattle are wild and indomitable creatures. She will not realise the horrid strength of passivity and inertia which is almost the preponderant force in domesticated creatures, men and beast alike. There are fowls too in various coops—flappy and agitated these.

At last, at about half past seven the train from the island arrived, and the people surged out in a mass. We stood hanging over the end of the upper deck, looking down. On they poured, in a thick mass, up the gangway, with all conceivable sorts of luggage: bundles, embroidered carry-alls, bags, saddle-bags—the q-b lamenting she had not bought one—a sudden surging mass of people and goods. There are soldiers too—but these are lined upon the bit of a quay, to wait.

Our interest is to see whether there will be any more first-class passengers. Coming up the wide board which serves as gangway each individual hands a ticket to the man at the top, and is shooed away to his own region—usually second class. There are three sorts of tickets—green first-class, white second, and pink third. The second-class passengers go aft, the third class go forward, along the passage past our cabins, into the steerage. And so we watch and watch the excited people come on board and divide. Nearly all are second-class—and a great many are women. We have seen a few first-class men. But as yet no women. And every hat with ospreys gives the q-b a qualm.

For a long time we are safe. The women flood to the second-class. One who is third, begs and beseeches to go with her friends in the second. I am glad to say without success. And then, alas, an elderly man with a daughter, first-class. They are very respectable and pleasant looking. But the q-b wails: "I'm sure she will be sick."

Towards the end come three convicts, chained together. They wear the brownish striped homespun, and do not look evil. They seem to be laughing together, not at all in distress. The two young soldiers who guard them, and who have guns, look nervous. So the convicts go forward to the steerage, past our cabins.

At last the soldiers are straightened up, and turned on board. There almost at once they start making a tent: drawing a huge tarpaulin over a cross rope in the mid-deck below us, between the first and second class regions. The great tarpaulin is pulled down well on either side and fastened down, and it makes a big dark tent. The soldiers creep in and place their bundles.

And now it is the soldiers who fascinate the q-b. She hangs over the bar above, and peers in. The soldiers arrange themselves in two rows. They will sleep with their heads on their bundles on either side of the tent, the two rows of feet coming together inwards. But first they must eat, for it is eight o'clock and more.

Out come their suppers: a whole roast fowl, hunks of kid, legs of lamb, huge breads. The fowl is dismembered with a jack-knife in a twinkling, and shared. Everything among the soldiers is shared. There they sit in their pent-house with its open ends, crowded together and happy, chewing with all their might and clapping one another on the shoulder lovingly, and taking swigs at the wine bottles. We envy them their good food.

At last all are on board—the omnibus has driven up from town and gone back. A last young lout dashes up in a carriage and scuffles aboard. The crew begins to run about. The quay-porters have trotted on board with the last bales and packages—all is stowed safely. The steamer hoots and hoots. Two men and a girl kiss their friends all round and get off the ship. The night re-echoes the steamer's hoots. The sheds have gone all dark. Far off the town twinkles very sparsely. All is night-deserted. And so the gangway is hauled up, and the rope hawsers quickly wound in. We are drifting away from the quay side. The few watchers wave their white handkerchiefs, standing diminutive and forlorn on the dark little quay, in the heart of the dark, deserted harbour. One woman cries and waves and weeps. A man makes exaggerated flag-wagging signals with his white handky, and feels important. We drift—and the engines begin to beat. We are moving in the land-locked harbour.

Everybody watches. The commander and the crew shout orders. And so, very slowly, and without any fuss at all, like a man wheeling a barrow out of a yard gate, we throb very slowly out of the harbour, past one point, then past another, away from the encircling hills, away from the great lump of Tavolara which is to southward, away from the outreaching land to the north, and over the edge of the open sea.

And now to try for a cabin to ourselves. I approach the steward. Yes, he says, he has it in mind. But there are eighty second-class passengers, in an accommodation space for forty. The transit-controller is now considering it. Most probably he will transfer some second-class women to the vacant first-class cabins. If he does not do so, then the steward will accommodate us.

I know what this means—this equivocation. We decide not to bother any more. So we make a tour of the ship—to look at the soldiers, who have finished eating, sitting yarning to one another, while some are already stretched out in the shadow, for sleep. Then to look at the cattle, which stand rooted to the deck—which is now all messy. To look at the unhappy fowls in their coops. And a peep at the third-class—rather horrifying.

And so to bed. Already the other three berths in my cabin are occupied, the lights are switched off. As I enter I hear one young man tenderly enquiring of the berth below: "Dost thou feel ill?" "Er—not much—not much!" says the other faintly.

Yet the sea is like glass, so smooth.

I am quickly rolled in my lower berth, where I feel the trembling of the machine-impelled ship, and hear the creaking of the berth above me as its occupant rolls over: I listen to the sighs of the others, the wash of dark water. And so, uneasily, rather hot and very airless, uneasy with the machine-throbbing and the sighing of my companions, and with a cock that crows shrilly from one of the coops, imagining the ship's lights to be dawn, the night goes by. One sleeps—but a bad sleep. If only there were cold air, not this lower-berth, inside cabin airlessness.

VIII. BACK

The sea being steady as a level road, nobody succeeded in being violently sick. My young men rose at dawn—I was not long in following. It was a gray morning on deck, a gray sea, a gray sky, and a gray, spider-cloth, unimportant coast of Italy not far away. The q-b joined me: and quite delighted with her fellow-passenger: such a nice girl, she said! who, when she let down her ordinary-looking brown hair, it reached rippling right to her feet! Voilà! You never know your luck.

The cock that had crowed all night crowed again, hoarsely, with a sore throat. The miserable cattle looked more wearily miserable, but still were motionless, as sponges that grow at the bottom of the sea. The convicts were out for air: grinning. Someone told us they were war-deserters. Considering the light in which these people look on war, desertion seemed to me the only heroism. But the q-b, brought up in a military air, gazed upon them as upon men miraculously alive within the shadow of death. According to her code they had been shot when re-captured. The soldiers had unslung the tarpaulin, their home for the night had melted with the darkness, they were mere fragments of gray transit smoking cigarettes and staring overboard.

We drew near to Cività Vecchia: the old, mediaeval looking port, with its castle, and a round fortress-barracks at the entrance. Soldiers aboard shouted and waved to soldiers on the ramparts. We backed insignificantly into the rather scrubby, insignificant harbour. And in five minutes we were out, and walking along the wide, desolate boulevard to the station. The cab-men looked hard at us: but no doubt owing to the knapsack, took us for poor Germans.

Coffee and milk—and then, only about three-quarters of an hour late, the train from the north. It is the night express from Turin. There was plenty of room—so in we got, followed by half a dozen Sardinians. We found a large, heavy Torinese in the carriage, his eyes dead with fatigue. It seemed quite a new world on the mainland: and at once one breathed again the curious suspense that is in the air. Once more I read the Corriere della Sera from end to end. Once more we knew ourselves in the real active world, where the air seems like a lively wine dissolving the pearl of the old order. I hope, dear reader, you like the metaphor. Yet I cannot forbear repeating how strongly one is sensible of the solvent property of the atmosphere, suddenly arriving on the mainland again. And in an hour one changes one's psyche. The human being is a most curious creature. He thinks he has got one soul, and he has got dozens. I felt my sound Sardinian soul melting off me, I felt myself evaporating into the real Italian uncertainty and momentaneity. So I perused the Corriere whilst the metamorphosis took place. I like Italian newspapers because they say what they mean, and not merely what is most convenient to say. We call it naïveté—I call it manliness. Italian newspapers read as if they were written by men, and not by calculating eunuchs.

The train ran very heavily along the Maremma. It began to rain. Then we stopped at a station where we should not stop—somewhere in the Maremma country, the invisible sea not far off, the low country cultivated and yet forlorn. Oh how the Turin man sighed, and wearily shifted his feet as the train stood meaningless. There it sat—in the rain. Oh express!

At last on again, till we were winding through the curious long troughs of the Roman Campagna. There the shepherds minded the sheep: the slender-footed merino sheep. In Sardinia the merinos were very white and glistening, so that one thought of the Scriptural "white as wool." And the black sheep among the flock were very black. But these Campagna were no longer white, but dingy. And though the wildness of the Campagna is a real wildness still, it is a historic wildness, familiar in its way as a fireside is familiar.

So we approach the hopeless sprawling of modern Rome—over the yellow Tiber, past the famous pyramid tomb, skirting the walls of the city, till at last we plunge in, into the well-known station, out of all the chaos.

We are late. It is a quarter to twelve. And I have to go out and change money, and I hope to find my two friends.—The q-b and I dash down the platform—no friends at the barrier. The station moderately empty. We bolt across to the departure platforms. The Naples train stands ready. In we pitch our bags, ask a naval man not to let anyone steal them, then I fly out into town while the q-b buys food and wine at the buffet.

It no longer rains, and Rome feels as ever—rather holiday-like and not inclined to care about anything. I get a hundred and three lira for each pound note: pocket my money at two minutes past twelve, and bolt back, out of the Piazza delle Terme. Aha, there are the two missing ones, just descending vaguely from a carriage, the one gazing inquiringly through his monocle across the tramlines, the other very tall and alert and elegant, looking as if he expected us to appear out of the air for his convenience.

Which is exactly what happens. We fly into each other's arms. "Oh there you *are*! Where's the q-b? Why are you here? We've been to the arrival platform—no *sign* of you. Of course I only got your wire half an hour ago. We *flew* here. Well, how nice to see you.—Oh, let the man wait.—What, going on at once to Naples? But must you? Oh, but how flighty you are! Birds of passage *veramente*! Then let us find the q-b, quick!—And they won't let us on the platform. No, they're not issuing platform tickets today.—Oh, merely the guests returning from that Savoy-Bavarian wedding in the north, a few royal Duchesses about. Oh well, we must try and wangle him."

At the barrier a woman trying in vain to be let on to the station. But what a Roman matron can't do, an elegant young Englishman can. So our two heroes wangle their way in, and fall into the arms of the q-b by the Naples train. Well, now, tell us all about it! So we rush into a four-branched candlestick of conversation. In my ear murmurs he of the monocle about the Sahara—he is back from the Sahara a week ago: the winter sun in the Sahara! He with the smears of paint on his elegant trousers is giving the q-b a sketchy outline of his now *grande passion*. Click goes the exchange, and him of the monocle is detailing to the q-b his trip to Japan, on which he will start in six weeks' time, while him of the paint-smears is expatiating on the thrills of the etching needle, and concocting a plan for a month in Sardinia in May, with me doing the scribbles and he the pictures. What sort of pictures? Out flies the name of Goya.—And well now, a general rush into oneness, and won't they come down to Sicily to us for the almond blossom: in about ten days' time. Yes they will—wire when the almond blossom is just stepping on the stage and making its grand bow, and they will come next day. Somebody has smitten the wheel of a coach two ringing smacks with a hammer. This is a sign to get in. The q-b is terrified the train will slip through her fingers. "I'm frightened, I must get in."—"Very well then! You're sure you have everything you want? Everything? A fiasco of vino? Oh *two*! All the better! Well then—ten days' time. All right—quite sure—how nice to have seen you, if only a *glimpse*.—Yes, yes, poor q-b! Yes, you're quite safe. Good-bye! Good-bye!"

The door is shut—we are seated—the train moves out of the station. And quickly on this route Rome disappears. We are out on the wintry Campagna, where crops are going. Away on the left we see the Tivoli hills, and think of the summer that is gone, the heat, the fountains of the Villa D'Este. The train rolls heavily over the Campagna, towards the Alban Mounts, homewards.

So we fall on our food, and devour the excellent little beef-steaks and rolls and boiled eggs, apples and oranges and dates, and drink the good red wine, and wildly discuss plans and the latest news, and are altogether thrilled about things. So thrilled that we are well away among the romantic mountains of the south-centre before we realise that there are other passengers besides ourselves in the carriage. Half the journey is over. Why, there is the monastery on its high hill! In a wild moment I suggest we shall get down and spend a night up there at Montecassino, and see the other friend, the monk who knows so much about the world, being out of it. But the q-b shudders, thinking of the awful winter coldness of that massive stone monastery, which has no spark of heating apparatus. And therefore the plan subsides, and at Cassino station I only get down to procure coffee and sweet cakes. They always have good things to eat at Cassino station: in summer, big fresh ices and fruits and iced water, in winter toothsome sweet cakes which make an awfully good finish to a meal.

I count Cassino half way to Naples. After Cassino the excitement of being in the north begins quite to evaporate. The southern heaviness descends upon us. Also the sky begins to darken: and the rain falls. I think of the night before us, on the sea again. And I am vaguely troubled lest we may not get a berth. However, we may spend the night in Naples: or even sit on in this train, which goes forward, all through the long long night, to the Straits of Messina. We must decide as we near Naples.

Half dozing, one becomes aware of the people about one. We are travelling second class. Opposite is a little, hold-your-own school-mistressy young person in pince-nez. Next her a hollow-cheeked white soldier with ribbons on his breast. Then a fat man in a corner. Then a naval officer of low rank. The naval officer is coming from Fiume, and is dead with sleep and perhaps mortification. D'Annunzio has just given up. Two compartments away we hear soldiers singing, martial still though bruised with fatigue, the D'Annunzio-bragging songs of Fiume. They are soldiers of the D'Annunzio legion. And one of them, I hear the sick soldier saying, is very hot and republican still. Private soldiers are not allowed, with their reduced tickets, to travel on the express trains. But these legionaries are not penniless: they have paid the excess and come along. For the moment they are sent to their homes. And with heads dropping with fatigue, we hear them still defiantly singing down the carriage for D'Annunzio.

A regular officer went along—a captain of the Italian, not the Fiume army. He heard the chants and entered the carriage. The legionaries were quiet, but they lounged and ignored the entry of the officer. "On your feet!" he yelled, Italian fashion. The vehemence did it. Reluctantly as may be, they stood up in the compartment. "Salute!" And though it was bitter, up went their hands in the salute, whilst he stood and watched them. And then, very superb, he sauntered away again. They sat down glowering. Of course they were beaten. Didn't they know it. The men in our carriage smiled curiously: in slow and futile mockery of both parties.

The rain was falling outside, the windows were steamed quite dense, so that we were shut in from the world. Throughout the length of the train, which was not very full, could be felt the exhausted weariness and the dispirited dejection of the poor D'Annunzio legionaries. In the afternoon silence of the mist-enclosed,

half-empty train the snatches of song broke out again, and faded in sheer dispirited fatigue. We ran on blindly and heavily. But one young fellow was not to be
abashed. He was well-built, and his thick black hair was brushed up, like a great
fluffy crest upon his head. He came slowly and unabated down the corridor, and
on every big, mist-opaque pane he scrawled with his finger W D'ANNUNZIO
GABRIELE—W D'ANNUNZIO GABRIELE.

The sick soldier laughed thinly, saying to the schoolmistress: "Oh yes, they are
fine chaps. But it was folly. D'Annunzio is a world poet—a world wonder—but
Fiume was a mistake you know. And these chaps have got to learn a lesson.
They got beyond themselves. Oh, they aren't short of money. D'Annunzio had
wagon-loads of money there in Fiume, and he wasn't altogether mean with it."
The schoolmistress, who was one of the sharp ones, gave a little disquisition to
show *why* it was a mistake, and wherein she knew better than the world's poet
and wonder.

It always makes me sick to hear people chewing over newspaper pulp.

The sick soldier was not a legionary. He had been wounded through the lung.
But it was healed, he said. He lifted the flap of his breast pocket, and there
hung a little silver medal. It was his wound-medal. He wore it concealed: and
over the place of the wound. He and the schoolmistress looked at one another
significantly.

Then they talked pensions: and soon were on the old topic. The schoolmistress had her figures pat, as a schoolmistress should. Why, the ticket-collector,
the man who punches one's tickets on the train, now had twelve thousand Lira
a year: twelve thousand Lira. Monstrous! Whilst a fully-qualified *professore*, a
schoolmaster who had been through all his training and had all his degrees, was
given five thousand. Five thousand for a fully qualified *professore*, and twelve
thousand for a ticket puncher. The soldier agreed, and quoted other figures. But
the railway was the outstanding grievance. Every boy who left school now, said
the schoolmistress, wanted to go on the railway. Oh but—said the soldier—the
train-men—!

The naval officer, who collapsed into the most uncanny positions, blind with
sleep, got down at Capua to get into a little train that would carry him back to
his own station, where our train had not stopped. At Caserta the sick soldier got
out. Down the great avenue of trees the rain was falling. A young man entered.
Remained also the schoolmistress and the stout man. Knowing we had been
listening, the schoolmistress spoke to us about the soldier. Then—she had said
she was catching the night boat for Palermo—I asked her if she thought the
ship would be very full. Oh yes, very full, she said. Why, hers was one of the last
cabin numbers, and she had got her ticket early that morning. The fat man now
joined in. He too was crossing to Palermo. The ship was sure to be quite full by

now. Were we depending on booking berths at the port of Naples? We were. Whereupon he and the schoolmistress shook their heads and said it was more than doubtful—nay, it was as good as impossible. For the boat was the renowned *Città di Trieste*, that floating palace, and such was the fame of her gorgeousness that everybody wanted to travel by her.

"First and second class alike?" I asked.

"Oh yes, also first class," replied the school-marm rather spitefully. So I knew she had a white ticket—second.

I cursed the *Città di Trieste* and her gorgeousness, and looked down my nose. We had now two alternatives: to spend the night in Naples, or to sit on all through the night and next morning, and arrive home, with heaven's aid, in the early afternoon. Though these long-distance trains think nothing of six hours late. But we were tired already. What we should be like after another twenty-four hours' sitting, heaven knows. And yet to struggle for a bed in a Naples hotel this night, in the rain, all the hotels being at present crammed with foreigners, that was no rosy prospect. Oh dear!

However, I was not going to take their discouragement so easily. One has been had that way before. They love to make the case look desperate.

Were we English? asked the schoolmistress. We were. Ah, a fine thing to be English in Italy now. *Why?*—rather tart from me. Because of the *cambio*, the exchange. You English, with your money exchange, you come here and buy everything for nothing, you take the best of everything, and with your money you pay nothing for it. Whereas we poor Italians we pay heavily for everything at an exaggerated price, and we can have nothing. Ah, it is all very nice to be English in Italy now. You can travel, you go to the hotels, you can see everything and buy everything, and it costs you nothing. What is the exchange today? She whipped it out. A hundred and four, twenty.

This she told me to my nose. And the fat man murmured bitterly *già! già!*—ay! ay! Her impertinence and the fat man's quiet bitterness stirred my bile. Has not this song been sung at me once too often, by these people?

You are mistaken, said I to the schoolmistress. We don't by any means live in Italy for nothing. Even with the exchange at a hundred and three, we don't live for nothing. We pay, and pay through the nose, for whatever we have in Italy: and you Italians see that we pay. What! You put all the tariff you do on foreigners, and then say we live here for nothing. I tell you I could live in England just as well, on the same money—perhaps better. Compare the cost of things in England with the cost here in Italy, and even considering the exchange, Italy costs nearly as much as England. Some things are cheaper here—the railway comes a little cheaper, and is infinitely more miserable. Travelling is usually a misery. But other things, clothes of all sorts, and a good deal of food is even more expensive here than in England, exchange considered.

Oh yes, she said, England had had to bring her prices down this last fortnight. In her own interests indeed.

"This last fortnight! This last six months," said I. "Whereas prices rise every single day here."

Here a word from the quiet young man who had got in at Caserta.

"Yes," he said, "yes. I say, every nation pays in its own money, no matter what the exchange. And it works out about equal."

But I felt angry. Am I always to have the exchange flung in my teeth, as if I were a personal thief? But the woman persisted.

"Ah," she said, "we Italians, we are so nice, we are so good. Noi, siamo così buoni. We are so good-natured. But others, they are not buoni, they are not good-natured to us." And she nodded her head. And truly, I did not feel at all good-natured towards her: which she knew. And as for the Italian good-nature, it forms a sound and unshakeable basis nowadays for their extortion and self-justification and spite.

Darkness was falling over the rich flat plains that lie around Naples, over the tall uncanny vines with their brown thongs in the intensely cultivated black earth. It was night by the time we were in that vast and thievish station. About half-past five. We were not very late. Should we sit on in our present carriage, and go down in it to the port, along with the schoolmistress, and risk it? But first look at the coach which was going on to Sicily. So we got down and ran along the train to the Syracuse coach. Hubbub, confusion, a wedge in the corridor, and for sure no room. Certainly no room to lie down a bit. We *could* not sit tight for twenty-four hours more.

So we decided to go to the port—and to walk. Heaven knows when the railway carriage would be shunted down. Back we went therefore for the sack, told the schoolmistress our intention.

"You can but try," she said frostily.

So there we are, with the sack over my shoulder and the kitchenino in the q-b's hand, bursting out of that thrice-damned and annoying station, and running through the black wet gulf of a Naples night, in a slow rain. Cabmen look at us. But my sack saved me. I am weary of that boa-constrictor, a Naples cabman after dark. By day there is more-or-less a tariff.

It is about a mile from the station to the quay where the ship lies. We make our way through the deep, gulf-like streets, over the slippery black cobbles. The black houses rise massive to a great height on either side, but the streets are not in this part very narrow. We plunge forwards in the unearthly half-darkness of this great uncontrolled city. There are no lights at all from the buildings—only the small electric lamps of the streets.

So we emerge on the harbour front, and hurry past the great storehouses in the rainy night, to where the actual entrances begin. The tram bangs past us. We scuffle along that pavement-ridge which lies like an isthmus down the vast black quicksands of that harbour road. One feels peril all round. But at length we come to a gate by the harbour railway. No, not that. On to the next iron gate of the railway crossing. And so we run out past the great sheds and the buildings of the port station, till we see a ship rearing in front, and the sea all black. But now where is that little hole where one gets the tickets? We are at the back of everywhere in this desert jungle of the harbour darkness.

A man directs us round the corner—and actually does not demand money. It is the sack again. So—there, I see the knot of men, soldiers chiefly, fighting in a bare room round a tiny wicket. I recognise the place where I have fought before.

So while the q-b stands guard over sack and bag, I plunge into the fray. It literally is a fight. Some thirty men all at once want to get at a tiny wicket in a blank wall. There are no queue-rails, there is no order: just a hole in a blank wall, and thirty fellows, mostly military, pressing at it in a mass. But I have done this before. The way is to insert the thin end of oneself, and without any violence, by deadly pressure and pertinacity come at the goal. One hand must be kept fast over the money pocket, and one must be free to clutch the wicket-side when one gets there. And thus one is ground small in those mills of God, Demos struggling for tickets. It isn't very nice—so close, so incomparably crushed. And never for a second must one be off one's guard for one's watch and money and even hanky. When I first came to Italy after the war I was robbed twice in three weeks, floating round in the sweet old innocent confidence in mankind. Since then I have never ceased to be on my guard. Somehow or other, waking and sleeping one's spirit must be on its guard nowadays. Which is really what I prefer, now I have learnt it. Confidence in the goodness of mankind is a very thin protection indeed. *Integer vitae scelerisque purus* will do nothing for you when it comes to humanity, however efficacious it may be with lions and wolves. Therefore, tight on my guard, like a screw biting into a bit of wood, I bite my way through that knot of fellows, to the wicket, and shout for two first-class. The clerk inside ignores me for some time, serving soldiers. But if you stand like Doomsday you get your way. Two firsts, says the clerk. Husband and wife, say I, in case there is a two-berth cabin. Jokes behind. But I get my tickets. Impossible to put my hand to my pocket. The tickets cost about a hundred and five francs each. Clutching paper change and the green slips, with a last gasp I get out of the knot. So—we've done it. As I sort my money and stow away, I hear another ask for one first-class. Nothing left, says the clerk. So you see how one must fight.

I must say for these dense and struggling crowds, they are only intense, not violent, and not in the least brutal. I always feel a certain sympathy with the men in them.

Bolt through the pouring rain to the ship. And in two minutes we are aboard. And behold, each of us has a deck cabin, I one to myself, the q-b to herself next door. Palatial—not a cabin at all, but a proper little bedroom with a curtained bed under the porthole windows, a comfortable sofa, chairs, table, carpets, big wash-bowls with silver taps—a whole *de luxe*. I dropped the sack on the sofa with a gasp, drew back the yellow curtains of the bed, looked out of the port-hole at the lights of Naples, and sighed with relief. One could wash thoroughly, refreshingly, and change one's linen. Wonderful!

The state-room is like a hotel lounge, many little tables with flowers and peri-odicals, arm-chairs, warm carpet, bright but soft lights, and people sitting about chatting. A loud group of English people in one corner, very assured: two quiet English ladies: various Italians seeming quite modest. Here one could sit in peace and rest, pretending to look at an illustrated magazine. So we rested. After about an hour there entered a young Englishman and his wife, whom we had seen on our train. So, at last the coach had been shunted down to the port. Where should we have been had we waited!

The waiters began to flap the white table-cloths and spread the tables nearest the walls. Dinner would begin at half-past seven, immediately the boat started. We sat in silence, till eight or nine tables were spread. Then we let the other people take their choice. After which we chose a table by ourselves, neither of us wanting company. So we sat before the plates and the wine-bottles and sighed in the hopes of a decent meal. Food by the way is not included in the hundred-and-five francs.

Alas, we were not to be alone: two young Neapolitans, pleasant, quiet, blond, or semi-blond. They were well-bred, and evidently of northern extraction. Afterwards we found out they were jewellers. But I liked their quiet, gentle manners. The dinner began, and we were through the soup, when up pranced another young fellow, rather strapping and loud, a commercial traveller, for sure. He had those cocky assured manners of one who is not sure of his manners. He had a rather high forehead, and black hair brushed up in a showy wing, and a large ring on his finger. Not that a ring signifies anything. Here most of the men wear several, all massively jewelled. If one believed in all the jewels, why Italy would be more fabulous than fabled India. But our friend the bounder was smart, and smelled of cash. Not money, but cash.

I had an inkling of what to expect when he handed the salt and said in English "Salt, thenk you." But I ignored the advance. However, he did not wait long.

Through the windows across the room the q-b saw the lights of the harbour slowly moving. "Oh," she cried, "are we going?" And also in Italian: "*Partiamo?*" All watched the lights, the bounder screwing round. He had one of the fine, bounderish backs.

"Yes," he said. "We—*going.*"

"Oh," cried she. "Do you speak English?"

"Ye-es. Some English—I speak."

As a matter of fact he spoke about forty disconnected words. But his accent was so good for these forty. He did not speak English, he imitated an English voice making sounds. And the effect was startling. He had served on the Italian front with the Scots Guards—so he told us in Italian. He was Milanese. Oh, he had had a time with the Scots Guards. Wheesky—eh? Wheesky.

"Come along *bhoys!*" he shouted.

And it was such a Scotch voice shouting, so loud-mouthed and actual, I nearly went under the table. It struck us both like a blow.

Afterwards he rattled away without misgiving. He was a traveller for a certain type of machine, and was doing Sicily. Shortly he was going to England—and he asked largely about first-class hotels. Then he asked was the q-b French?—Was she Italian?—No, she was German. Ah—German. And immediately out he came with the German word: "Deutsch! Deutsch, eh? From Deutschland. Oh yes! Deutschland über alles! Ah, I know. No more—what? Deutschland unter alles now? Deutschland unter alles." And he bounced on his seat with gratification of the words. Of German as of English he knew half a dozen phrases.

"No," said the q-b, "Not Deutschland unter alles. Not for long, anyhow."

"How? Not for long? You think so? I think so too," said the bounder. Then in Italian: "La Germania won't stand under all for long. No, no. At present it is England über alles. *England über alles.* But Germany will rise up again."

"Of course," said the q-b. "How shouldn't she?"

"Ah," said the bounder, "while England keeps the money in her pocket, we shall none of us rise up. Italy won the war, and Germany lost it. And Italy and Germany they both are down, and England is up. They both are down, and England is up. England and France. Strange, isn't it? Ah, the allies. What are the allies for? To keep England up, and France half way, and Germany and Italy down."

"Ah, they won't stay down for ever," said the q-b.

"You think not? Ah! We will see. We will see how England goes on now."

"England is not going on so marvellously, after all," say I.

"How not? You mean Ireland?"

"No, not only Ireland. Industry altogether. England is as near to ruin as other countries."

"Ma! With all the money, and we others with no money? How will she be ruined?"

"And what good would it be to you if she were?"

"Oh well—who knows. If England were ruined—" a slow smile of anticipation spread over his face. How he would love it—how they would all love it, if England were ruined. That is, the business part of them, perhaps, would not love it. But the human part would. The human part fairly licks its lips at the thought of England's ruin. The commercial part, however, quite violently disclaims the anticipations of the human part. And there it is. The newspapers chiefly speak with the commercial voice. But individually, when you are got at in a railway carriage or as now on a ship, up speaks the human voice, and you know how they love you. This is no doubt inevitable. When the exchange stands at a hundred and six men go humanly blind, I suppose, however much they may keep the commercial eye open. And having gone humanly blind they bump into one's human self nastily: a nasty jar. You know then how they hate you. Underneath, they hate us, and as human beings we are objects of envy and malice. They hate us, with envy, and despise us, with jealousy. Which perhaps doesn't hurt commercially. Humanly it is to me unpleasant.

The dinner was over, and the bounder was lavishing cigarettes—Murattis, if you please. We had all drunk two bottles of wine. Two other commercial travellers had joined the bounder at our table—two smart young fellows, one a bounder and one gentle and nice. Our two jewellers remained quiet, talking their share, but quietly and so sensitively. One could not help liking them. So we were seven people, six men.

"Wheesky! Will you drink Wheesky, Mister?" said our original bounder. "Yes, one small Scotch! One Scotch Wheesky." All this in a perfect Scotty voice of a man standing at a bar calling for a drink. It was comical, one could not but laugh: and very impertinent. He called for the waiter, took him by the button-hole, and with a breast-to-breast intimacy asked if there was whisky. The waiter, with the same tone of you-and-I-are-men-who-have-the-same-feelings, said he didn't think there was whisky, but he would look. Our bounder went round the table inviting us all to whiskies, and pressing on us his expensive English cigarettes with great aplomb.

The whisky came—and five persons partook. It was fiery, oily stuff from heaven knows where. The bounder rattled away, spouting his bits of English and his four words of German. He was in high feather, wriggling his large haunches on his chair and waving his hands. He had a peculiar manner of wriggling from the bottom of his back, with fussy self-assertiveness. It was my turn to offer whisky.

I was able in a moment's lull to peer through the windows and see the dim lights of Capri—the glimmer of Anacapri up on the black shadow—the lighthouse. We had passed the island. In the midst of the babel I sent out a few thoughts to a few people on the island. Then I had to come back.

The bounder had once more resumed his theme of l'Inghilterra, l'Italia, la Germania. He swanked England as hard as he could. Of course England was the top dog, and if he could speak some English, if he were talking to English people, and if, as he said, he was going to England in April, why he was so much the more top-doggy than his companions, who could not rise to all these heights. At the same time, my nerves had too much to bear.

Where were we going and where had we been and where did we live? And ah, yes, English people lived in Italy. Thousands, thousands of English people lived in Italy. Yes, it was very nice for them. There used to be many Germans, but now the Germans were down. But the English—what could be better for them than Italy now: they had sun, they had warmth, they had abundance of everything, they had a charming people to deal with, and they had the *cambio*! Ecco! The other commercial travellers agreed. They appealed to the q-b if it was not so. And altogether I had enough of it.

"Oh yes," said I, "it's very nice to be in Italy: especially if you are not living in an hotel, and you have to attend to things for yourself. It is very nice to be overcharged every time, and then insulted if you say a word. It's very nice to have the *cambio* thrown in your teeth, if you say two words to any Italian, even a perfect stranger. It's very nice to have waiters and shop-people and railway porters sneering in a bad temper and being insulting in small, mean ways all the time. It's very nice to feel what they all feel against you. And if you understand enough Italian, it's very nice to hear what they say when you've gone by. Oh very nice. Very nice indeed!"

I suppose the whisky had kindled this outburst in me. They sat dead silent. And then our bounder began, in his sugary deprecating voice.

"Why no! Why no! It is not true, signore. No, it is not true. Why, England is the foremost nation in the world—"

"And you want to pay her out for it."

"But no, signore. But no. What makes you say so? Why, we Italians are so good-natured. Noi Italiani siamo così buoni. Siamo così buoni."

It was the identical words of the schoolmistress.

"Buoni," said I. "Yes—perhaps. Buoni when it's not a question of the exchange and of money. But since it is always a question of *cambio* and *soldi* now, one is always, in a small way, insulted."

I suppose it must have been the whisky. Anyhow Italians can never bear hard bitterness. The jewellers looked distressed, the bounders looked down their noses, half exulting even now, and half sheepish, being caught. The third of the *commis voyageurs*, the gentle one, made large eyes and was terrified that he was going to be sick. He represented a certain Italian liqueur, and he modestly asked us to take a glass of it. He went with the waiter to secure the proper brand. So we drank—and it was good. But he, the giver, sat with large and haunted eyes. Then he said he would go to bed. Our bounder gave him various advice regarding seasickness. There was a mild swell on the sea. So he of the liqueur departed.

Our bounder thrummed on the table and hummed something, and asked the q-b if she knew the *Rosencavalier*. He always appealed to her. She said she did. And ah, he was passionately fond of music, said he. Then he warbled, in a head voice, a bit more. He only knew classical music, said he. And he mewed a bit of Moussorgsky. The q-b said Moussorgsky was her favourite musician, for opera. Ah, cried the bounder, if there were but a piano!—There is a piano, said his mate.—Yes, he replied, but it is locked up.—Then let us get the key, said his mate, with aplomb. The waiters, being men with the same feelings as our two, would give them anything. So the key was forthcoming. We paid our bills—mine about sixty francs. Then we went along the faintly rolling ship, up the curved staircase to the drawing room. Our bounder unlocked the door of this drawing room, and switched on the lights.

It was quite a pleasant room, with deep divans upholstered in pale colours, and palm-trees standing behind little tables, and a black upright piano. Our bounder sat on the piano-stool and gave us an exhibition. He splashed out noise on the piano in splashes, like water splashing out of a pail. He lifted his head and shook his black mop of hair, and yelled out some fragments of opera. And he wriggled his large, bounder's back upon the piano stool, wriggling upon his well-filled haunches. Evidently he had a great deal of feeling for music: but very little prowess. He yelped it out, and wriggled, and splashed the piano. His friend the other bounder, a quiet one in a pale suit, with stout limbs, older than the wriggler, stood by the piano whilst the young one exhibited. Across the space of carpet sat the two brother jewellers, deep in a divan, their lean, semi-blond faces quite inscrutable. The q-b sat next to me, asking for this and that music, none of which the wriggler could supply. He knew four scraps, and a few splashes— not more. The elder bounder stood near him quietly comforting, encouraging, and admiring him, as a lover encouraging and admiring his *ingénue* betrothed. And the q-b sat bright-eyed and excited, admiring that a man could perform so unself-consciously self-conscious, and give himself away with such generous wriggles. For my part, as you may guess, I did not admire.

I had had enough. Rising, I bowed and marched off. The q-b came after me. Good-night, said I, at the head of the corridor. She turned in, and I went round the ship to look at the dark night of the sea.

Morning came sunny with pieces of cloud: and the Sicilian coast towering pale blue in the distance. How wonderful it must have been to Ulysses to venture into this Mediterranean and open his eyes on all the loveliness of the tall coasts. How marvellous to steal with his ship into these magic harbours. There is something eternally morning-glamourous about these lands as they rise from the sea. And it is always the Odyssey which comes back to one as one looks at them. All the lovely morning-wonder of this world, in Homer's day!

Our bounder was dashing about on deck, in one of those rain-coats gathered in at the waist and ballooning out into skirts below the waist. He greeted me with a cry of "It's a long, long way to Tipperary." "Very long," said I. "Good-bye Piccadilly—" he continued. "Ciao," said I, as he dashed jauntily down the steps. Soon we saw the others as well. But it was morning, and I simply did not want to speak to them—except just Good-day. For my life I couldn't say two more words to any of them this morning: except to ask the mild one if he had been sick. He had not.

So we waited for the great *Città di Trieste* to float her way into Palermo harbour. It looked so near—the town there, the great circle of the port, the mass of the hills crowding round. Panormus, the All-harbour. I wished the bulky steamer would hurry up. For I hated her now. I hated her swankiness, she seemed made for commercial travellers with cash. I hated the big picture that filled one end of the state-room: an elegant and ideal peasant-girl, a sort of Italia, strolling on a lovely and ideal cliff's edge, among myriad blooms, and carrying over her arm, in a most sophisticated fashion, a bough of almond blossom and a sheaf of anemones. I hated the waiters, and the cheap elegance, the common *de luxe*. I disliked the people, who all turned their worst, cash-greasy sides outwards on this ship. Vulgar, vulgar post-war commercialism and dog-fish money-stink. I longed to get off. And the bloated boat edged her way so slowly into the port, and then more slowly still edged round her fat stern. And even then we were kept for fifteen minutes waiting for someone to put up the gangway for the first class. The second class, of course, were streaming off and melting like thawed snow into the crowds of onlookers on the quay, long before we were allowed to come off.

Glad, glad I was to get off that ship: I don't know why, for she was clean and comfortable and the attendants were perfectly civil. Glad, glad I was not to share the deck with any more commercial travellers. Glad I was to be on my own feet, independent. No, I would *not* take a carriage. I carried my sack on my back to the hotel, looking with a jaundiced eye on the lethargic traffic of the harbour front. It was about nine o'clock.

Later on, when I had slept, I thought as I have thought before, the Italians are not to blame for their spite against us. We, England, have taken upon ourselves for so long the rôle of leading nation. And if now, in the war or after the war, we have led them all into a real old swinery—which we have, notwithstanding all Entente cant—then they have a legitimate grudge against us. If you take upon yourself to lead, you must expect the mud to be thrown at you if you lead into a nasty morass. Especially if, once in the bog, you think of nothing else but scrambling out over other poor devils' backs. Pretty behaviour of great nations!

And still, for all that, I must insist that I am a single human being, an individual, not a mere national unit, a mere chip of l'Inghilterra or la Germania. I am not a chip of any nasty old block. I am myself.

In the evening the q-b insisted on going to the marionettes, for which she has a sentimental passion. So the three of us—we were with the American friend once more—chased through dark and tortuous side-streets and markets of Palermo in the night, until at last a friendly man led us to the place. The back streets of Palermo felt friendly, not huge and rather horrible, like Naples near the port.

The theatre was a little hole opening simply off the street. There was no one in the little ticket box, so we walked past the door-screen. A shabby old man with a long fennel-stalk hurried up and made us places on the back benches, and hushed us when we spoke of tickets. The play was in progress. A serpent-dragon was just having a tussle with a knight in brilliant brass armour, and my heart came into my mouth. The audience consisted mostly of boys, gazing with frantic interest on the bright stage. There was a sprinkling of soldiers and elderly men. The place was packed—about fifty souls crowded on narrow little ribbons of benches, so close one behind the other that the end of the man in front of me continually encroached and sat on my knee. I saw on a notice that the price of entry was forty centimes.

We had come in towards the end of the performance, and so sat rather bewildered, unable to follow. The story was the inevitable Paladins of France—one heard the names *Rinaldo! Orlando!* again and again. But the story was told in dialect, hard to follow.

I was charmed by the figures. The scene was very simple, showing the interior of a castle. But the figures, which were about two-thirds of human size, were wonderful in their brilliant, glittering gold armour, and their martial prancing motions. All were knights—even the daughter of the king of Babylon. She was distinguished only by her long hair. All were in the beautiful, glittering armour, with helmets and visors that could be let down at will. I am told this armour has been handed down for many generations. It certainly is lovely. One actor alone was not in armour, the wizard Magicce, or Malvigge, the Merlin of the Paladins. He was in a long scarlet robe, edged with fur, and wore a three-cornered scarlet hat.

So we watched the dragon leap and twist and get the knight by the leg: and then perish. We watched the knights burst into the castle. We watched the wonderful armour-clashing embraces of the delivered knights, Orlando and his bosom friend and the little dwarf, clashing their armoured breasts to the breasts of their brothers and deliverers. We watched the would-be tears flow.—And then the statue of the witch suddenly go up in flames, at which a roar of exultation from the boys. Then it was over. The theatre was empty in a moment, but the proprietors and the two men who sat near us would not let us go. We must wait for the next performance.

My neighbour, a fat, jolly man, told me all about it. His neighbour, a handsome tipsy man, kept contradicting and saying it wasn't so. But my fat neighbour winked at me, not to take offence.

This story of the Paladins of France lasted three nights. We had come on the middle night—of course. But no matter—each night was a complete story. I am sorry I have forgotten the names of the knights. But the story was, that Orlando and his friend and the little dwarf, owing to the tricks of that same dwarf, who belonged to the Paladins, had been captured and immured in the enchanted castle of the ghastly old witch who lived on the blood of Christians. It was now the business of Rinaldo and the rest of the Paladins, by the help of Magicce the *good* wizard, to release their captured brethren from the ghoulish old witch.

So much I made out of the fat man's story, while the theatre was filling. He knew every detail of the whole Paladin cycle. And it is evident the Paladin cycle has lots of versions. For the handsome tipsy neighbour kept saying he was wrong, he was wrong, and giving different stories, and shouting for a jury to come and say who was right, he or my fat friend. A jury gathered, and a storm began to rise. But the stout proprietor with a fennel-wand came and quenched the noise, telling the handsome tipsy man he knew too much and wasn't asked. Whereupon the tipsy one sulked.

Ah, said my friend, couldn't I come on Friday. Friday was a great night. On Friday they were giving I Beati Paoli: The Blessed Pauls. He pointed to the walls where were the placards announcing The Blessed Pauls. These Pauls were evidently some awful secret society with masking hoods and daggers and awful eyes looking through the holes. I said were they assassins like the Black Hand. By no means, by no means. The Blessed Pauls were a society for the protection of the poor. Their business was to track down and murder the oppressive rich. Ah, they were a wonderful, a splendid society. Were they, said I, a sort of camorra? Ah, on the contrary—here he lapsed into a tense voice—they hated the camorra. These, the Blest Pauls, were the powerful and terrible enemy of the grand camorra. For the Grand Camorra oppresses the poor. And therefore the Pauls track down in secret the leaders of the Grand Camorra, and assassinate them, or bring them to the fearful hooded tribunal which utters the dread verdict of the Beati Paoli. And when once the Beati Paoli have decreed a man's death—all over. Ah bellissimo, bellissimo! Why don't I come on Friday?

It seems to me a queer moral for the urchins thick-packed and gazing at the drop scene. They are all males: urchins or men. I ask my fat friend why there are no women—no girls. Ah, he says, the theatre is so small. But, I say, if there is room for all the boys and men, there is the same room for girls and women. Oh no—not in this small theatre. Besides this is nothing for women. Not that there is anything improper, he hastens to add. Not at all. But what should women and girls be doing at the marionette show? It was an affair for males.

I agreed with him really, and was thankful we hadn't a lot of smirking twitching girls and lasses in the audience. This male audience was so tense and pure in its attention.

But hist! the play is going to begin. A lad is grinding a broken street-piano under the stage. The padrone yells *Silenzio!* with a roar, and reaching over, pokes obstreperous boys with his long fennel-stalk, like a beadle in church. When the curtain rises the piano stops, and there is dead silence. On swings a knight, glittering, marching with that curious hippety lilt, and gazing round with fixed and martial eyes. He begins the prologue, telling us where we are. And dramatically he waves his sword and stamps his foot, and wonderfully sounds his male, martial, rather husky voice. Then the Paladins, his companions who are to accompany him, swing one by one onto the stage, till they are five in all, handsome knights, including the Babylonian Princess and the Knight of Britain. They stand in a handsome, glittering line. And then comes Merlin in his red robe. Merlin has a bright, fair, rather chubby face and blue eyes, and seems to typify the northern intelligence. He now tells them, in many words, how to proceed and what is to be done.

So then, the glittering knights are ready. Are they ready? Rinaldo flourishes his sword with the wonderful cry "Andiamo!" let us go—and the others respond: "Andiamo". Splendid word.

The first enemy were the knights of Spain, in red kirtles and half turbans. With these a terrible fight. First of all rushes in the Knight of Britain. He is the boaster, who always in words, does everything. But in fact, poor knight of Britain, he falls lamed. The four Paladins have stood shoulder to shoulder, glittering, watching the fray. Forth now steps another knight, and the fight recommences. Terrible is the smacking of swords, terrible the gasps from behind the dropped visors. Till at last the knight of Spain falls—and the Paladin stands with his foot on the dead. Then loud acclamations from the Paladins, and yells of joy from the audience.

"*Silenzio!*" yells the padrone, flourishing the fennel-stalk.

Dead silence, and the story goes on. The Knight of Britain of course claims to have slain the foe: and the audience faintly, jeeringly hisses. "He's always the boaster, and he never does anything, the Knight of Britain," whispers my fat friend. He has forgotten my nationality. I wonder if the Knight of Britain is pure tradition, or if a political touch of today has crept in.

However, this fray is over—Merlin comes to advise for the next move. And are we ready? We are ready. *Andiamo!* Again the word is yelled out, and they set off. At first one is all engaged watching the figures: their brilliance, their blank, martial stare, their sudden, angular, gestures. There is something extremely suggestive in them. How much better they fit the old legend-tales than living people would do. Nay, if we are going to have human beings on the stage, they should be masked and disguised. For in fact drama is enacted by symbolic creatures formed out of human consciousness: puppets if you like: but not human *individuals*. Our stage is all wrong, so boring in its personality.

Gradually, however, I found that my eyes were of minor importance. Gradually it was the voice that gained hold of the blood. It is a strong, rather husky, male voice that acts direct on the blood, not on the mind. Again the old male Adam began to stir at the roots of my soul. Again the old, first-hand indifference, the rich, untamed male blood rocked down my veins. What does one care? What does one care for precept and mental dictation? Is there not the massive brilliant, out-flinging recklessness in the male soul, summed up in the sudden word: *Andiamo!* Andiamo! Let us go on. Andiamo!—let us go hell knows where, but let us go on. The splendid recklessness and passion that knows no precept and no school-teacher, whose very molten spontaneity is its own guide.

I loved the voices of the Paladins—Rinaldo's voice, and Orlando's voice: the voice of men once more, men who are not to be tutored. To be sure there was Merlin making his long speeches in rather a chuntering, prosy tone. But who was he? Was he a Paladin and a splendour? Not he. A long-gowned chunterer. It is the reckless blood which achieves all, the piff-piff-piffing of the mental and moral intelligence is but a subsidiary help, a mere instrument.

The dragon was splendid: I have seen dragons in Wagner, at Covent Garden and at the Prinz-Regenten Theater in Munich, and they were ridiculous. But this dragon simply frightened me, with his leaping and twisting. And when he seized the knight by the leg, my blood ran cold.

With smoke and sulphur leaps in Beelzebub. But he is merely the servant of the great old witch. He is black and grinning, and he flourishes his posterior and his tail. But he is curiously inefficacious: a sort of lackey of wicked powers.

The old witch with her grey hair and staring eyes succeeds in being ghastly. With just a touch, she would be a tall, benevolent old lady. But listen to her. Hear her horrible female voice with its scraping yells of evil lustfulness. Yes, she fills me with horror. And I am staggered to find how I believe in her as *the* evil principle. Beelzebub, poor devil, is only one of her instruments.

It is her old, horrible, grinning female soul which locks up the heroes, and which sends forth the awful and almost omnipotent malevolence. This old, ghastly woman-spirit is the very core of mischief. And I felt my heart getting as hot against her as the hearts of the lads in the audience were. Red, deep hate

I felt of that symbolic old ghoul-female. Poor male Beelzebub is her loutish slave. And it takes all Merlin's bright-faced intelligence, and all the surging hot urgency of the Paladins, to conquer her.

She will never be finally destroyed—she will never finally die, till her statue, which is immured in the vaults of the castle, is burned.—Oh, it was a very psychoanalytic performance altogether, and one could give a very good Freudian analysis of it.—But behold this image of the witch: this white, submerged *idea* of woman which rules from the deeps of the unconscious. Behold, the reckless, untamable male knights will do for it. As the statue goes up in flame—it is only paper over wires—the audience yells! And yells again. And would God the symbolic act were really achieved. It is only little boys who yell. Men merely smile at the trick. They know well enough the white image endures.

So it is over. The knights look at us once more. Orlando, hero of heroes, has a slight inward cast of the eyes. This gives him that look of almost fierce good-nature which these people adore: the look of a man who does not think, but whose heart is all the time red hot with burning, generous blood-passion. This is what they adore.

So my knights go. They all have wonderful faces, and are so splendidly glittering and male. I am sorry they will be laid in a box now.

There is a great gasp of relief. The piano starts its lame rattle. Somebody looking round laughs. And we all look round. And seated on the top of the ticket office is a fat, solemn urchin of two or three years, hands folded over his stomach, his forehead big and blank, like some queer little Buddha. The audience laughs with that southern sympathy: physical sympathy: that is what they love to feel and to arouse.

But there is a little after-scene: in front of the drop-curtain jerks out a little fat flat caricature of a Neapolitan, and from the opposite side jerks the tall caricature of a Sicilian. They jerk towards one another and bump into one another with a smack. And smack goes the Neapolitan, down on his posterior. And the boys howl with joy. It is the eternal collision between the two peoples, Neapolitan and Sicilian. Now goes on a lot of fooling between the two clowns, in the two dialects. Alas, I can hardly understand anything at all. But it sounds comic, and looks very funny. The Neapolitan of course gets most of the knocks. And there seems to be no indecency at all—unless once.—The boys howl and rock with joy, and no one says Silenzio!

But it is over. All is over. The theatre empties in a moment. And I shake hands with my fat neighbour, affectionately, and in the right spirit. Truly I loved them all in the theatre: the generous, hot southern blood, so subtle and spontaneous, that asks for blood contact, not for mental communion or spirit sympathy. I was sorry to leave them.

BIOGRAPHICAL TIMELINE

1885   David Herbert Lawrence is born on September 11 in the small coal town of Eastwood, Nottinghamshire, England, to Arthur John Lawrence, a nearly illiterate coal miner, and Lydia Beardsall Lawrence, who trained as a schoolteacher but took manual work in a lace factory due to her family's financial difficulties.

1891–01   Lawrence attends the Beauvale Board School where he becomes the first local pupil to win a county council scholarship to Nottingham High School in nearby Nottingham.

At the age of sixteen, Lawrence leaves school and starts working as a junior clerk at a Haywood's surgical appliances in Nottingham to support his family financially, but is unable to continue work due to a case of severe pneumonia.

1902–06   While recovering from pneumonia, visits the Haggs Farm nearby and begins an intense friendship with Jessie Chambers.

Serves as a pupil-teacher, a training program in use as an apprentice system for teachers, at the British school in Eastwood.

1906   Begins attending University College, Nottingham.

1907   Wins a short story competition in the *Nottinghamshire Guardian*, the first time that he gains any wider recognition for his literary talents.

1908   Receives a teaching certificate from University College, Nottingham (then an external college of University of London).

Moves to London and begins teaching at Davidson Road School, in Croydon, a town in South London, where he continues writing.

1909   Begins romantic relationship with Jessie Chambers; Chambers submits some of Lawrence's poetry to Ford Madox Ford (then known as Ford Hermann Hueffer), editor of *The English Review*.

1910–11   Ends relationship with Chambers in August.

Proposes to Louise Burrows, an old friend from his days in

Nottingham and Eastwood.

Lawrence's mother dies of cancer.

Ford publishes Lawrence's short story "Odour of Chrysanthemums" in *The English Review*.

The White Peacock, Lawrence's first novel, is published.

Resigns position after lengthy bout of pneumonia.

1912   *The Trespasser* (novel).

Breaks off engagement with Louie Burrows.

Meets Frieda Weekley (née von Richthofen), a woman with three children and the wife of his former modern languages professor at University College Nottingham. They elope to Germany.

During their stay Lawrence is falsely arrested for spying; after the intervention of Frieda's father, he is released and leaves for a small hamlet to the south of Munich where he is joined by Frieda.

From Germany, they walk southwards across the Alps to Italy.

1913   *Love Poems and Others* (poetry); *Sons and Lovers* (novel) is published and becomes Lawrence's first major literary success. The novel establishes Lawrence as a prominent author.

The couple return briefly to Britain and meet and befriend New Zealand-born short story writer Katherine Mansfield before returning to Italy.

1914   Following Frieda's divorce, Lawrence and Frieda return to Britain and are legally married on July 13, 1914; they remain married for the rest of Lawrence's life. She loses custody of her children.

World War I breaks out on July 28.

The War confines the couple to England. During the war years, associates with T. S. Eliot, Ezra Pound, and others connected with *The Egoist*, an important Modernist literary magazine that published some of his work. Frieda's German parentage and Lawrence's pacifism cause them to be viewed with suspicion and they live in near-destitution during wartime Britain, moving from place to place.

1915   *The Rainbow* (novel).

1916   *Twilight in Italy and Other Essays* (travel writing).

1917   House is raided by the police and the Lawrence's are expelled from Cornwall.

1919   Nearly dies of the Spanish Flu.

In November, permanently leaves Britain returning only twice for brief visits. For the next several years, travels with Frieda to Italy, Austria, and Southern Germany.

1920   *Women in Love* and *The Lost Girl* (novels).

1921   *Sea and Sardinia* (travel writing); *Movements in European History* and *Psychoanalysis and the Unconscious* (nonfiction).

1922   *Aaron's Rod* (novel); *Fantasia of the Unconscious* (nonfiction).

In February, the Lawrences leave Europe with the intention of immigrating to the United States. They first visit Ceylon (now Sri Lanka) and Australia; they arrive in the United States in September.

1923   *Kangaroo* (novel); *Studies in Classic American Literature* (essays).

The Lawrences settle in Taos, New Mexico, where they befriend Mabel Dodge Luhan and other prominent artists; makes frequent visits to Mexico.

1924   *The Boy in the Bush*, coauthored with M.L. (Mollie or Molly) Skinner (novel).

Acquires a 160-acre ranch in Taos, New Mexico, now called the D. H. Lawrence Ranch.

Travels to England, France, Switzerland, Germany, and Austria before returning to Mexico, then Taos.

1925   Suffers a near-fatal attack of malaria and tuberculosis, necessitating his return to Europe for health reasons; settles in a villa near Florence, Italy.

1926   *The Plumed Serpent* (novel)

1927   *Mornings in Mexico and Other Essays* (travel writing); writes *Sketches of Etruscan Places* (travel writing).

1928   *Lady Chatterley's Lover* (novel) published privately; thereafter, pirated copies of the novel appear. A full unexpurgated edition will not be published until 1959 in the United States and 1960 in England.

Lawrence's health deteriorates rapidly due to tuberculosis.

1929   *The Escaped Cock*, republished as *The Man Who Died* (novel).

An exhibition of his paintings at the Warren Gallery in London is raided by the police and several works are confiscated.

Moves to the south of France.

1930   On March 2, shortly after being discharged from treatment in Vence, France, D. H. Lawrence dies of tuberculosis.

By the time of his death Lawrence had written twelve novels and, collectively, more than three dozen collections of short stories, volumes of poetry, plays, works of nonfiction, and travel books. He also translated books from Russian and Italian. He is widely acknowledged as one of the most influential English writers of the twentieth century.